BRINGING

BACK

A

HERO

BY

ROBERT D. JORNLIN
CAPTAIN OF LST 325

Chania   Souda   Iraklion

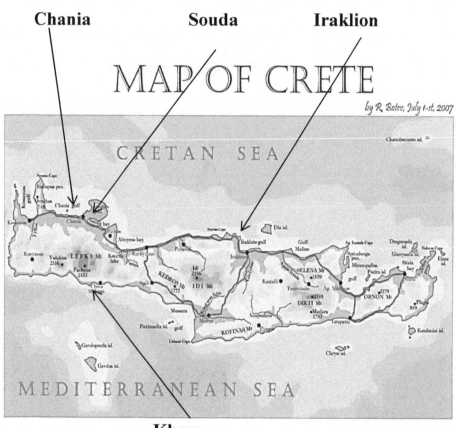

Khora

CONTENTS

THIS BOOK IS DEDICATED TO:

Jackson L. Carter, CDR U.S. Navy, my Executive Officer, who passed away a short six weeks after our return. He was instrumental in the success of restoring and returning the LST 325. I still miss him today.

The twenty-nine men (later named the Gold Crew) who brought the LST back to life sailed her for forty-two days across the Mediterranean Sea and North Atlantic to the USA.

The wives, significant others, and families left behind. Although they remained at home, they sailed every mile with us, gave us their full support, and prayed for our safety.

This book is also enthusiastically dedicated to my wife, Lois, who allowed me to do this, took care of the farm, harvested the crops, and navigated through the government farm programs while I was gone. She sold seed corn to everyone I had sold to the previous year – and sold more and just by the telephone! She was alone at home, experienced a terrible early winter in northern Illinois, and was snowbound most of December while I was with the crazy guys who were going to bring this "Hero Ship" home. When I left for Greece, I told her I would not be gone not more than six weeks! Actually, it took four months and ten days.

Captain Bob

GOLD (SAILING) CREW

THE CAST OF CHARACTERS

	AGE	DUTY STATION	HOME
JAMES BARTLETT	69	CHIEF ENGINEMAN	Marble Falls TX
JOHN CALVIN	75	WHEEL HOUSE	Dunnellon FL
JACK CARTER	71	EXECUTIVE OFFICER	Rancho Palos Verdes CA
DON CHAPMAN	73	CHIEF ELECTRICIAN	Moline IL
JIM EDWARDS	74	ENG. OFFICER	Canton TX
CORBIN FOWLKES	69	ENGINEMAN	Bethleham PA
WILLIAM HILL	75	ENGINEMAN	Surprise AZ
NORVAL JONES	74	CORPSMAN	Auburn Hills MI
ROBERT JORNLIN	61	CAPTAIN	Earlville IL
DON LOCKAS	73	HELMSMAN	Marseilles IL
GARY LYON	68	ELECTRICIAN	Roseville MN
RON MARANTO	68	AUX ENGINE RM	Metairie LA
JIM MCCANDREW	69	ENGINEMAN	Sebastian FL
DICK MEYERS	75	HELMSMAN	Lincoln NE
JOE MILAKOVICH	74	ENGINEMAN	Wauwatosa WI
DON MOLZAHN	74	HELM/STORE KEEPER	La Crosse WI
HIKE NEDEFF	75	HELMSMAN	Dayton OH
BILL NICKERSON	73	QUARTERMASTER	Margate FL
DOMINICK PERRUSO	74	SHIP FITTER	Cresco PA
JOE SADLIER	73	CHIEF COOK	Ketchikan AK
HAROLD SLEMMONS	74	ENGINEMAN	Lone Oak TX
PAUL STIMPSON	77	ENGINEMAN	New Haven PA
EDWARD STROBEL	77	HELMSMAN	Decatur, IL
DEWEY TAYLOR	75	HELMSMAN	W Palm Beach FL
BRUCE VOGES	74	BOATS'N MATE	Ogden, IL
ALBERT WHITE	73	LAUNDRY	Roswell NM
LOREN WHITING	76	CHIEF ENGINEMAN	Baker NY
BAILEY WRINKLE	71	AUX ENGINE RM	McKenzie TN
GLENN GREGG	40	PHOTOGRAPHER	Pine Brook NJ

EDITED BY: DL LARSON
DL WORDSMITH
EDITING SERVICE
4478 E. 1675 RD
EARLVILLE, ILLINOIS 60518

Cover design: Sean Schubert
Art Department,
Lake Screen Printing, Inc.
1924 Broadway
Lorain, OH 44092

Library of Congress Control number 2014913548
ISBN: 978-0-9907492-3-3 Paperback
ISBN: 978-0-99074-92-2-6 E-Book

Purchase copies of book from the following:

USS LST SHIP MEMORIAL, INC.
 840 LST Drive, Evansville, IN 47713   (A Non- Profit Corp.)
E-mail: 325office@lstmemorial.org   Phone 812-435-8678
Web page: www.lstmemorial.org (ship's store)

Amazon andother great book retail outlets and from Author at

**** Bringing Back A Hero - 4763 E.10th Rd., Earlville, IL 60518
Web page: www.lst325heroship.com

Printed in the USA updated 8/15

PROLOGUE

The LST was a dream of Winston Churchill as his army was being pushed off the European Continent by the Germans at Dunkirk, France in late May of 1940. He had no means of getting his heavy equipment off the beach, in fact had a very hard time removing 350,000 men! During this evacuation, Mr. Churchill was envisioning how heavy equipment, tanks, and hefty artillery might be placed back on European soil in order to defeat the Germans. He knew the ports would be mined and heavily fortified by the Germans. It had to be a unique ship.

Churchill brought his idea to America for a ship that could slide up on the beach and unload equipment. A submarine designer, John Niedermeier, drew a diagram of a ship capable of driving right onto the beach, and deposit troops, heavy equipment, and Sherman tanks through its bow onto dry sand. It's been said this diagram was drawn on a napkin in only fifteen minutes time. I have secretly wished he had spent another fifteen minutes an made it better!

One thousand and fifty-one Landing Ship Tanks (LSTs) were built in a short three-year period and used during WWII! All of these ships were HEROES. The LST ships could not launch aircraft as aircraft carriers did, nor could they sink into the ocean like submarines. They were not fast as destroyers and cruisers which could outrun and outmaneuver their enemies. They didn't have big guns like battleships; they had to stand and fight and fight they did!

General Dwight D. Eisenhower held back the European Invasion waiting for more LSTs to come out of the shipyards in the Midwest and sail to England.

Mr. Winston Churchill, Prime Minister of England, once said and I quote, "Let there be built great ships, which can cast upon a beach in any weather, large numbers of the heaviest tanks." His later quote, "Two great empires depend on some goddam thing

called an LST." Those that worked and served on LSTs truly believed they were *the ships that won the war!*

The search for a restorable, operational LST took men from all over the U.S. looking in our mothball fleets. When none were found in the USA, the search went to Taiwan, which had twenty-three LSTs. The Chinese promised one to the town of Seneca, Illinois; this LST had to be abandoned as it was not capable of sailing. Finally our search ended in Greece in 1995 when a ship was found. The State Department had said no to an operational LST; they determined it was a 'significant piece of military equipment' and the Memorial could not have one, even though most had been destroyed or given away. It took four years to pass a bill through Congress that gave this LST to the USS LST SHIP MEMORIAL.

It was *deja vu* for these veterans going to retrieve a ship like the one they served on. Most of these men were in their 70's going off to a far away place, giving up six months or more of their lives away from their families, fully aware they may experience health problems and the dangers of sailing an old ship across the North Atlantic in the winter. Several of the crew, as one might expect at their age, had health problems before they left for Greece. With their wives' approval, off they went.

Out of some seventy-two men who originally signed up to go in 1990 after the LST 859 in Taiwan, only fifty actually made the passage to Souda, Crete to help in the restoration and reclaiming of the LST 325. In this story, one will read about the determination and unrelenting pursuit of this crew of veterans to acquire a working, operational LST for a Museum. This LST was not to be a stationary museum ship that spends its remaining years in some distant, stagnant harbor or backwater bay left to rust, but an operational LST. Many of these historic museum ships will never run again, never shear through the emerald-green waters, or the never-ending waves of our great oceans.

These giants of men wanted a real, operating, engine throbbing, exhaust smoking, wave making ship they could sail to different cities and demonstrate to the people how they worked and retracted from the beaches. They wanted to prove to the uninformed there was such a ship they grew into manhood on, and actually made invasions on the beaches in the Pacific and Atlantic Oceans. This was a vessel that went wherever needed, carried everything the allies required, and deposited the tanks and supplies on dry sand right in the middle of the fight. LSTs received the second most Battle Stars in WWII. Destroyers earned the most; these more heavily armed and faster ships escorted and guarded the LSTs against attack by Submarines and E-boats across the oceans and onto the hostile beaches. We never had a sufficient number of the Landing Ship Tanks, but not a single invasion was unsuccessful after the LSTs entered into the fight. Was the LST important? Why were they forgotten?

The crew that persevered and kept working under dreadful conditions and against enormous odds were truly men made of granite. I am proud to have worked with this crew and have them as friends. All were of the 'Greatest Generation,' even though only eighteen were WWII. Personally, I wanted an LST for a Museum to be able to tell its story, a narrative to keep the memories alive and a testimony to the important heroic role these one of a kind ships played in the wars. I am writing this book to record events I was closely involved in. As the Captain, I alone was responsible, but my crew members were the ones who accomplished this feat. After giving over 600 talks on this adventure, I have been told by many in attendance that I should write a book and a movie should be made! So here is the book and the movie will not be far behind.

Only a few know the difference between *a Fairy Tale* and *a Sea Story?* A *Fairy Tale* starts out, 'Once upon a time,' while a *Sea Story* begins simply with, _THIS IS NO SHIT_!

<u>PART I</u>

FROM THE

'BONE-YARD'

TO

OPERATIONAL

CHAPTER 1

LET THE JOURNEY BEGIN

MEN OF STEEL FOR A STEEL SHIP

ATTENTION!

To all LST fans, trains on the tracks and all the ships at sea: We are after a WWII LST, one of the last of its class in original military configuration as it came out of the shipyards in 1942. We need a crew of men to restore and operate it. Men to fly to Greece on their own dime, leave home for an unknown amount of time, and sail her, a 58-year-old hero, back home. Men who have been successful enough to afford a $600 plane ticket, $1600 for their share of fuel and food needed for a trip of some 6500 nautical miles to an unknown port in the USA! Only STOUT-HEARTED MEN need apply.

This was a true adventure, a real *Sea Story* - a term used to describe tall tales about ships and sailors. This one topped them all. A story not about a time of war, but about brave men with one goal in mind - to bring back an operational WWII LST, a Landing Ship Tank.

The normal compliment for an LST averaged one hundred enlisted men and ten officers in wartime. Since we hoped not to be shot at, nor in fact shoot at anyone else, there was no need for gunners' mates. We eliminated signalmen and a few men in all departments. We figured a crew of seventy-two ample, which left room for expected loss when the bell rang to head for whatever country a ship was found. We greatly underestimated the loss of crew; *Father Time* always remained our enemy.

Like me, most answered the call after reading a small story in the *Scuttlebutt,* our National LST Association's newspaper. This announcement told of plans to sail an LST back from Taiwan, then requested volunteers. I placed a phone call to San Diego and asked to ride the Taiwan LST from Peoria to Seneca, Illinois, on the Illinois River - one short ride for the memories. One should be careful of making phone calls! The rest of the crew came along by word of mouth, through continued updates in the *Scuttlebutt,* and/or information from other LST sailors given out at the US LST Conventions.

WE HAVE AN LST!

It was on the Island of Crete, Greece, some six thousand five hundred miles away across the Mediterranean Sea (which in Latin means in the middle of land), and the Atlantic Ocean.

In 1995, after eight years searching for a WWII LST known as the *workhorse* of the Navy, Ed Strobel stumbled on one located in Greece. It took four more years before it became the Memorial's LST by an act of Congress. Twenty-nine veterans faced the challenge to sail back this 1942 vintage LST 325, a genuine WWII Hero. LST 325 had played an important role in the invasions of Sicily, Salerno, and Normandy. Nineteen years later, it was loaned to a foreign country, Greece, and used in the Hellenic Navy for thirty-five years from 1964 till 1999. Taken out of service, the ship was to be buried in their boneyard of dead ships, then and there forgotten. These men wanted to rescue the LST 325 and sail her back home to the United States to make her an operating museum.

Navy veterans came forward to form a crew from some seventeen different states. Most had never met each other. Six from Illinois met at Starved Rock Lodge in Utica, Illinois, in early July of 2000 to meet and talk about the trip. All of these men were gung-ho to sail a vintage ship home. I was surprised at the enthusiasm each exhibited. Every one of these men (except for me) served in WWII. The Illinois men in attendance: Bruce Voges, slated to be the Bos'n Mate (deck chief), looked to be sixty-five years old, not his actual age of 74. Don Lockas, who emphatically noted Lockas with one 'S', a Seaman first Class in WWII, who became my helmsman and resident singer and always asked me for a promotion. Lockas spent his career at Libby-Owens Ford making windshields so the media proclaimed we had a glass blower aboard! Ed Strobel went to school in Seneca, IL and was the person who found the LST in Greece while on vacation there with his wife, Eileen. Don Chapman, an electrician from Moline, and Dave Baird, who for health reasons did not make the trip to Greece, rounded out the group. Illinois had two other crewmembers not able to attend this meeting; George White, our only Marine and 'Lover Boy' and Roald Zvonik, a retired supervisor at Rock Island Arsenal.

Most of the 72 crew joined up back in 1990 when the plan was to go to Taiwan and sail back an LST. The men of this crew had aged ten years, but kept the faith we would still find an LST somewhere. We had looked extensively in the United States for an LST before going to foreign countries where our government had loaned LSTs after WWII.

The crew was a gathering of ordinary men who rose up to become exceptional and extraordinary. They had two things in common: one, a love for their country and two, a kinship for a unique type of ship they served on in WWII, Korea, or Vietnam. The men in this story are real; names have not been changed to protect the innocent because no one was blameless in this tale! Ten additional men were added to the roster after a plea for engineers on our web page after we were in Greece when our numbers dipped dangerously low for sailing. Everyone was to call CWO Melcher, placed in charge by a retired Navy Reserve Captain in San Diego who headed up the Taiwan LST project for the town of Seneca. Melcher continued the project of looking for an LST after he and I inspected the Taiwan LST and gave it a failing grade. Our State Department also gave it thumbs down.

CWO also formed a non-profit corporation, *United Service Navy, Inc.* This corporation, with no assets, was to sail the LST home and assume all liabilities. The name was a small change from the United States Navy to the *United Service Navy.* Each crewmember submitted a picture, a fingerprint, plus rank, blood type, date of birth, and serial number while in the Navy. Each individual accepted received an ID card which looked very similar to a real Navy ID. All hands were to attend the National LST conventions and wear the khaki uniform each one had to purchase from the Navy Uniform shop.

I had briefly met several of the crewmembers at Conventions. One, Jim Edwards from Canton, Texas, who eventually was appointed Engineering Officer, persuaded his Congressman from Texas, the Honorable Ralph Hall, to help us pass a Bill through Congress. Hall's aide, Priscilla Thompson Roberts, helped persuade other representatives to co-sponsor the bill giving the LST 325 to the LST Memorial. Priscilla, the one single person I credit with *carrying the mail* for the LST Bill, relentlessly pursued individuals for approval believing fully in our mission to obtain an operational LST. This Bill, on the second try, finally passed in the fall of 1999.

Plans were to fly on July 17, 2000 to Greece to bring the LST home. We had an impressive route to sail; a great sailing plan all worked out with courses, speeds and times including quite a few port visits. We wanted to beat the winter storms in the North Atlantic, be across before the Atlantic turns rough. We hoped the ship did not need a ton of repair work in order to sail. Seven men were to go over on July 17 and place the LST into livable condition - the ship cleaned up, electricity, water hooked up, toilets working, and bunks with mattresses in place. Each of the crew had to bring his own sheets, towels, shaving gear, and personal items. Remember, this ship had been in the 'Bone Yard' for seventeen months.

On August 1, the second group of twenty was to fly to Crete. This group consisted of engineers to check all the operating equipment, cooks to bring food and supplies on board, turn on the reefers, and make sure the Galley had a sufficient number of dishes, silverware, and cooking utensils. Deck hands were needed to check the mooring lines, the bow doors, ramp, anchors, and clean more spaces. In two to three weeks or when the ship was ready to sail, the balance of the crew was to come over, some forty-five men if they hadn't gotten cold feet, developed health problems, or their wives said, "No, you don't." With arrival of the last crew, the mooring lines would be pulled aboard and we would sail for home. Actually, the plan was for the first twenty-seven to sail the ship to Athens where the third group would come aboard. Now does that sound like a very workable plan? Everyone who went to Crete believed one-hundred percent in this plan, except for me. My first clue things were not on schedule came when I was instructed to bring the last group of men to Crete; the ship would not be in Athens the first of September as planned.

The 325 was still in the 'Bone Yard' when the first group arrived. I guess the Hellenic (Greek) Navy had not gotten word through channels the LST 325 belonged to the Memorial! After a week, the Greeks decided to help and moved the LST to a nice pier in the Repair Base, then hooked it up to electricity and water. They also brought alongside an oil barge to pump bilge oil out of the engine rooms and oily water out of the shaft alleys.

One problem on board was the cockroaches. While cleaning, someone picked up a few bags of rotten potatoes and out scurried a couple hundred roaches which of course spread to all parts of the ship! One of the men, Ron Maranto, who lived in Metairie close to New Orleans, had experience with killing roaches. He made up a special concoction of poison and went to work placing it where those elusive devils run. He positioned this bait all over the ship. By the time I arrived at the end of August, Ron had them pretty well under control; in fact I never saw one roach on the ship. He kept bait out the entire time. This problem made the web page and then the newspapers. The LST Bridge became a Cockroach Hotel.

The first group, the 'Magnificent Seven' I call them, found many things broken and equipment missing on the ship. After complaining to our Embassy, they received instructions to fire off a list through the Greek command for possible replacement. The list, presented to the Greek Commander at the Repair Base in triplicate, went through the Greek command structure to the top, then was sent to our embassy and back down to Souda with everything crossed off or noted as not available. This process took ten days.

Meanwhile the next twenty crewmembers made their way over. However, since they did not receive notification or a 'heads up' of more crew arriving, the Greek Navy Officers were upset. This did not lend to increased cooperation.

More men did not necessarily increase or speed up the process towards the ship sailing. In fact, work slowed almost to a stop. With no evidence or visible signs of progress, after a few days some of the second group left and returned home. Several reasons hastened their departure. Temperature in Souda was a factor as the thermometer hit one hundred to one hundred ten degrees every day in August. Due to the high heat, many from the Country of Greece go on vacation for the entire month of August!

Standing watch was necessary for safety, but when ordered to stand watch in uniform with shined shoes, well that was another thing. Watches were set for around-the-clock in three-duty sections. The watches were for four hours, and started at 0800 in the morning and continued for twenty-four hours, the same as a regular US Navy watch.

In order to help tolerate the extreme temperature, the men asked to get up early when it was not so hot, work in the cool of the morning and knock off at 1300. This plan was immediately rejected by the current CO, and the work continued seven days a week 0800 to 1700. Also, for the first two weeks, everyone had to buy meals uptown. The crew started eating at *Nick's Place*, the closest restaurant to the ship. Walking that mile up to town and back did not lend to good morale either.

After trying to lower the ramp one evening with no help from crew, CWO Melcher hit the up button to stop the fast fall of the ramp since no one was manning the brake. This sudden stop snapped the huge drive shaft which lowered and raised the ramp. Since they needed permission to remove parts off the LST moored outboard, the repair crew waited until after dark, then crossed over to the *Kriti* carrying their few tools. This meager tool list consisted of one ten inch crescent wrench, slip-nose pliers, and a hammer! Somehow, they were able to unbolt the shaft and pulley, and managed to move it out of the ramp machinery room, a very narrow compartment with small access hatches located above the bow doors directly under the forward 40mm gun. They had to carry the equipment to the 325, remove the broken shaft, and install the new one!

At first the crew was not allowed to buy tools. Of the few tools on board, one of the crew had checked out a hacksaw, but proceeded to break the blade and lose the pin that held the blade in place. This crewman was afraid to tell Melcher, so Bruce Voges or 'Boats' as we called him, volunteered to go see the CWO. Boats first offered to buy a new one, but then managed to fix it with a nail substituted for the pin. As the days went on some of the men bought a few tools using their own money.

More crew continued to leave. One was Dominick Perruso, the ship's plumber. He left because he could not work without tools and wasn't allowed to buy a pipe wrench. The crew desperately needed him, as the toilets were all the *Greek Bomb Sights* and needed to be upgraded to a flush type of American toilet. If one had not experienced these, a big surprise was coming. To use them, one simply aimed and went - no seat and not even a place for one! It was difficult and unpleasant for anyone, but for older men, simply terrible! If one did not already have a reason to drop out of this project, these facilities were reason enough!

Even after hearing of the rather unpleasant happenings from Greece, the twenty-four crew left at home were undaunted, still ready, bags packed, with passports in hand. Mr. John Horvath in Chicago, with Greek Olympic Airlines, handled all tickets. Everyone had to be in New York's JFK airport on August 28, 2000 at 2200 to catch the flight for Athens and fly towards destiny.

I HAD FULL INTENTIONS OF LEADING THIS LAST GROUP TO THE PROMISED SHIP.

CHAPTER 2

MY INCREDIBLE NIGHTMARE TRIP

MY TRIP TO GREECE STARTED from my farm in rural Earlville, IL. I headed out for O'Hare Airport in Chicago via a shuttle bus service out of Rockford, Illinois. My scheduled flight was from Chicago to New York to join and lead the last group of crew to Greece. My wife dropped me and my several bags off and said, "Good luck Honey, please be careful." I had given her reasons more than once for her to add *be careful.* I already knew I needed all the luck I could hope for, but it ran out fast at O'Hare. My arrival for the 1330 hour flight was all go at that point. I checked my bags and got my boarding pass. I had allowed eight and one half hours to get to JFK to not only catch my flight to Greece, but to meet the rest of the crew as they arrived at the airport.

I spotted a restaurant in the corner of the lobby that did not seem very busy, wandered in and sat down, ordered a grilled cheese sandwich and black coffee. When I came out thirty minutes later, I checked the big status board; my flight had a big red cancel sign. I quickly got in the long line for the next American Airline's flight to LaGuardia; this had a 1430 departure. After finally reaching an airline attendant, I learned this flight and the 1530 both were cancelled; no reason given. A flight to Newark, NJ was the only flight available for me to arrive in time via a shuttle over to JFK airport, to catch my Athens flight.

I tried hard to get my bags back from the first flight since past flying experiences told me there was a whopping good chance of never seeing them again. The airline people assured me my bags would be in Newark when I arrived. The attendant indicated to me the computer would switch my bags and she conveyed this with a smile! The Newark flight boarded at 1630 hour (4:30 PM) right on time, but sat at the gate for a while. This flight by some means missed its turn and after reaching the runway, sat on the tarmac for about three hours! I realized I was not going to get to JFK in time to catch my Greek flight, as the minutes slipped into hours!

After the cancellation of the first three possibilities, I had called Mr. Horvath at Olympic Airlines and told him of my troubles. He did a wonderful job of obtaining the information on my Newark flight, and when that flight was delayed, he cancelled my Athens flight, and re-booked me for August 29 at 2200, the same flight, at the same time, only a day later!

My baggage did not arrive. I went to the hotel board, paid for a room and stayed the night in Newark. The next morning, I went back to the airport and the baggage claim office to look for my bags – not there. I asked the baggage claim man to check LaGuardia. He called - no bags there either. I decided to take the bus to LaGuardia hoping my bags had arrived or would arrive there. The baggage claim person knew at this point I was not happy and gave me a courtesy pass good for a one-way fare on the shuttle bus. On arriving at LaGuardia the baggage claim person said, "No sir, your bags have not arrived." I hated to take NO for an answer. I pushed back through the line of people formed behind me, and noticed out to the side of this baggage claim cubbyhole, a high mound of unclaimed baggage. Underneath several duffle bags lay my bags. I was at this moment very happy and proceeded to go to the first restaurant I came to and ordered up my favorite breakfast. I wondered if the other crewmembers had made the flight.

Arriving at JFK International Airport I gave the cabbie a good tip. Now all I had to do was check my bags, get my boarding pass and wait until 2200. Once I was able to check my bags for Greece, I was free to wander around in the airport. I made a call to the ship and said I would be late. Then I called the Olympic Airlines and thanked Mr. Horvath for all of his help.

So far I figured one year of my life was lost from the pressure and anxiety of finally getting to a point about one tenth of the way to my destination. I sure hoped that my Olympic flight would leave on time! I had no idea what lie ahead for me, but was soon to find out. I had an inkling that more problems were in store. Had I known how many snags, I might well have caught a plane back home. I thought this part was to be fun.

I had enough adventure already for this small town boy from the Midwest. This reminded me of another place and another time: *I flew out of Chicago in 1961 for Navy OCS in Newport RI. I. To this point, I had no experience of flying in anything but a piper cub airplane that had not left the visibility of Earlville. Here I was off in a big jet, and had signed my life away for seven years to the US Navy.*

My plane landed in Athens after noon. I retrieved my bags and headed for customs and immigration. When I presented my passport, they handed me a note with a phone number. Please call a Mr. Dan O'Grady, First Secretary to Ambassador Burns. Making a phone call may sound easy, except in Greece one needed a phone credit card to make a call at a public phone. My Master Card did not work! As a result, I tried to buy a credit card at the money exchange window but could not.

I went back to the row of phones contemplating what to do, and there in one of the phones, I noticed a phone card sticking out of the slot - unbelievable. I figured it was a dead soldier, all used up. To my surprise it worked, in fact worked for days! Now as I look back, who left their phone card for me? Who can cancel all three of my planes and lose my luggage and why? A coincidence, good luck, or just bad luck! Some kind of power possibly wanted me separated from the other crewmembers, and then that same power gave me a phone calling card when it became obvious I could not make a call!

When I dialed the number, I reached a very friendly voice belonging to Dan O'Grady, who quickly asked me how I was and did I have a good flight? I did not explain, saying to myself do not go there! Then he thanked me for calling and got to the point. Could I catch a cab and come down to the US Embassy? The Ambassador would like to talk with you! How many US Ambassadors call someone and want him or her to stop by in the afternoon for a little chat? I was anxious to get to the ship.

I explained, "I have a flight for Crete in two hours."

O'Grady told me, "Don't worry I will change your flight until tomorrow, and the Ambassador will put you up tonight."

"*Right,*" I said to myself, "*the Ambassador is going to put me up for the night!*" I thought that something rotten happened at the ship. Did it sink at the pier? I had written the Ambassador a couple of times asking him to help the boys out with the repairs and missing equipment. I was merely trying to move the project ahead.

I left the airport and went out to the taxi stand. A driver helped load my bags in the trunk and asked, "Where to?"

He was using very good English, so I replied, "To the US Embassy please." The driver took off making several turns and then settled on a main thoroughfare. We soon stopped in front of a small building with another huge sand-colored building behind it. A high black wrought iron fence wrapped around the entire building, or so it looked. In front of the fence, protecting it and the building were large cement blocks.

I went in through the large iron gate in the fence into the small building where a Greek guard held out his hand. He asked to see my passport, and then asked what business I had at the embassy. Next, they wanted my baggage and motioned me through a metal detector. After putting everything back into my pockets, they pointed me out through another door into a framed metal walkway leading into the American Embassy.

The Greek Guards did all of the security checks. The Americans greeted me on entering and asked me the same questions! I handed over my passport which I thought I might not see again. Dan greeted me, introduced himself, and indicated the Ambassador was waiting. He ushered me into the Ambassador's meeting room, a powerfully furnished area with big comfortable chairs, thick carpet, lots of pictures of U.S. Presidents, the White House, the famous picture of the six Marines putting up the flag on Iwo Jima, and one LST hat on a small shelf! I learned later, Mr. Peter Leasca had given the hat to the Ambassador Burns right after the congressional bill passed.

I first met Ambassador Burns and then Mr. O'Grady introduced me to two US Navy Officers. They were Captain Ted Venable and Captain Dale Benson of the ODC, the Office of Defense Coordination with Greece. Asked to sit down, the Ambassador told me about the shortfalls of our project regarding the return of LST 325, specifically the methods used by our leader, CWO Melcher. The Ambassador alluded to Melcher running his point of contact, a Greek Officer named Ensign Mardakis, off the ship and other problems with the Greek Navy. This took a little while!

The Ambassador then pointed out very plainly that the Greeks, the Navy, and the State Department intended to pull their support from the LST unless the leadership changed. I thought to myself, what support?

The next question from the Ambassador, "Can you get rid of Melcher and take charge?" Now just how was my trip going? I have had two bad days, an all-night flight with little sleep. I arrived a day late. I had worn the same clothes for two days and I needed a shave and shower. I sat in a room with four strangers, two had the rank of Captain that I worshiped in the Navy, and one of course was the American Ambassador to Greece. Can I add that I was in some kind of fortress with nowhere to run and hide! As best I could, I answered all their wild, off the cuff questions.

I explained I had gotten along with Melcher for ten years. We had gone to Taiwan looking for LSTs. I traveled up the Alcan Highway riding in one of his WWII army vehicles in 1992. (This is another story for a different book). We had met at the US LST conventions every year and talked mostly about acquiring this LST or one like it. Melcher had stopped in Ottawa, Illinois and called me sometimes as late as 10:00 PM to drive twenty miles to see him. He was the main reason this project had stayed alive, and he had rounded up the crew including me. I could see on the two Captains' faces this was not what they wanted to hear, so I quickly added that I could turn him around, and convince him to go down in the engine room where his real expertise supposedly was.

The four men were not convinced this would work. They very emphatically stated, "We think he would still cause problems."

I then climbed out on a very high, long, and downward pointing tree limb and informed them that, if necessary, I could remove him and take over since the crew was behind me! This was what they wanted to hear. I could tell by the faint smiles on their faces. Pressure and more pressure mounted! Would it ever let up?

The two Captains then asked about my ability to bring an LST back through the Mediterranean Sea and across the Atlantic Ocean. I thought of telling them how I had navigated for years through the small and large towns of Illinois, turning up the many blacktop roads with tall corn on both sides just to see where they would lead me. I had always found my way home! I decided not to be smart and avoided that impulse. Their questions went on, "What courses will you take? How much fuel will you need? How many crew? Can you navigate after a thirty-five year absence from the Navy?" They did not stop there.

As truthfully as I could, I answered all their questions, expounding on my abilities and my experiences that I could come up with spontaneously while sitting in the hot seat. I started with my understanding of their apprehensions about my capabilities. To most, I have always bragged that I was not a 90 day but a 120-day wonder! In WWII, one trained 90 days to become a naval officer! I did not graduate from the Academy, but was an OCS graduate, achieved Lieutenant Rank and was an Engineering Officer on an LST for 3 years. I asked, "Have you read my fitness reports from when I was in the Navy?" (Your commanding Officer made one out evaluating your performance every six months.)

They immediately said, "No."

I answered back, "I haven't bothered to read them either!" The two Captains gave a quick smile and a short laugh erupted from the Ambassador and O'Grady. "However, each of the three different Captains I served under told me my fitness reports were superb. In addition, our Squadron Commander offered me an Executive Officer position if I would stay in the Navy. I honestly thought if the Vietnam War heated up, and if I was recalled, I would have stayed in the Navy. One of the reasons I decided to leave the Navy was the fact my fellow officers and friends were all leaving."

I continued, "We expect to have a crew of around forty. I only know a few of these men, but I have read all of their resumes. These men all served on LSTs in war, all for three years or more. Most achieved very successful positions in their civilian lives. One other important thing – they want to bring back an LST come hell, rough water, or high winds!"

The Navy did a very good job training me. I also learned from hands on experience in the operation of an LST. My first Chief Engineman on LST 825 was drunk at 0900, so I learned the inner workings of the LST, how to start and run the main engines and generators. I know the important things in Damage Control to keep a ship afloat and firefighting to keep it from burning having gone through the navy schools on Treasure Island. I know how to ballast and transfer fuel. I assisted in bringing a WWII LST out of mothballs in San Diego after the Cuban Missile Crisis. As the Engineering Officer, and with only five officers and thirty-five enlisted men, we navigated the LST 825 from San Diego down through the Panama Canal, across the Gulf of Mexico into Guantanamo Bay, through the Windward Passage up the East Coast, and into the Amphibious Base at Little Creek, VA.

My third Captain, Lieutenant John Sterling, allowed us to handle the ship frequently underway, and he volunteered the ship for everything the Navy or Army requested. If we were not volunteering, we sailed on R&R to New York City or down to Fort Lauderdale, Florida for more training. HE WAS BIG ON DRILLS!

"It will take fifty thousand gallons of #2 diesel fuel to get her home and one thousand gallons of 30W lube oil. I have a Garmin 12 GPS to navigate wherever we want to go. I have a Quartermaster who has the charts for the Mediterranean Sea and Atlantic Ocean and they are updated." I pulled from my suitcase the detailed ship's navigation plans. These plans had waypoints, distances, times, courses both magnetic and gyro, and estimated speeds.

I emphasized, "Gentlemen, my strongest asset was being able to work with people. With my sales experience working with American farmers, average age sixty, and possessing at least a fair personality, I can get along with about anyone. I will try hard to make friends with the Greek Officers, sailors, and our US Navy. These unique assets are why Melcher picked me to be the Executive Officer."

I continued, "We will get this ship repaired and running. I will make sure we fix everything properly, and we will not sail until in a condition essential to travel all the way to the US. Remember, I have a great experienced crew to actually repair this ship for underway sailing and keep her going."

I must have done an adequate job of dazzling my skeptics because they seemed very satisfied with my answers. They shook my hand and said, "Good luck. We do admire what you are trying to do." They informed me I would be staying at the operations or assistant Ambassador's house for the night.

I was ushered out the back door, put into a big black Mercedes, and given a fast, wild ride changing streets almost every block. In about twenty minutes we ended up at a large house. I learned that security never takes the same route to an Ambassador's home or anywhere they drive. This was for everyone's safety. We went through another steel gate with Greek guards and drove up by the house. My bags came right behind me. A very nice woman greeted me and she introduced herself as the assistant Ambassador's wife. She informed me dinner was to be ready soon. I was ushered up to my room for the night on the second floor. The bedroom was a large, but very plainly furnished room with a double bed and a connecting bathroom. My bags were placed just inside the door. "Please make yourself at home and after you freshen up, please come downstairs."

My schedule tomorrow started at 0700 with the Embassy car picking me up. The Assistant Ambassador volunteered to wake me up when he rose at around 0600 and we would have breakfast before I left.

Meeting Ambassadors and a drilling by our Navy was not something I did every day for enjoyment. I needed a shower and after that, I hit the bed and fell right to sleep, never moving until 0700 when the Asst. Ambassador beat on my bedroom door. He said he was sorry but had overslept and my ride would be there any minute. Great, I said to myself. My plane was scheduled to leave at 0830 for Crete! I put myself in high gear fearing Dan might think I was the one who overslept. I shaved, put on my Navy blue sport coat, a fresh white shirt, and a tie since now I was going to see the Captain of the US Naval Support Base located close to Souda Bay where the LST 325 was moored.

The car waited. Checking my watch, I was only fifteen minutes late. We made a quick stop at the Embassy because they neglected to give me my passport back. This took a little time to scan the bottom of the car, look in the trunk, under the hood, check us out and then proceed a short way to the back door. I ran in and retrieved my passport. We arrived at the airport I thought in plenty of time, but not soon enough it seemed - they had sold my seat! Mr. O'Grady and I waited for about an hour and a half for the next flight. To this day, I am not much for flying! The pressure of new surroundings, no coffee, a botched wake up call, a missed flight, and only 0830! What next? No coffee is a serious thing!

Arriving in Souda, a US Navy car waited to pick us up, and out to the naval base we went. Again, we maneuvered through two security gates and weaved through cement blocks placed to keep a fast moving car with a bomb from getting up any amount of speed, or maybe pushed together would serve for a roadblock in case of word on a possible assault. I learned that all of our bases in foreign countries were actually NATO bases and guarded by the host country's soldiers, security forces, etc. Our gate, the second gate of course, was guarded by the US Marines – no, not really - just our Navy MPs. I gave them my ID card made for me as a Commander in the USN – United Service Navy. The Navy Guards at the gate asked me, "What kind of an ID is this?"

I told them, "It's a special identification card and only about seventy existed." They just uttered, "Oh," and waved us through into our Naval Support Base at Souda.

I soon met the CMC - the Command Master Chief Rabb, whom I would talk to many times over the next weeks. He took us into the Captain's Office. They first introduced me to the base's Executive Officer. I could tell by his genuine smile and his looking me square in the face, he was OK. The CMC quickly added he was a short timer. I found out later he had bought a 40-foot sailboat, and he and his wife were going to sail around the Mediterranean Sea and across the Atlantic in the late spring of next year.

The Captain introduced himself as Captain Einsider and invited us to come in and please sit down. He got right to the point, saying, "Mister, you have to get rid of the guy in charge at the LST. Can you do that? That man Melcher's going around masquerading as a full Navy Commander. We have checked on him and he retired from the Army as a Warrant Officer! Further, he has set back our relations with the Greeks here in Souda by at least ten years! You have no idea how hard we have worked to keep up good relations with the Greek Navy, and, if I say so myself, we were making some progress until he showed up. Sir, can you get rid of this guy?"

I again told him my plan, "I can get him to stay in the engine room with the help of the crew who are not fond of him either. If I have to, I can relieve him as Captain."

Captain Einsider added, "I understand that the crew believes him to be a reincarnation of Captain Bligh and Captain Queeg all rolled into one." He then gave me a handshake and said, "Good luck. What you and the Navy veterans are trying to do is commendable."

I am now certain after this talk with the base Captain that I had dropped bodily into a super colossal disaster in progress. Dan and I left and headed for the ship. I was excited and in a hurry to get a glimpse of LST 325. So far, this had been so enjoyable! I now fully had the big picture. Everything I heard back home from the men that had left the project and from the many phone calls from Edwards was true; the LST project was in trouble.

ON TO THE BIG TOWN OF SOUDA, AND LST 325

CHAPTER 3

SOUDA BAY, CRETE, GREECE

Mr. O'Grady and I arrived at the Hellenic Navy Repair Base on August 31, 2000 in the small dusty town of Souda, on the northwest corner of the Island of Crete in the Mediterranean Sea. It was a bright sunny day and the temperature was ninety degrees and rising. We came into town from the west, having arrived about 1100 at the airport in the ancient walled Venetian city of Chania (pronounced Hania.) We had made a short stop at the US Navy Support Base for thirty minutes or so. The road narrowed with many curves, but existed as the main entrance and exit highway for the town.

I spent ten years anticipating this day, but not all the time believing I would ever be here. Over these ten years from 1990 until this day, I never thought we would find an LST. In addition, I had quad heart bypass surgery in 1995 and for a time had decided against doing this – bring back a WWII LST from Greece to the USA or from any place.

This was a quiet little town all of three or four blocks long, with most of the stores on my right as we entered. There were several bars, coffee shops, a pizza restaurant, several merchandise stores, a Greek Bank, a drug store, grocery store, a couple of bakeries, and Nick's Restaurant at the very east end of the business area, with rooms to rent upstairs as the sign in front read. To my left and opposite of Nick's, a divided street with a park in the middle led down to the waterfront a distance of about a city block, to the very west end of Souda Bay, a small inlet of blue water with the same name as the town. I wondered which name came first - the town or the bay.

Dan told me the ferry boats from Athens and several other Greek Islands come in the bay and stop at the Souda dock. They load and unload cars and passengers, then proceed on to the next destination. Many tourists visited Crete, and then moved on to other Islands in the Mediterranean Sea. Crete was the biggest Greek Island with history dating back to four thousand years BC.

People walked along the sides of the road as most merchants and restaurants had tables and merchandise displayed on the sidewalk that paralleled the building fronts. A short way past Nick's on my right, Dan told me, stood a bookie joint. It was a small house-like building with four or five older men sitting out front at a small table playing cards or counting their money!

Dan disclosed what he had heard at the navy base; the odds of the Americans restoring the ship and moving it away from the pier were seven to one against them.

I asked him, "On which side do you have your money?" He smiled but did not answer. Across the street was a travel agency, next to it a hardware store, and about two hundred feet farther past a row of parked cars which were angled straight in, popped up the main gate to the Greek Base where Dan told me the LST 325 was docked.

We rode through the gate in the blue US Navy car that picked us up at the airport. The Secretary and I had no problem getting into the Greek base. Evidently he had called ahead! On the right side of the gate was a guard shack; to our left a sidewalk burrowed in paralleling the road for about fifteen feet. At its end, one stepped down about twelve inches onto gravel. Farther to the left and a little beyond the sidewalk, a Greek Naval Officer, fully dressed in his white uniform, stared at us out the door of his post as we passed through. He did not move or say anything, but his eyes followed us. Potholes filled the road, and the pavement, now reduced to almost gravel, must have broken up a long time ago. The entire base looked run down and unkempt. Being a long time repair base was some of the reason for its dismal appearance. Quite a few dogs ran loose on the base. They were all Heinz 57 variety of different shapes, colors, and size; our driver slowed as several ran in front of us.

Ahead of us the Greeks had displayed a big ship's anchor in a neatly groomed center portion of the road, with a tall ship's mast sticking up. The mast displayed a blue and white Greek flag waving in the hot breeze from its yardarm. I recognized a couple of gray ships, former American Navy ships, tied up at different dock areas. We drove deeper into the base past some long low buildings scattered throughout.

These buildings were home to the supply department, pipe shop, engine shop, welding shop, and other repair facilities. A few Greek sailors walked on the side of the road or on the partial sidewalks that started and ended abruptly. The sun was growing hotter, now close to dead overhead, as we navigated the winding road.

We drove almost a mile deeper into the base. To our right, up on top of a hill Dan pointed out the main Base Headquarters with another Greek flag waving from another ship's mast. Almost directly in front and very close to the headquarters stood a white cylinder-like building about fifteen feet in diameter and thirty feet high, with a slight list. It reminded me of the pictures I have seen of the *Leaning Tower of Pisa*. I would soon learn this was the pilot's station for the bay pilots on call for ships moving in or out of the harbor. A curving stairway led up to the entrance on the second floor of the building. It looked like they had a nice vantage point to view the ships coming or going, and a panoramic view of everything on the base.

Three LSTs were opposite the pilots' building and Headquarters. Dan pointed out the Syros L144, formerly the LST 325. What a sight! It was moored parallel to the dock and tied up starboard side too! The Headquarters building was two hundred feet up a very steep hill from the ship. A cement five-foot wide stairway led down to the road and the one hundred-fifty foot flat area along the side of the LSTs.

Right behind the stern of the LST was an LCI, and to the starboard side of the LCI another LST, a Terrebonne class, built in the early 1950's. Both of these vessels moored bow first or in 'Mediterranean mooring,' used almost exclusively by the Greeks. The third LST was tied outboard of the 325.

On reaching the ship, I could see an accommodation ladder that extended from the 325's main deck, then turned aft 90 degrees against the side of the ship and sloped down sharply to a foot above the dock and one foot away from the dock. I could see one had to step off the pier towards the ship and up onto the ladder to climb aboard.

Jim Edwards and Ed Strobel tromped down the gangway to greet us. I had met both of them before but only briefly. Jim had called me at home several times and brought me up to date on some of the problems at the ship and the lack of fundamental progress, always pleading for me to come early. They shook my hand and Dan's and said, "Welcome to Souda!" Then they grabbed my bags and we started the process of getting our feet on the ladder and climbing aboard.

The ship did not have lettering for LST 325 on the bow or stern, but L-144, the Greek number. They also had given L-144 the name *Syros*. Dan explained, "All Greek ships are named after a Greek Island." A name was something our Navy had not given to LSTs in WW II - only numbers. In 1955, LSTs were given names after state counties and then only the Navy Landing Ship Tanks in active military service at that time.

The LST 325 did not receive an American name since it was not in active military service to the Navy at the time, but served in the Sea Transport Service (sort of an ocean-going Army Corps of Engineers). The 325 was reactivated in 1951 and labored putting up early warning radar units in Iceland, Greenland, and Northern Canada, and serviced these installations for ten years. It was placed out of service one more time in 1961, then in 1964 reactivated again for the third time and loaned to the Greek Navy. The Hellenic Navy used the 325 for thirty-five years until the spring of 1999 when it was again placed out of service for its third and (they all thought) final time!

In the fall of 1999, it became the property of a non-profit corporation the USS LST SHIP MEMORIAL, INC., by an act of Congress.

As I stepped on the gangway, the loose bottom gave me a very unsteady feeling. As I started to climb up, the cable handrails were loose and they gave way some when I tried to steady myself. I yelled back, "Dan be careful, this is not very rigid!"

Half way aboard, my thoughts shifted back in time to San Diego, back to when I was on active duty and a little younger! Back to that fateful day when I first saw my second duty ship, the Hickman County, LST 825. *I was driving a Navy Jeep along the pier in the area where the Navy Base kept the mothballed fleet. A fellow officer and I were on a mission to find a part for our ship on one of the LSTs entombed there. We were enjoying the warm sunshine of Southern California. It was early March 1963, and the 825 had been withdrawn a few days earlier from being mothballed and like the 325, was to be reactivated. Five months after the Cuban Missile Crisis there was a threat from Fidel Castro not to remove the missiles installed on his island country. The U.S. was going to invade Cuba and remove them and in order to do this the LSTs again were needed.*

LST 825 had rust, lots of rust; dull faded haze-gray paint was peeling in big chunks off its sides and superstructure. It had about a 3-degree list to port. I remember saying to Ensign John R. Smith, riding shotgun next to me, "I really feel sorry for anyone who pulls duty on that thing!" He agreed completely!

That very night the ship's radioman came into the wardroom where I stood my duty officer watch proclaiming, "Sir, your orders are here!" Then he added, "Sir, they really are!" My orders to report aboard as Engineering Officer on <u>LST 825</u> *had just come in from Naval Headquarters!*

The LST 325 did not have the list that the 825 had, but otherwise, it was almost identical in appearance. The quote often used in the Navy, 'Haze Gray and Underway' came to mind. I prayed at that moment, please God let it be so, let us get this ship running. On deck, several other crewmembers came over and Jim Edwards was eager to tell them who I was – the XO, Mr. Jornlin. I greeted and shook hands with these crewmembers and introduced them all to the First Secretary.

Evidently, Edwards had told them to wait and hold on until I arrived and I would magically straighten out the problems. One man was the ship's Chief Boatswain, 'Boats' for short. I had met him earlier. Bruce Voges lived in Oakwood, Illinois. He was a U.S. Navy man with twenty-one years of experience. He had served on several different ships starting late in WWII on an LST. As a matter of fact, he had been on the first LST that beached at Iwo Jima in February of 1945. His ship, he said, gave the Marines the big ceremonial flag that became famous in the picture by the Associated Press photographer, Rosenthal, of the flag being raised on Mt. Suribachi. Boats, of course, had a vast knowledge with all his naval experience and I bounced many decisions off him for his opinion. He worked hard painting the deck and sides, and did most of our proper navy protocol. Boats could pipe dignitaries and high-ranking Officers aboard and off the ship. His knowledge of ships and his uncanny ability to motivate his men to work and get things accomplished without really raising his voice, amazed me. He preferred Destroyer duty and always bragged about how squared away the crews were on Destroyers.

I stopped and looked the ship over from the main deck, then noticed a faded white painted helicopter landing square about amidships in the center of the deck with L-144 printed on the aft end, about fifteen feet square, not round like the US Navy landing circles. This ship looked just like all of the LSTs that I had been aboard; plainly painted in one light haze gray for the sides and superstructure, a much darker deck gray for the main deck. One small difference jumped out at me, a very visible 'sunburst' about fourteen by fourteen inches. With a bright blue background, the yellow round sun had fire-like streaks radiating from it. This painting appeared conspicuous on the forward gun director. Edwards noticed my stare and quickly explained, "That is a Greek good luck symbol that dates back to *Alexander the Great*, and if we take it off or paint over it, the ship will sink according to the Greeks!"

I quickly replied, "Let's not take it off!"

Edwards also told me the Greeks called their ships a HE not a SHE as we do. He also said the Greeks believed a ship has a SOUL; it was alive. They never cut their ships up or in essence, kill them. Tied outboard of the 325, Edwards told me, nestled our parts ship the *Kriti L171*. We could get parts from it to fix the 325 as needed. Smiling to myself, I wondered if the Greeks thought the 325 might need repairs! The parts ship's state and appearance looked about the same as the 325's. I followed Edwards into 'Officer's Country,' and I thought to my stateroom, the XO's room on the starboard side of the ship. The 325's interior was not a whole lot better in appearance, but it looked clean.

Mr. O'Grady decided his job was over for now and he needed to catch his plane back to Athens. He shook my hand, whispered to me, "Good-bye and good luck," and then added, "I believe you are going to need a lot of it!"

Smiling, I quickly told him, "Hey Dan, on your way back to your plane, stop at the bookie joint and put some money on us Americans! We are going to get this ship away from the pier! You can bank on it!"

Again, he just smiled. He gave me a cell phone that would work in Greece and his number. He asked to be kept informed on our progress or if I needed something. At this point in time, I liked him. He seemed to be generally interested in helping and seemed to be on our side. This was something refreshing, since the State Department had not been so inclined in this venture so far.

CWO Jack Melcher came out of the Captain's cabin. He mumbled, "Well you finally made it. Get yourself settled and I will show you the ship."

The CWO, dressed in Navy khakis looked thinner and older to me, and tired. He was unshaved and sported a short stubble of whiskers.

I answered him by saying, "That would be fine. I want to see all of the ship and the progress you have made in getting it to run!"

Jim Edwards, from the big Texas town of Canton east of Dallas, had worked and retired from a Texas phone company, and lived on a small farm he owned with his wife, Doris. If anyone wanted to take his picture, he always said, "Don't take my picture, I'm wanted in Texas!" I asked what he meant by that and he replied, "My wife, Doris, wants me back home!" He had conveyed to me on his several phone calls that I was going to have my work cut out for me, and they needed me to take over the running of the ship. It was never my ambition nor even in my thoughts to take over.

Yesterday, Ambassador Burns had told me the same thing, "You must replace him."

Today the Captain of the Naval Base had made it quite plain, "Melcher must go!"

In 1990, I had gone to Taiwan with Melcher looking for an LST. A Taiwan Navy Admiral was going to give an LST to the town of Seneca, located on the Illinois River, close to my home. The small town of Seneca built one hundred fifty-seven LSTs in WW II. I had spent almost twelve days with Melcher in San Diego and then Taiwan. He and I thoroughly and painstakingly went through the LST 859 from top to bottom, moored in a boneyard at the Chinese Naval Base at Kaohsiung. We both decided it would never run or make it back to the U.S.

I also went with him and a reenactment group up the Alcan Highway in 1992 driving WWII vehicles; this trip commemorated fifty years of the building of that highway. Melcher had asked me to drive one of his WWII army trucks. I had gotten along with him pretty well for now on ten full years. I hoped to convince him to let me handle the men, and for him to concentrate on the ship making it operational, so we could head for home. From all he had said about himself, he was a good mechanic. My six weeks I had told the wife I would be gone, were ticking away.

Jack Carter, acting XO for the past month, came up the passageway from the galley, shook my hand, introduced himself, and said, "Welcome aboard." Jack, I learned as time went on, was one of the best men on the crew. I had not met him or talked to him before. He was a Korean War veteran and had made full Commander in the Reserves after that war. He had served as Senior Watch Officer on his LST in 1951-53. He had many miles of sailing under his belt. He was a HAM radio operator, and could send e-mails and get weather reports through a special overseas radio operator in Florida.

Carter was dressed in light blue striped faded coveralls, and had a beat up, washed-out baseball cap on his head. He had a full, partially gray beard. If it were not for the officer's emblem on the front of his hat, I would not have guessed he was an officer and especially not a full Commander. He was a thin man about six feet two inches tall, had a smile and friendly eyes. He and I were the only true naval officers on board the 325. I did not know at the time he was a Commander and outranked me if we were in the Navy.

I had no knowledge of Carter, because he was from the Los Angeles, California area, a long distance from most of the crew, including me. I do not recall seeing him at any of the LST conventions either, but with a crew of seventy-two signed up and maybe forty or so at a convention plus four hundred others, I could have missed this seemingly quiet man. After our short conversation, he mentioned, "I suppose you would like my cabin? I am in the XO's cabin."

I nodded my head yes, while saying, "I certainly would."

I had occupied that stateroom as the engineering officer on the LST 825, even though on most all LSTs the Executive Officer made it his stateroom. It was the largest stateroom, actually somewhat larger than the Captain's, but did not have the Captain's private bath!

He unhappily responded, "Sir, I will move my things into the next stateroom before you unpack your stuff."

I quickly answered him, "Thank you Jack." Jack Carter and I were soon to become the best of friends, and I relied heavily on his expertise, especially with radios. I let him formulate and send out all of the daily postings to the ship's web page. I regretted that only a couple of times! I am not exactly sure how, but he made friends easily with the Greek sailors and shipyard workers and could persuade them to do most anything. This was very important in making the 'T' run. He had an easygoing demeanor, learned to say good morning in Greek, and with his unkempt look, the Greeks liked him. He was somewhat like them. For the most part the crew liked Jack also and respected him.

As promised, CWO Melcher gave me a tour of the ship. Mr. Carter tagged along. We started forward on the main deck, went down through the port doghouse one deck into the bow machinery room. From there we maneuvered aft through the port side troop berthing going around and over the troop bunks, then down to visit the auxiliary and main engine rooms, both shaft alleys. To reach all of these spaces one must take a twenty foot ladder straight down to access them and needed to keep his hands on the sides of the ladders to avoid the grease and dirt on the rungs deposited there from the engineer's shoes as they climbed out. Melcher lead us back to aft steering, and up and out through the Galley past the three thousand pound stern anchor that helped pull the ship off the beach and up to the 01 level, alongside the 40mm guns, into the wheelhouse, and aft to the radio room. Then we climbed up the steep two ladders to the 03 level and CONN located at the very top of the ship. *CONN* is short for Conning Tower.

The CONN is a space about seven by eight feet where the officers controlled all operations during periods the ship was underway. It held the radar and gyro repeater along the starboard side. A flat shelf extended across the front about two feet deep that could hold the navigational charts. Under the shelf the rudder angle indicator was located and the Greek engine order telegraph peeked out, plus the marine radio. A three inch brass voice tube that ends in the wheelhouse below went through the shelf; the Officers used this tube to order steering commands to the men in the wheelhouse. The CONN had great visibility forward and to the sides (there were windows all around) and was forty-six feet above the water. This space had one chair – the captain's chair. In the US Navy no one but the Captain was allowed to sit down period, and never let him catch you in his chair!

Oh, yes! Melcher showed me the 'spy shack,' a space eight by twelve feet, located right aft of the CONN. It was NOT a standard compartment on any LST. The 325, I believe, could have been a listening ship or *spy ship* with this extra radio room and the many radio antennas placed everywhere on the ship - some quite tall. This ship may have picked up radio transmissions from the Russians through their ships at sea and who knows from where else. Could *'Radio Free Europe'* have broadcast from this very ship? Who knows! The spy shack was a real detriment to navigating the ship because it gave the OOD (Officer of the Deck) a large blind spot aft from the CONN. The OOD could not see anything aft, especially traffic that might be close in or overtaking the ship when we sail! One could see behind by going to either side on the outboard wings.

CWO Melcher had declared, "The ship was 80% ready to sail! We will sail in six days after the remainder of crew arrives." He had told me this about a week before I came aboard.

The balance of the crew was some thirty-four men out of the original seventy-two. Eleven had cancelled out! I had spread the word to those standing by to sail her home. Out of these men, I was only able to convince twenty-four to *'Come Sail with Me!'* A couple had serious health problems, so I talked them out of going. Eight refused to go since they believed the crewmembers who had left the ship and came home, saying, "The ship will never sail; don't waste your money."

Melcher had been instrumental in keeping the project alive since 1990. He had picked the crew, made out a sailing plan, made up study guides to refresh the crew on the ship operations, seamanship, and engineering. He gave tests on these subjects, and tests on emergency procedures of fire fighting, man overboard, abandon ship, and others. He had made several trips to Greece looking at LSTs. He also helped push the LST Congressional Bill until it passed through Congress and President Clinton signed it giving the LST 325 to the Memorial. This process took four years! He had spent his own money and put in countless hours working to get to this day – the day when we finally had an LST and a crew to sail her home. Now having toured the ship and talked to Edwards and Carter, I learned little had been accomplished over the past six weeks, except maybe loss of crew! I started to believe the Bookies that we would not get this ship running.

I looked around the ship a bit more, and then moved into my cabin after Carter removed his things. I had missed my coffee, breakfast and lunch, so I joined Don Chapman, our Chief Electrician, and some of the crew heading uptown for dinner. Don and I talked as we walked the long road up to Nick's Restaurant. Don brought me up on some of the happenings and conditions of the ship. Several of the crew had to stop and rest along the way, both going and coming back.

I had no idea what to order. One of the crew said try the Iowa pork chop. An Iowa pork chop in Greece? I tried it, and never tasted a better one - nice, thick, and juicy. I also tried a couple of cold glasses of Greek draft beer in a frosted mug, as did most of the crew. Need I say more? We sat at tables outside on the sidewalk because the restaurant and stores did not have air conditioning. The crew took up all of Nick's tables out front. One could see almost the whole town and everyone who walked in the street. I imagine the crew was a curiosity and topic of conversation the first week or so sitting there three times a day, every day. I had spent the whole month of August at home worrying about the ship and crew. I had received several calls from the few crewmembers I had met before they left for Greece. One of the main concerns was they wanted meals prepared on the ship since they had paid Mr. Edwards $1600 to cover their share of the fuel and food costs for the trip and $600 for the slop fund.

In answer to their requests, I had called Chief Warrant Officer Melcher from home and explained that some of the men were short of money. A few of the crew started to run out of money since their instructions in what to bring only suggested a couple hundred dollars for extra spending money. Then they found out they were spending six or seven dollars three times a day, with no end in sight. I asked why he was not serving food. Melcher explained, "I want the Greeks to feel sorry for us so they will give back the items they took off the ship. They have removed all of the silverware, plates, and kitchen utensils."

"The crew has pre-paid for food," I told him. "You have a cook, so why not have the cook buy some paper plates, plastic forks and knives for now, and feed these guys? How much time in man-hours are you wasting while they walk up town and back three times a day?"

Eventually two meals were prepared and served daily; breakfast at 0700 followed by lunch at 1300 hours.

It cooled off at night, but it took until midnight to make that happen with all portholes and hatches opened and one of the tank exhaust blowers turned on. The blower moved air like a fast moving train and helped immensely to lower the temperature in the ship. The tank blowers on LSTs were used to remove the carbon monoxide from the tank deck produced from the Sherman tanks exhausts when the army started and warmed them up before a landing. The blowers were to have another purpose soon.

THIS DAY DID NOT MAKE ME LOOK FORWARD TO THE NEXT!

CHAPTER 4

ONE PERCENT READY TO SAIL

FIRST FULL DAY ABOARD

0800 QUARTERS

Reveille was at 0600 and breakfast for the crew at 0700. As I joined the men in the line going through the galley, I met our cook, Joe Sadlier, from Ketchikan, Alaska. He joked with the men. This morning he picked on Ed Strobel for not keeping up in the line. A few of the crew gave it right back to him - his coffee, they complained, was way too strong, and he was out of sugar! Cookie's menu this morning was pancakes and bacon, my favorite breakfast! He introduced himself first, and then shouted from the back of the stove, "Welcome to my Galley! Thank you for that nice big luggage carrier you brought me, a Cadillac!" I was asked to bring a heavy luggage carrier by Edwards, since Cookie didn't have a good one to haul back groceries from the local market.

Someone yelled back, "Sadlier, your pancakes are a little lumpy this morning."

He answered, "Says who? You know I had a girlfriend like that once!" I learned Cookie didn't have a serious bone in his body.

"Now Hear This: Quarters, Quarters on the main deck."
Then, "First call, first call to Colors." Five minutes later. . .
"Colors, - all hands, attention, attention to Colors."

The crew formed up on the port side, amidships, in three rows - ten in the front, and twelve and fourteen, in the back two rows. They stood at attention and the bugle, through the public-address system, played Colors while our flag was raised. About the same time, the Greeks raised their flag. We all stood at attention while the Greek Headquarters high up on the hill raised their flag on that ship's mast. The LST 325 also flew *John Paul Jones's* flag (with the snake and the words '*Don't Tread on Me*') on the Jack Staff up on the bow. In the Navy, only the oldest commissioned ship could display the Jones flag (the *USS CONSTITUTION)*. After 9/11, all Navy ships could. The crew thought the LST 325 was old enough to qualify. The Jack staff flag had only flown when moored in port or the ship was at anchor.

Mr. Carter and I stood in front facing the crew. At this time, we had thirty-seven crewmembers on board the ship. Only fifty-one of the original seventy-two that signed up volunteering to be crew, made the trip all the way to Souda. In the last five weeks, we had lost eighteen; three were from my group that arrived two days ago! We were inching towards the danger of not having enough crew to sail the ship. I knew this could not continue. Carter and Edwards informed me last night at dinner there were now an additional six crewmembers packing their bags, checking the airlines, and making ready to take the Ferry back to Athens. They all had enough of waiting around, saw no progress, and made their minds up that the ship would never sail. They believed it was a waste of their time and money to stay.

My first speech as XO was short. I simply introduced myself and told them, "There will be some changes made fast. I hope all of you will give me a day or two to accomplish a complete change of direction. I only know a few of your problems from your side, and nothing from Melcher's side or why he has moved slowly on starting the engines and making other repairs. We need every one of you to accomplish refurbishing this great fifty-eight year-old ship to running condition, and every last one of you is important, especially if we sail. No, when we sail!" I asked, "Does anyone have a question? Please make the questions easy!" I tried to get a laugh but failed. No one had any questions and I was glad of that. The entire crew remained silent looking at Carter and me. I am sure they all hoped for change and that I would do what I said. "So let's get to work; you are all DISMISSED."

Having missed yesterday's quarters, I knew I had my job cut out for me today. They told me CWO Melcher had given the men quite a speech. After the lecture Mr. Peltier, billeted as Deck Officer and new on board, went below, packed his bags, and with two other friends in tow left the ship. They headed back home; Peltier forgot his passport and his blue blazer in his haste!

Melcher's speech was delivered to the whole crew, but I assume aimed at the twenty-four new arrivals; it must have been demoralizing, intimidating, and frightening. I wished someone had recorded it so I knew exactly what had been said. Jim Edwards told me he had tried several times to talk to Melcher about his unusual treatment of the men, the Greeks, and our Navy, but got nowhere. CWO Melcher had told me once that Engineers (he considered himself as one) were not big on tact, diplomacy, or sensitivity.

A few of the crew with a little more nerve than most had bought a palm tree and placed it on the 01 level. At quarters, they presented the CWO with a couple of big roller bearings for him to roll together in the palm of his hand just as *Captain Queeg,* from the 1954 movie, *The Cain Mutiny,* did under pressure or when chastising his men. Melcher, not having a clue, thought it actually funny; the crew just grit their teeth!

The ship's storekeeper, Don Molzahn, from La Crosse, Wisconsin, and our only Coast Guard crewmember, did not have to handle money. He just had to keep track of who bought what. The charges for items were subtracted individually from the $600 each man paid for incidentals from the ship's store. Melcher had promised some of the men the return of their money, or stock certificates in the ship, their choice, when and if the ship reached the United States. Non-profit corporations cannot issue stock. I wondered where he was going to get money to pay everyone back.

On my tour of the ship, I saw easily quite a few things that needed to be fixed, cleaned, and checked. I decided to hold a meeting of key people to bring me up to date as to the ship's status. Included in this meeting were Jack Carter, Don Chapman, Boats, and Jim Edwards. I painfully learned that the main engines had not been run to date or even turned over, let alone started! There were no batteries, diesel fuel or lube oil on board to start and operate anything! Not one of the three generators had been started so they could be checked to see if they would produce electricity! Only one of the two fire and flushing pumps worked.

The stern tubes I had observed on the tour leaked water, and I noticed the packing bolts all turned in tight on the flanges against the stops, making it necessary to repack these tubes. This would involve divers to plug the shafts back by the propellers behind the cutlass bearings. These shafts were nine feet below the surface of the water.

The ten ring bearings that carried the main drive shafts to the stern tubes and on to the propellers were full of water. I learned both shaft alleys port and starboard had salt water above the bearings when the crew came aboard. Pumping out this water contaminated with the oil from the bearings was one of the few major jobs done before I arrived. To make sure the bearings have oil in them free from water, they needed to be flushed out thoroughly with clean oil first, then the bearings refilled with oil to the right depth on the oil dipsticks. The crew had removed most of the bilge oil and water from the main and auxiliary engine rooms.

On the 01 level, the two motor-generators, (a DC motor driving an AC generator) which produced the ship's AC electricity for the radar, rudder angle indicators, and radios, were both basket cases – wiring was pulled out of the regulating panels. This ship ran on DC, but needed the motor generators for AC current. The Radar didn't work nor the Gyro according to Carter. I wondered if anything was operational!

Jim Edwards stated the oil texture in the engines looked similar to road tar. Evidently, over the last several years, they never changed the oil, just added new oil. Chapman said, "It appeared they drained the used oil right into the bilges."

We needed to check the steering system. The main reefers (refrigerators) needed to be test operated to pull the boxes down to their proper temperatures. How would we keep food for a forty day trip for thirty-five men if the big reefers did not work? We had no quantity of food on board except for a day or two as Cookie went to the store as needed hauling what he could on my luggage carrier. No food was stored or even a menu planned for the amounts and kinds of food needed for the trip. I finally had to ask them, "What have you guys been doing over here for the past six weeks?" I jokingly asked, " Do we have any cold beer aboard?"

Edwards immediately answered, "Yes!"

Bruce Voges piped in with, "We will need more!"

To continue this nightmare, I learned the anti-aircraft guns had not been demilitarized which was necessary to come out of international waters into the U.S. waters. No paperwork signed or produced, transferring the ship to us from the Greeks. The magnetic compasses were missing, also necessary to sail, and no LCVPs on board, our four landing boats that were to go with the ship. Had anyone tested the anchor or the running lights? The bow doors were open and the ramp was down. I wondered if we would be able to close them. The ship was about 1% ready to sail, nowhere close to the 80% Melcher said. This advisory meeting added more pressure to that already placed on me by the US Navy and US State Department.

The Galley didn't have utensils or pots or pans, most removed by the Greeks. The P500 pumps and P250 pumps for emergency fire fighting and pumping flood water were unaccounted for. All blankets, bunk bottoms, brooms, painting equipment, all of the hand tools, and many other things too numerous to mention here, were broken or gone astray.

Edwards informed me the port engine starter was broken and needed replacing. We had a spare starboard starter but no port spare. Carter explained, "Since the starboard engine turned clockwise and the port engine turned counter-clockwise, the spare starter would not work." That much I knew from my previous experience with the Hickman County.

Chapman joined in with, "Both starter controllers for the main engines were worn out. The carbon contacts actually had no carbon left on them, just bare metal." There were no life rafts or a sufficient number of Coast Guard approved life jackets on board; actually only a few non-CG approved Greek life jackets were there, according to Boats. All of the CO_2 Bottles were empty and most needed to be pressure tested - a big cost. No one would fill them until given a new test. I looked at several bottles; did not find any in compliance.

Ordered by Melcher in early August, Cookie went up to the Greek Headquarters and asked for permission to go to their warehouse and retrieve the ship's galley equipment. A Greek Officer took him out to the city dump and advised him, "You can have anything out here, help yourself!" Joe told me that he was very disturbed with the Greek Navy and very insulted by them dragging him to a city dump. I never learned what Greek Officer took him out there, but this was an indication of the poor relationship we now had with the Greek Navy. I knew we needed their help. I had to fix this relationship.

My Boatswain mate then added in all of his wisdom, "You should also know Boss, you do not have a pier or even a port to sail this ship to!"

I cried, "You have to be kidding me!"

"No, I am not. The original owner of the pier Melcher had lined up in Lake Pontchartrain for the LST, sold it and no one bothered to talk to him for five years. The present new owner says the depth of water at this pier is only about five feet deep; besides, he was using it!" The ship needs at least 10 feet of water to dock.

To add a little more pressure, I received a call from the Command Master Chief at the Navy Base telling me he was bringing twelve or fifteen sailors over Saturday to work on the ship.

After my heart by-pass in 1995, my Cardiologist advised me to stay away from stress and pressure! Well, so much for that advice!

I asked Carter, "Do we have an ABANDON SHIP BILL to get off this ship?"

Jack said, "We do, but you can't use it!"

I HAD FEW OPTIONS AND LITTLE CHOICE.

CHAPTER 5

HOW DID I GET INTO THIS MESS?

My first thought of this venture, and very little thought at that, I believed to be something doable. First, I thought it would be fun and one great experience! After all, I was not to be in charge, just help sail her back. Secondly, this hero ship was supposed to be ready to sail when the last group of crew climbed aboard, and third, we were to have a port and a pier to go to!

When I graduated with a major in Geology and a minor in Math and Chemistry from Monmouth College, Monmouth, IL in May of 1961, I immediately became number six on the draft list for LaSalle County, my home county. According to the Draft Board, a male, age 22, healthy and single, would be drafted in October or November. I could volunteer for the Navy and enter into the Navy Officers Candidate School or dig ditches in the army for two years! If I graduated from OCS, I would have seven years in the US Navy – three years, four months active duty and then four years in the reserves, and as they promised, I would see the world.

I had little choice for my immediate future. I delayed my plans to expand my father's farming operation, joined the US Navy, and in November entered their prestigious OCS program. I was not behind the plow, but in the Navy now! I went to college to see what the other ninety-eight percent of the world had to offer! I asked myself would I now see the other two percent.

In April of 1962 I graduated as an Ensign in the US Navy, and sent to beautiful and picturesque, San Francisco, 'The City by the Bay!' I was to have three more months of schooling and training on Treasure Island, in the Bay, right next to Alcatraz. On completion, I received my orders to report to the *USS Jerome County, LST 848*, home ported in San Diego, billeted as their Damage Control Officer. I flew to Hawaii, hitchhiked on a navy jeep to Pearl Harbor, and climbed aboard my LST which was to be my home, I thought, for the next three years.

The ship's schedule called for the 848 to be in Oahu for another week. I had dreams of a whole week in Hawaii, just one of the places this country boy hoped to visit some day! After reporting aboard the *Jerome County*, I learned it was leaving in the morning for San Diego! I could have one night to go on liberty in Waikiki Beach!

I and three other Officers made the most of that one night! About 0830 the next morning, my roommate shook me awake and informed me that I had missed Quarters, the ship was underway and out past the breakwater of Pearl Harbor, and also the Captain wanted to meet his new officer if I could work it into my schedule.

Instead of three years, I only served seven months on the LST 848; I received orders to transfer to the Hickman County (LST 825). The navy brought out ten LSTs from mothballs in several shipyards. I was to report aboard and be the Engineering Officer and be part of the re-commissioning crew. This was rather a big promotion to go from DC Officer, past Assistant Engineering Officer directly to the top spot as Chief Engineer! My Captain said he could pull some strings and keep me on the *Jerome* if I wanted him to. I turned him down, instead looking forward to the challenge.

The *Hickman* departed in early June 1963, sailed south, then through the Panama Canal and east across the Gulf of Mexico. (I found out the Panama Canal does not run west to east). We had our share of engineering problems that trip which quickly forced me to learn about the mechanics of LSTs. Part of our orders were to pick up a Sherman tank the Marines ran into the Gulf at Guantanamo Bay, since we were sailing right by anyway. The tank needed cleaning and the salt water removed.

After my experience with the Hickman County, getting another LST from the 'bone yard' of a foreign country and sailing it home didn't seem impossible, in fact very feasible! How wrong can one man be? My change in duty to help place an LST back in commission in 1963 was valued as the one single accomplishment that propelled me upward as an expert in ship reactivation - long forgotten by me! This sole act in all of my sixty-one years placed me in this very predicament in Souda. I had no idea agreeing to help bring an LST back home would alter my current life forever, take me out of my comfort zone and into a complicated and stressful 'hell hole,' but here I was.

To put this undertaking in perspective, think about going to a foreign country, in this case Greece, and physically pull an old 1942 Chevrolet automobile out of the junk yard. Pump up the tires, but use the old ones; fill the gas tank, put in new spark plugs, water in the radiator, and a new battery. Your brother-in-law had used this car for the past thirty-five years. He thought it too expensive to fix, and in addition, too old, so he hauled it to the junk yard. One washed off most of the dirt, pushed on the starter button - it started! With a quick turn around the block, the brakes sort of worked, then one headed out for home across a desert (ocean in this case - can't drink the water). Home was six thousand four hundred miles of rocky road. To make it more interesting, winter has set in because of forced delays by the government in issuing a license. By the way, your driver just turned seventy-two years old. Really, how feasible will this be? Think about it! I did!

My friends generally were divided on this project. About sixty percent thought I was stark raving mad and declared, "You old guys will never, ever do it. It can't be done!" The rest thought it would be one heck of an adventure and they wished their wives would let them go!

One of my friends, who came for coffee somewhat frequently in the morning to my farm, simply told my wife after I had left, "He should be home farming!" I thought bringing back an LST was important. I agreed with Jim Edwards when he said, "It was something to do, something to accomplish, and it will be my last hurrah!"

The original plan was to sail the ship around June 1st stopping in Athens, Gibraltar, Rota, Spain, Normandy, France, and Portsmouth, England. Then we would sail it across the Atlantic to Boston. If time allowed, we would travel from Boston up to the Saint Lawrence Seaway, then down to Buffalo, NY. (This was where the US LST Association was having their convention in the middle of September of

2000). This would have fit into my farming schedule very well as planting should be over before I left, the CO-OP Elevator could put on chemicals for weed and insect control, and I would easily be back in plenty of time to harvest my corn and beans. I was never planning on going to Buffalo!

Actually, if the first congressional LST Bill had gone through (1997) we could have participated in the making of the movie *Private Ryan.* They asked the Memorial if they would consider that possibility; of course we considered it. Not only would this have paid our bills, the LST would have received a ton of advertising. How grand would that have been to be in a movie with Tom Hanks? How great for the LST 325 to land on Normandy and unload troops and Sherman Tanks some 56 years later. Just imagine it!

Back to reality now, I set out to find each of the six men who planned to leave and talk them into staying. I knew their concerns and asked them individually to stay aboard. I also told each one I needed his help. Each of them agreed to my requests and said they would stay a little longer, but warned me that if things did not improve, they would be gone. Under my breath, I thought I would probably be with them on the plane.

The temperature soared to about 100° and that was in the shade, not on the steel deck. The crew all had water with them as they were told to keep drinking fluids. One of the men, Dewey Taylor, a 'deck ape' and Boats' right hand man, told me that he hadn't gone to the bathroom all day even though he had drank several gallons of water. He guessed he perspired so much there was nothing left. His shirt was wet, his pants were wet, even his socks and his shoes were soaked. Dewey is married to a woman by the name of Elizabeth, so he alleged he married Liz Taylor.

I told Dewey back when I was on active duty, Les Boyer (from OCS and now in the same Navy School) and I were watching TV when the actress Liz Taylor came on. He jabbed me with his arm saying, "I am going to marry her."

I replied, "You must be joking."

He said, "No, the way she is going through men, she will have to get to me some day!"

Dewey had served on a 'Flag' LST (a ship that carries the Admiral) that was the first ship to beach on Leyte in WWII. The beach was not secured as they had thought and several Japanese mortars took aim. This mortar fire hit the forward 40mm gun, one of the 20 mm and hit the CONN killing the XO. Dewey was on the other forward 20mm trying to neutralize the mortars. Navy planes were called in and were successful in eliminating the mortars.

I ran into Boats Voges. I told him about the US Navy volunteers from the base coming on board in the morning. I asked him if he could line up some work for them. He smiled as he spoke, "That will be easy." I also talked to Carter, Edwards, and Chapman to find out things the Navy crew could work on. Then I gave Cookie a heads up about lunch for an additional fifteen, and he would take care of it.

The time had come to talk to CWO Melcher and work things out; we needed an understanding. It had been weighing on my nerves long enough. I found him in his stateroom sitting at the desk. He asked me to sit down on the couch and started in with some small talk mostly about how they arrived picking the LST 325 out of six other LSTs. I changed the subject and got down to the lack of progress and the departure of crew.

I started out by telling him we needed to change gears and it was imperative to allow me to take charge over the crew, the Navy, the Greeks and do the talking with the State Dept. I emphasized, "Your reason for me being your XO was simply because I can get along with people and honestly, because you can't!"

Energized, I continued, "Jack, you have been here for over six weeks and have very little accomplished. Your crew is leaving because there's no substantial progress. It is impossible to make a foreign country or its people for that matter feel sorry for Americans! You can lose this crew and starve to death before they will feel sorry for any of us."

Jack's response was a dissertation about not trusting the State Department or our Navy. Then he stated he had received a warning the State Department had sent a man here to take over this project! I just countered with my best argument to prove that man was not me, "I have not received any checks from the government!" I tried to reason with him that we have to treat everyone with respect and be courteous, particularly the Greeks. He knew we required a sizeable amount of help to get the ship's equipment running, like the AC converters, radar, and gyro to name a few.

I was surprised when Melcher finally agreed to try it my way, but said factually it would not work.

I turned and left saying to him, "You should go down below and get the main engines running. Chief, please lay off the crew, the two of us cannot sail this ship back to the USA alone. This crew did not sign on for this project for it to last the rest of their lives, nor did I. For one, I signed on to bring her home in six weeks and a couple more days if necessary."

The rest of that day went smoothly; several of the men worked on the countless jobs that needed done. Several checked running lights, the anchor windless, some on the #2 fire and flushing pump. They were not doing anything that would make the ship sail, except for one younger crewmember who worked for the railroad. Edward Whitman could not have been more than thirty or thirty-five years old. He had confided in me that the railroad had threatened to fire him, and he already had lost his girlfriend. He claimed he had run out of money also, so a few of us were giving him money to buy dinner at night. He was reported to be a good engineman and important as a young crewmember keeping our average age down to look good for the Navy and our State Department. Whitman had found about thirty-five hundred to forty-five hundred gallons of diesel fuel located in a fuel tank in the belly of the *Kriti,* our parts ship. Don Chapman and Edwards had gone over on the *Kriti* to help figure out how to transfer the diesel fuel from that ship into the LST 325's fuel tanks.

Chapman and Edwards devised a plan. They would drop one end of the parts ship's shore power cable, a large rubber electric cord about two hundred feet long and three inches in diameter, down the engine room's escape trunk, and hook it up to that ship's fuel transfer pump; the other end made fast to the power supply connections on the 325. Whitman was to climb into the diesel tank, a centerline tank immediately below the tank deck just forward of the Auxiliary Engine room. He took a roll of duct tape in his back pocket and, with a large blower blasting air into the tank, down the inspection ladder into the tank he went. Ed walked, stepping on the ballast pipes, drainpipes, and other fuel lines over to the suction pipe with the hole.

Lying on his belly on top of a ballast pipe, he put several turns of tape around the rusted hole in the two-inch suction line. The Greeks evidently thought they had pumped that diesel out. However, when the level of the fuel got as low as the hole in the suction line, it quit pumping because it sucked air. The Greeks had not checked to see if there was any diesel left, maybe thinking the tank was empty or as empty as it was going to get. Ed had gone over and sounded the fuel tanks in the hope of finding fuel, and to his surprise, he did! Ed's problem was how to retrieve it. Jim Bartlett, one of our talented enginemen, knew a lot about the fuel systems. He hooked a fuel hose from the parts ship's transfer connection on the main deck to one of our diesel tank fill pipes located on our main deck and was ready for fuel. He signaled Don Chapman who pushed the start button on the fuel transfer pump. Much to our surprise, fuel gurgled out and transferred into the LST 325. The tank we pumped out of had about twelve inches of diesel. This large fuel tank's capacity is fifty-five thousand gallons of diesel when full. This figures out somewhere around four hundred seventy gallons to the inch. The suction line has an air gap of two-inches so one does not pump water, rust or dirt from the bottom of the tank. I watched this operation very closely. We needed to get some diesel so we could run the engines and maybe go on a sea trial someday. I figured when the pump sucked air again, we had retrieved about four thousand gallons of high priced diesel.

One job the men needed to accomplish was retrieve a sizable number of mattresses off the parts ship and bring them back aboard the LST 325. The crew had taken these forty spotted and dirty mattresses over to the parts ship earlier. On learning what they had done, Melcher ordered them to haul the mattresses back to the 325! He wanted those mattresses to host Boy Scouts and other groups staying overnight for a fee, after arrival back to the USA. I would never want to sleep on any of those filthy mattresses.

THE US NAVY IS COMING, GANGWAY!

CHAPTER 6

A MUTINY OF SORTS

The Command Master Chief (CMC) Rabb, from the US Navy base on Souda called at 0730 reminding me he was bringing fifteen sailors aboard that morning; they would be happy to do some of the heavy work or whatever we needed done. I should line up some jobs for them since he wanted his sailors to be kept busy. We had numerous heavy lifting jobs to do and I knew we could use a day with strong young Navy men. The younger navy men and women liked to hear the crew's *War Stories!* Well maybe the term 'Sea Story' was more appropriate, but they enjoyed coming on the ship.

The morning was sunny - just like the last several days. It was now September 2nd and I was looking for a little cooler temperature. Breakfast this morning was eggs to order, bacon, toast, and different kinds of dry cereal. Cookie always had fruit - apples and plenty of bananas. Bananas were full of potassium and helped in preventing a 'Charlie Horse' or cramps in the legs. After climbing up and down ladders all day, the men were prone to leg cramps at night. Cookie, with his continued humor, was doing a marvelous job of cooking except I thought his coffee, just like in the Navy, was a little too strong. I quickly learned in the Navy one does not criticize the cook if one wants to continue to eat well. Cookie was certainly no exception to that rule!

The navy arrived at 0830 and I gave the CMC a list of jobs we needed accomplished. He sent several men over to the parts ship. After some serious grunting, pushing, and a few choice words, they managed to move the large stainless two-door reefer (refrigerator) out of the chief's quarters located on the starboard side forward. Fortunately, they only had to go forward one compartment, make a one hundred-eighty degree turn, and maneuver up one level to reach the main deck of the parts ship. The ladder (stairway) was steep and narrow.

Our ship's crew had obtained another stainless steel refrigerator out of somewhere on the LST 325, most likely from our Chief's Quarters. This one had poor fitting doors, but worked. The parts ship reefer had good doors but was out of Freon. The Navy personnel were to exchange doors and put the repaired one into the Officer's pantry, at least that was the plan.

We also hoped the Navy would move a large quantity of machinery parts out of the parts ship and down to the main engine storage room located off the tank deck just forward of the aft bulkhead on the 325's port side. The Navy would have to carry the many boxes up two decks to the main deck of the parts ship, not a small feat, go forward on the weather deck almost one hundred feet, travel over the *Kriti's* main deck, then cross on the gangway constructed between the two ships. Next they would turn right walking aft about one hundred feet, and down two decks! It was not a job for the weak! These parts for the main engines were large, bulky, and heavy.

The *Kriti* had a huge storeroom with not only parts for the 12-567 GM engines, but also for the generators, ballast pumps, reduction gears, and most of the other LST equipment. It also had a shelf full of armatures and parts for electric motors. We expanded the parts storage to two compartments, knowing we were getting a number of valuable, hard to find parts that could be priceless to get the ship home. We commandeered them all adding to the parts already on board.

In this fine looking work party were two women, who the CMC and Boats assigned to working on exchanging the reefer doors and assigned the men to transferring the parts.

The CMC came into the wardroom after getting a cup of coffee from the Galley. He sat down and then asked me how things were going. I told him all things considered they were going very well. I explained Melcher and I had a talk and he agreed to changes in the way things were being done on the LST.

CMC Rabb, with a smirk on his face, responded, "I'll believe it when I see it." After coffee, he went out and started to tour first the *Kriti* and then the LST 325.

The Navy, rather than each carry a part the entire distance, had started an assembly line augmented by some of our crew passing the parts from one sailor to the next. I told the CMC that we had bottled water for everyone. It was important to keep everyone hydrated and I could see the sweat starting to roll off the faces of several young sailors, not to mention those of my crew.

Cookie provided all of them a good lunch, ham and cheese sandwiches, potato salad, and pineapple upside down cake, Cookie's favorite dessert. We had lemonade and a red fruit punch to drink, along with coffee and water.

The women struggled exchanging the doors on the reefers. Even though the doors looked the same, the measurements were evidently different. Whatever the reason, the doors did not fit once they tried to relocate them on the other reefer. The women were instructed to place the doors back on the first reefer! Some new refrigerant was found, Freon 24 that replaced Freon 12. I am sure the old reefers used Freon 12, and everyone believed that. Neither the Navy nor our crew could find any 12. Several of the engineers decided the Freon 24 would work for a while, but not for very long. The Freon 24 needed different seals on the compressors and would eventually eat through the old seals and slowly cause Freon to leak out. Nevertheless, we put in the Freon 24 in the reefer, plugged the cord in the electric outlet, and it ran and turned cold. The Navy guys placed that reefer in the passageway right in front of the officer's pantry located between the Captain's Quarters and the Wardroom. We then asked if the Navy would take the other reefer and carry it over to the *Kriti*, which they did.

Cleaning and repairing the 325 had accumulated quite a large amount of rubbish of all kinds, stored in the tank deck. To keep the Navy sailors busy, Boats assigned them to remove that junk from the tank deck, carry the rubbish out to the dumpster on the pier, and haul the iron and other metals over on the *Kriti*. It was now late afternoon, and looking for something more to do, Carter and Boats with the help of two sailors and the CMC himself, decided to move the reefer in the passageway into the officer's pantry. They had to use a couple of big four by fours to raise it up and slide it over the five-inch doorsill, into a space just big enough for it to fit along the forward bulkhead outboard of the sink.

Five big men and the limited space didn't leave room for me. I first went below to be sure the trash was properly separated in the removal process. When I returned back up to the Galley passageway, Cookie stopped me.

He asked, "Should I submit a menu every week for approval?" I told him, "No, you are the cook; make up a menu and buy the necessary food, but if I find you buying too many T-Bone steaks, or having 'SOS' every day I may change my mind." SOS does not mean 'special on Sunday', or the 'emergency help signal!'

"I may give you a list of foods that I like and don't like!" I laughed. That seemed to make his day! I also asked him to put together a list of food that we would need for a crew of thirty-five men for forty days.

He said, "I'm already working on it."

CDR Melcher, after the men squeezed the reefer into the pantry, walked out of his stateroom and noticed the reefer's position in the pantry. Not seeing anyone, he stormed down the officer's passageway yelling for me. Cookie and I both heard him coming and I could see this gleam develop on the Cook's weathered Alaskan face. He whispered, "XO you are in trouble."

I said "I believe you may be right."

Shortly a sober faced Melcher wanted to know why I had the Navy move the reefer into the pantry when he wanted it in the Galley. I quickly told him, "I had absolutely nothing to do with putting the reefer in the Pantry (entirely true.) Mr. Carter and Boats, with the help from the Navy personnel wrestled it in there. Chief, I thought you wanted it there and I know they thought so, too. You should have heard all the noise from the struggle placing it in there and said something." He turned around on his heel and headed back up the passageway now yelling for Carter.

My curiosity made me follow him; I sort of moseyed up forward towards my cabin and the pantry. I could see that Melcher had found Jack Carter and their faces were approximately two inches apart. I heard him say, "Why did you put the reefer in there, pointing in the pantry?"

Jack, God bless him, very calmly articulated, "Well Sir, the reefer was sitting in the passageway right in front of the pantry. For that reason, Sir, it was assumed that the reefer was meant to go into that space and that is where it went." Knowing the chat was probably over, I quickly returned to the passageway in front of the galley right by the 'grinning' Alaskan hiding behind his pots and pans. The CWO called for me again.

Cookie quietly said, "You are really going to get a licking now!"

I just mocked him, by saying, "You know I had a girl like that once." Melcher came down the passageway around the corner and right up to me. He made a cardinal mistake when giving an order – giving an 'either/or' mandate. If the person does not do the command given him, you must do the OR ELSE!

He demanded, "Sir, I want you to have the Navy remove the reefer from the pantry right now or I will be off this ship in five days."

In my most polite voice I replied, "Chief, I am not going to have the Navy move the reefer right now."

He had now put himself in a box and had to answer, "OK, I will be off of this ship in five days." He then turned sharply and went back to his cabin.

From behind me I heard Cookie say, "Did I hear that right?" A sort of echo came out of the galley resounding off the metal exhaust hood.

I felt no relief. At this moment, the weight of the whole ship, some three thousand tons of it, along with the success or failure of getting underway was mine. This burden was multiplied by all the stress, strain, tension, worry and hassles that I guessed were coming. I believed three things had come into play and the reefer had little to do with it.

1. Melcher wanted to embarrass me with the Navy.
2. The Navy had come aboard to see if I had taken charge.
3. Melcher wanted to show them he was still the boss.

CWO Melcher came back in a little while with a written piece of paper addressed to all concerned parties:

"This letter will serve to document that on September 2, 2000 at 1600 hour local Crete, Greece time that I, J. Melcher Sr., Cdr., have passed command of M/V LST Memorial to R. Jornlin, Cdr. He now has

full command and authority to conduct ship's business in accordance with the title 33 and 47 of the US Code." He signed it: J. Melcher, Cdr.

He also had stamped the ship's seal on the bottom of the paper, I guess to make it look official. He asked me to sign on the bottom, gave me a copy, then turned around and went back to his stateroom.

The CMC came into the Wardroom just as I sat down to ponder my new predicament and told me he and his crew were leaving. He had this same smirked smile again on his face. I believe, in fact I am sure, he heard or someone told him what had just taken place. I knew Cookie was spreading the word. I thanked the CMC and said I hoped he would bring his crew back again soon, and off he went to call the ODC, I suspect. As time went on, I learned that the CMC reported regularly to the Ambassador and the ODC on everything that went on aboard and maybe off the LST.

I pondered CWO Melcher's ultimatum to abandon the ship. I think he knew we had serious problems and he believed we would fail. If he left me in charge, it would be my fault! I have searched my mind for another reason but can't come up with one.

I needed to do something, so I looked in the galley to see if a good place existed for the reefer. I quickly observed a large hole would have to be cut enlarging the hatch going into the galley for the reefer to slide in and part of the port ladder railing removed. Moving the reefer out of the pantry would be difficult, but getting it into the galley would be a major undertaking. I decided at this point that Cookie could walk up the passageway and grab whatever he needed from the reefer. I'm afraid that reefer was going to stay right there - possibly forever! Besides, it looked like it belonged there!

Someone had donated several cases of beer for the crew. We found out rather quickly over the next few days that the idea Boats had come up with to store beer in that reefer had a supreme flaw. This beer magically disappeared quickly. Up until this time, only four or five of the crew would sign beer out of the supply room and have it credited against their accounts. Now that there was FREE beer, two thirds of the crew suddenly drank beer! I had some ideas as to which men were drinking more than their share and it was not the four previously mentioned. When the supply ran out, this reefer no longer stored beer.

If one was a wagering man, the odds uptown this very night climbed to twelve to one against us.

I went back to talk to Don Chapman, our electrician. I often discussed current issues with him since I first climbed aboard the LST. He would give me straight answers and gave good reasons along with good advice. I didn't know half the crew, and the other half I knew only a little. Don was probably the smartest man that I have ever met, in particular with knowledge of DC electricity; very few men if any were of his caliber. Just to mention a few of his accomplishments, Don had put the elevators in the *Space Needle* out in Seattle in the state of Washington for the World's Fair in the early sixty's. He also helped design, engineer, and assist with the installation of the elevators in the St. Louis Arch, *The Gateway to the West*. These elevators start down in the bottom below the arch in a flat horizontal configuration. As the elevator (actually eight small separate compartments that hold five people each) moves up through the arch, the compartments remain flat (level) all the way to the top. He had been Vice-President for Montgomery Elevator and Escalator Company in Moline, Illinois. Don helped build that company and was a key figure in its success. Though retired, the company periodically called him back on problems that no one else could solve. I had learned he had some good suggestions regarding our crew, our Greek friends, and our Navy.

The LST 325 had loads of electrical problems - the ones we knew about and the several hundred that cropped up as the electricians dug deeper. Our electricians on board were Don, Jim Edwards, Ron Maranto, their avid helper, and a fourth electrician, Bailey Wrinkle from McKenzie, TN. Bailey was owner of a hardware store and very handy. He had built a full size log cabin in his back yard for his granddaughter. He also had some nice pecan trees in his yard! These guys had worked every day on circuits, switches, fuse panels, replaced motor brushes, and of course the controllers for the different motors aboard ship.

Breakdowns happened with some frequency, some seemingly impossible to repair. Don would tell me he was not sure how he would fix it. He had looked all over first for a replacement part on the *Kriti* and in the parts rooms of the 325. Then not finding one, he looked for a substitute piece of equipment to replace the broken one, sometimes with no success. With Don, that problem would disappear in a day or two - all fixed. I am not sure what he did or how he did it, by making a new part or somehow fixing the old one, but Chapman, I learned, could do the impossible. Repairs to the electrical equipment were one thing I did not have to worry about on the ship.

"Are you ready for a beer? Did the Navy leave?" Don yakked at me. I had a key to the Supply Room, or ship's former office where we kept our beer supply. It was right across the passageway from Don's stateroom. I also knew I had to take at least two beers for him and one for me. Don would have the first one down before I had a chance to open mine! The beers opened, our discussion turned to all that happened, and we reviewed the work the Navy had done. I asked him what he thought about the wrong Freon in the reefer. He agreed it would work for a while. Did I mention Don was a man of few words!

We started our walk to go uptown to make our usual rounds and stop at Nick's for dinner. Boats and Dewey joined us. Don was not an alcoholic and I hope I am not making him out to be one. He generally stopped after only two. I wish I could say the same for Boats and Dewey! As we walked, they both wanted an update on my new role as the 'Person in Charge!'

CWO stayed aboard the ship for five more days as he said he would. He spent most of his time in the Captain's stateroom. Two of the crew approached me about asking Melcher to stay aboard as engineering officer and help us get the ship going. I told them to go ahead and try. Melcher informed both of them that he taught DOWN not UP, and that he was not going to stay aboard as a mere Engineman Chief.

The CWO would show up at Nick's every night to eat dinner. He would sit at a table most of the time by himself. Sometimes Dave Williams joined him. I know that Ed Strobel had approached Melcher to stay and so had Jim Edwards. I actually thought that the CWO would change his mind and maybe put it up to the crew for a vote as to who would be Captain. He did not do that. He did ask if he could promote a number of the men to Chief for their outstanding work under such hard working conditions. I told him no explaining we had enough Chiefs and not enough Indians now. Boats had told everyone to leave their rank at the gangway when they came aboard. We worked as a team and Carter and I kept them informed and listened to their suggestions and ideas. I went out to Quarters every morning, so the crew could ask me any questions and get my response.

When the fifth day came around, I did not see Melcher packing his bags or making any indication that he was leaving. I went to his stateroom and told him that his five days were up and I expected him off the ship today by 1800. He told me that he was not counting Sunday. I quickly told him, sorry, but I was. The crew worked last Sunday just like always.

Melcher said, "I can't possibly be packed and off the ship tonight by 1800."

I said, "Chief, I am not an unreasonable man. I will extend it until midnight."

Jack got very busy, packed his stuff, and walked around the ship. I am not sure why, except he did several loads of laundry. The crew told me they saw him in the engine room.

At midnight, Melcher carried off his luggage and several cardboard boxes. Not one of the crew helped him. A Greek sailor showed up with a car and loaded everything into the trunk and back seat then proceeded off the base. We figured he was probably going to the airport and fly home. This was not to be the case; he stayed in Souda for almost ten more days.

I quickly found out Melcher had taken all the ship's personnel records, including my own, and the medical physicals with the next of kin's phone numbers for emergencies. He also took the information we needed to de-mill the guns for the ATF. They had approved plans to render the guns inoperable. Also removed were the plans to change the overboard discharge of the ship's sewage to a ballast tank. It was now illegal to have raw sewage going directly overboard.

After ten days, we learned the CWO had climbed on a plane and flew back to Brady, Nebraska. This bit of news put me in the game. I had the ball at center court, with five seconds left. Do I shoot or pass? Everyone yelled shoot!

Shortly after Melcher's departure, the First Secretary Dan O'Grady called me. He told me a number of boxes had arrived at the Embassy. Evidently, Melcher mailed the boxes at the Navy Base to himself. It seems all he did was cross out the 'TO' and 'FROM' on the address label and wrote 'FROM' and 'TO' beside them. He had originally mailed them from his home in Brady to the US Embassy in Athens. Dan speculated to me the government postal employee did not see the change and sent them back to the US Embassy! He wanted to know if I wanted the boxes and I quickly told him yes. They contained a lot of information that should have never left the ship. I told Dan I hoped they were the boxes of the crew's personnel and medical records.

In a few days, Dan delivered the boxes back to the ship and upon opening the cartons, I found all the paperwork Melcher removed on his departure. This mail incident was one of those things that make me wonder about our US government, the CIA, or State Department in particular. Just how did those boxes get back to the Embassy really? When I looked at the mailing labels, it was clear to what the CWO had done; the boxes should have gone to Nebraska! Boats decided that we could not mention Melcher's name anymore or one would have to buy everyone present a beer. From then on, we used the abbreviation 'M-man' if we referred to him in conversation. Strobel slipped up saying his name more than the rest of us and bought several rounds of beer

I WAS TOLD TO MOVE INTO THE CAPTAIN'S CABIN

CHAPTER 7

CAPTAIN ASSUMES COMMAND

I didn't sleep well that night. Many thoughts wandered through my mind. I had done what almost everyone had asked, but at what expense? Who would sail the ship home now; how long was this going to take? These frightening, gut-wrenching thoughts kept me half-awake with the same name clinging to the top – mine! I had a quandary on my hands. Go home and combine 1200 acres of corn and soybeans or stay and help these guys with this long shot. Several in our crew believed this ship would never run, but were afraid to say it. I wondered, do the odds makers possibly know something that we on the ship do not?

I believed most of the crew never figured on it being this way. This was certainly not what I expected. I had dealt myself into a game of five card stud with a stacked and marked deck to play against!

After Melcher's departure, the men encouraged me to move into the Captain's cabin so I eventually did. I then told Carter he should move back into the XO cabin. He rolled his eyes, but made the move.

Morning finally arrived with reveille blasting through the ship's speakers. Not much talk at breakfast, the crew a little quieter than normal, or that was how it seemed to me. Cookie was making jokes as always.

I had phoned a few of the men that had left for good solid reasons. The men I called to come back, or those that called me and asked my permission to come and help were: Dominick Perruso, our plumber from Pennsylvania; Bill Nickerson, Quartermaster, Margate, Florida; James

McCandrew, a Radio man who became Perruso's helper, Sebastian, Florida; and a second ship fitter from the east coast, who left almost as soon as he arrived. Still on their way was William 'Rocky' Hill, enginemen from Surprise, Arizona; Gary Lyon, electrician, Roseville, Minnesota; and Joe Milakovich, enginemen, Wauwatosa, Wisconsin. When Joe arrived in Crete, he forgot the name of the town. The taxi cab driver gave him several choices; cost him a long ride and most of the night, and $95. 00. Joe was a good enginemen and a quiet man; missed his wife a lot.

When I phoned Perruso and asked him to come back, he made me promise him I would keep him busy! I told him to bring his plumbing tools with him – no small chore - and yes, I would keep him busy. He asked how busy? I said take a deep breath before you come aboard. It would be your last one for a very long time! The ship's plumbing was next to the electrical as needing the most work. Perruso was already back aboard and working.

Bill Nickerson purchased all of our navigational charts for the entire trip across the Mediterranean Sea and Atlantic Ocean. When the M-man found out he bought and paid for the charts instead of getting them donated free, he told Bill to stay home. By paying for them, Bill explained, all of the charts arrived updated and corrected with Navigational updates and changes. These changes are mostly shore navigational lights. With a stop watch you time the pause between flashes or the number of flashes every ten seconds for an example. Looking then on a chart you can find exactly where that light is located. By drawing a line to three lights, one could pinpoint the ship's location at the intersection of the lines. I agreed with him that his decision was better than spending many hours of quality time going through the correction books for every chart from Crete to home. That would have been a huge job.

Rocky Hill, an Engineman, and Gary Lyon, an electrician, had both read our need for enginemen that Jack Carter had placed on the web page. They were packing after I said, "Come on, we need you." I hoped they would be in Crete in three or four days ready for work.

At Quarters, I explained the new agenda and priorities. I wanted first for the engineers to go down to the main engine room and see that the main engines were ready to start when I found batteries. Change the oil filters and turn on the cooling water. Check the clutches, air compressors, and circulating motors for the reduction gears. Then when batteries arrived, they were to start those engines. Jack and I either were to look for batteries over on the Repair Base or purchase them from a store. Once we knew the main engines would run and run well, the engineers and electricians were to move to the generators. They must start them and make sure they produced electricity, and also change engine oil, oil filters, and fuel filters. If by chance the mains and generators did not run, I suggested cutting our losses and heading for home! I explained Mr. Carter and I planned to visit all of the shops and the Greek's main office after quarters.

"Now, here's the real important part for each and every one of us," I said. "Listen up!"

"I want every man to greet and say '*HI*' to every Greek, especially the sailors, even if he changed sides of the road trying to avoid you. We have shifted gears into high. If we can't locate things on the base or talk the Greeks out of them, we are going out and purchase what is needed. We must move at a much faster pace and make this ship run."

I sent two men out to buy tools, a complete set of wrenches and a big socket set for the engineers. I said to Voges, "Go out and buy scrapers, paint brushes, brooms, and a vacuum cleaner. I know you have been trying hard to spruce up the ship making it look good, but now we are going to work smarter using proper tools. Can you go over to our naval base and see if they can be talked out of some haze gray paint?"

He stepped forward saying, "Yes, I can."

I had seen the few Greek brooms left on the ship. Their handles are only two feet long and the bristles were spread out and bent backwards. If anyone could make them sweep, he would lose his back in about ten minutes.

Someone in the back yelled out, "How about American toilets?" I sent Perruso to buy some flush toilets. He went right out, purchased three toilets, and instantly became a real hero to the crew. I believed the crew worshiped him from then on! Perruso and McCandrew, who carried his tools and helped where he could, were two of the hardest workers aboard and, for this crew, that said something!

I then asked if anyone had a question. Mr. Perruso, a plumber for many years, stepped out and in his deep voice asked, "Sir you have run off Mr. M and now I'm told you are leaving us to go home and combine your corn crop. Who is going to sail this ship home?"

I told him in my 'command' voice, "First of all, I didn't run the M-man off. The ship's crew, which includes you, wanted him gone as well as the State Department and our Navy. He left on his own and was asked to stay as Chief Engineer but refused. I thought I would have to bring him out here and have a vote right here on this deck – him or me! I believe he knew the answer and that was why he left. All of you, as well as I, knew perfectly well that this ship was dead if things did not change. Time was running out. I am the poor sucker who got the blame, and I will accept it."

Perruso persisted, "Sir, you are going around the answer to my question."

I looked hard at all of their sunburned faces with their drooping chins. They all looked beaten and tired standing in their stained work pants that our modern laundry soap only hinted at cleaning anymore. These men had been through the worst weeks of maybe their entire lives. They came and found their prize - a worn out ship; a ship that when they fixed one thing, two more broke.

Most had an article in the local paper back home, with a picture or two of them, one at a young age and one now. How would they face those that said they would never do it? It was not their nature to fail or give up, for they all were American Navy veterans and damn proud of it!

I had fallen into the challenge of showing the Greeks, the bookies and our timid friends what Americans can do. Looking into the crew's hopeful staring eyes, they were all quiet, as if E. F. Hutton was about to speak and, because of a quirk in fate, I was it. I knew they wanted a ship. If I could guarantee this ship would sail back to the USA, they would gladly pay thousands of dollars. If the good Lord would help us restore this ship and sail her home, well NO amount of money could buy them the thrill of accomplishing this seemingly impossible task. A trip on a 58-year-old LST crossing the Atlantic – if we could pull it off, it would be this ship's fourth and greatest crossing of the Atlantic!

I must have been crazy and said, "OK, if one of you will call my wife and tell her I will not be home in six weeks, **I WILL STAY AND WE WILL TAKE THIS SHIP HOME!"**

No one called my wife, but they all instantly had happy faces with a grin from ear to ear. That was except me. I now had to call Lois!

I picked my Officers. Mr. Carter would be the Executive Officer or XO; Jim Edwards the Chief Engineer; Bruce Voges (Boats) would be the Deck Officer; and Don Chapman, Chief Electrician. I believed they were good choices. I also made it clear, "I will not be telling you how to do your job. I expect each one of you to do your best. All of you know what needs doing to get this ship running, but I want it done by the priorities I have laid out. My job and Mr. Carter's, will be to find you the materials, parts you need, and work with the Greeks, our Navy, and the State Department."

No one had any objections and they set to work. I believe they forgot their aches and pains, worked as they never had before. The odds were higher downtown when the word slipped out that there had been a Mutiny on the LST 325 and a new younger man was now in charge, and the M-man made to walk the plank so their story went! The men on the 325 would show those Greeks what Americans could do; all were behind this effort. The gauntlet thrown down, the race had started.

As I told my wife on the next phone call, they were climbing out of their bunks earlier and working harder. We were going to bring this ship home. It will take longer than six weeks and we will have to get someone to combine the corn and beans. Could she find someone? I gave her two names to call, one to combine beans and one to harvest the corn.

She commented that when I left she had a feeling I would be gone longer than six weeks, but said, "Don't take too long." She had told our landlords that I wouldn't be harvesting their crops, but they would be combined and put into the bins. One Landlord flew B-24's, or B-17's in WWII over Germany, another was a Marine. None of my landlords had a problem with my adventure and in fact, told my wife they were proud of me for trying to bring back a Hero. My Mother had her 90th birthday right after I left. Lois had an open house for her. A couple days later, Lois informed me Mom had fallen and broke her patella. Lois had a lot to handle at home. Similar things happened for all the crew.

When I had been on active duty all three of my Captains had respectfully been called the 'old man' because they were thirty or thirty five years old and the crew was nineteen or twenty. Last night I heard someone say, "Where is the kid?"

LET'S GET THE OLD GAL RUNNING

What Jack and I needed was trading stock to break the ice between us and the Greeks. I don't remember now who came up to show me his box of some three hundred blue wood pencils with a silver outline of an LST imprinted on them. I said to him, "I have to commandeer your pencils for the beneficial use of the ship. I am going to give them to the Greeks, officers in particular, to grease the skids and get their help and favors." He didn't argue at all. We all knew the Greeks did not drink coffee, which was the one sure way to get most anything done in the US Navy - give a can of coffee to the Chief. I also grabbed two bottles of 'Single Barrel' Scotch away from Jim Bartlett when he made the mistake of showing them to me. I now had trading power. Jim had said OK, but his look was as if I had hit his first-born child. Well, maybe if I had hit one of his two dogs, since he doesn't have children!

The XO and I went over to the base battery and gyro shop after quarters. The ship needed batteries for the main engines ASAP. We received looks from the Greek sailors, but Jack Carter and I just said 'Hi' and offered to shake their hands. I could see an immediate change in expressions. I asked one of the men who was in charge and he pointed to an Officer in the back at a desk. The Officer looked up, then away, until we approached him.

The Officer asked, "What do you two want?" I was certainly glad that most of the Officers could speak English. I handed him a fancy blue pencil. He stood up, pointing to the chairs next to him for us to sit, asking, "What can I do for you men?" His attitude changed immediately.

I explained, "Sir, we could use a little help. We need some twelve volt batteries to start the engines on the LST."

He answered, "Sorry, but we don't have batteries here, used or new. We get batteries thought to be no good from our ships. We test them, and try to charge them up. If we can, they go right back to the ship. If not, we turn in a supply chit for new batteries. The batteries are then sent directly from the supplier to the ship, we never see them. I wish I could help."

I told him, "I understand. We also could use some assistance with starting our gyro, and we need a magnetic compass; in fact, two were missing from our ship."

He told us, "The compasses off the mothballed ships would have been returned to Athens for safe keeping. Go talk with someone higher up about procuring the compasses. Our gyro man is in the shop; turn to the left going out. He has been in America attending gyro schools several times. He will help if he can." Jack and I thanked the Officer again, shook his hand one more time, then proceeded out to find the Greek gyro man.

Jack and I entered the adjacent building and were directed to a pleasant man in his late thirties or early forties. When he said his name after examining a pencil, it sounded like Francisco. At least that was what I called him from that day on. Jack explained our problem to him. He quickly agreed to come that weekend and look at the gyro. He stated, "I was fortunate to receive schooling in the U.S. on the Mark 14, which is the model of gyro on your ship." He added, "The Hellenic Navy has upgraded our ships to a much better, more reliable gyro."

Jack replied, "We are looking forward to seeing you this weekend." I thought maybe one of our problems was solved!

We continued on to the pipe shop – more pencils; the engine shop, the electric shop, and the general maintenance shop handing out wood pencils and shaking hands. I thought all of the base personnel we talked to were very receptive and told us they would lend a hand if they could.

Then we charged up to the Headquarters and walked in as if we belonged. Nobody paid much attention to us, but we did get in to see Commander Nikoldakis, the officer in charge of us. He was the man, the Officer we called on from this point for just about everything. I gave him three pencils, informed him that I had taken over command of the ship. That CDR Melcher – the M-man – turned the LST over to me. I gave him a copy of the command transfer paper with his signature and the ship's seal. Carter had been in the Commander's office several times before and it helped. Nikoldakis congratulated me. He indicated the Hellenic Navy wanted to help, "Captain, please come and see me with any problems or questions."

On the way out of the Hellenic Navy's Headquarters and just a short few steps away, we came to what I refer to as *The Leaning Tower of Pisa* or the pilots building, with this unique circular stairway to the entrance on the second floor. It had a large sign posted in Greek and English. The sign read 'authorized personnel only!' In all ports, unless a ship's homeport, all ships have to use a pilot to go in and out of the harbor.

Up the ladder I went, but Jack hesitated. I said, "Come on XO. They can only throw us out, and we will need a pilot to leave here." I showed him the pencils I still had in my back pocket. Jack was right behind me as I entered through the doorway and surprised the five pilots inside, and handed each a pencil.

One pilot, overcoming his initial shock, came up to us, shook our hands, and asked, "Would you two like some coffee?" We both knew what their coffee would be like, but we did what we have to do for our Country – or for the 325 in this case. They had a bird's eye view of our ship and therefore knew exactly who Jack and I were. I figured they had a lot of fun watching the old guys try to repair and fix the LST. I bet they wondered why we carried those mattresses back and forth every week or so! They invited us to sit down and soon the Greek coffee showed up. They drank instant coffee, very, very strong. It was no mystery to me why very few Greeks drank coffee, but they were fully aware we drink a lot of it.

A woman corrected me one time when I asked for American coffee in a restaurant. She said what I wanted was French Coffee. Jack and I drank our coffee and praised them, saying it was good. Only one Pilot in the room did not seem friendly; he never left the window on the far side and hardly looked at us. I rather thought that he had something against Americans, but what was one out of five? The rest asked us questions. They had already heard that a new man was in charge and guessed it must be me. Carter confirmed that information while trying to down his coffee.

The next question we would be asked many times, a question that was on the minds of most of the Greek sailors, "Are you going to have an escort?"

I answered, "No, we will sail alone." They all looked at us in disbelief, which we interpreted as 'you are brave or crazy men.'

I justified our visit saying, "Mr. Carter and I need a good pilot when the ship is repaired." They stared at each other and then almost together said, "Yes sir, no problem." The look on their faces told me they all had bets against us downtown.

I felt good about our stops, and in my mind thought maybe my sales experience of selling seed for thirty years was finally paying off. Jack also thought we had turned the corner. We did have Francisco coming aboard Saturday to help us with the gyro. We also learned we were not securing any batteries from the Greeks and the reasons why. We knew now we would have to go uptown or over to the big city of Chania to purchase them. This had been a productive day in the next life of the LST 325! Some time ago, a very good sales representative told me, *"If you want to sell, go see the people." How right he was!*

AN AMERICAN-GREEK VISITOR

The next day an American Sailor showed up on the ship. He said he could speak Greek and would like to help us in any way he could. His name was John Pournarakis. He was a good-looking sailor in a neat navy uniform, maybe six feet tall.

Jim Edwards jumped right in, "We can use your help. I have just the job for you, John. We need to buy main engine batteries as soon as possible to get the engines started. Do you know a place that sells them?"

John acknowledged he knew several places in Chania. After some discussion, he indicated he would return tomorrow to take us to some battery places and would be glad to talk to the Greek owners on our behalf. He wanted to know how many we needed and Edwards indicated about twenty of the twelve volt.

John said, "How many?" I knew we needed about six for each main engine and two each for the three generators. John probed, "Do you have that much money?"

I answered, "Of course we do. We want good batteries, a volume discount, and can they deliver?"

He countered, "We shall find out tomorrow, but I'm on duty as a Navy SP, Shore Patrolman. I have tomorrow off, but now I must get back to the base." John, we learned, was born in Greece, but his parents moved to America in his mid-childhood years. He received most of his schooling and spent his youth growing up in the states. John, after basic training, received orders to report to the US Naval Support Center on Crete! I was soon to find out he could speak better Greek than most of the Greeks themselves, causing them to believe he was one of their own! Above all, he thought our project to sail a WWII ship back home was exciting. He was going to give us all the help he could when off duty.

John, using his personal car, chaperoned Edwards and I to several places in Chania and we picked the batteries and price we liked! The business delivered them right to the ship the next day, which pleased the engineers no end. John also went with us up the hill to the Commander's Office, and asked in Greek about obtaining our equipment taken from the ship. He covered a host of items we had requested with our list sent to the *powers that be* in Athens. One item we needed in order to sail the LST was a magnetic Compass. One for the wheelhouse and we had a place for another on the flying bridge in front of the CONN. I kept quiet that we only needed one to sail the ship. It would be nice to have two.

We followed the same procedure as before making out a list, sent the list in triplicate through the Commander to Athens. It took nine or ten days again, and came back with the same results – zero! They did add that if we were able to get the ship operational, they would let us have one magnetic compass. At the bottom of the list they remarked, "Do not put the same items on future lists." The Commander explained that when our 'High Command' turns someone down on an item, that was final. He then mocked us, "What don't you understand about that?"

I smiled as I knew we had sent the M-man's list back and added some other things we found missing. Carter and I understood perfectly, but what the heck, we had nothing to lose. With John speaking fluent Greek, Nikoldakis finally softened by adding, "Maybe I can make arrangements for a few items to be returned." Jack and I joked about the comment, '*what don't you understand?*' We both repeated that from time to time and it was always followed by laughter. John knew where to get the CO2 bottles filled and booked the fire extinguisher company for the first of the week. They agreed to inspect our bottles to see if the last pressure test dates were done within the past ten years. If they were not out of date, they would fill them and attach an up-to-date inspection tag. John convinced them to fill all of them with CO2, but not stick tags on the ones out of date. That way they were not responsible and for practical reasons, they would work if we needed them. They agreed to do that for us. As time went by, John became a good friend of ours, and was a huge asset when talking to the Greeks. Jim always referred to him as 'Johnny' and he seemed to like that.

John Pournarakis' first enlistment was ending soon. Where did he want to have his reenlistment ceremony performed? Well, right on the main deck of the LST 325! Cookie made a special cake for the occasion. John and another sailor had a nice ceremony, both sworn in for another four years. Pictures of the men with the Commanding Officer of the Navy Support Base were taken, with the ship's superstructure in the background.

John told me that he knew a local TV anchor who would like to come to the ship and do an interview with me on the deck of the LST. Well, why not John, bring him on. "Maybe it will do us some good," I added.

John then explained more, saying "This guy has disdain for most Americans and especially our government. You will have to watch yourself and be very careful with what you say and how you answer his questions. This could help your cause or hurt it. Proven by the high odds against the ship, a large measure of local interest exists here in western Crete. This person's show was very popular and he will advertise this live interview. He will want to take pictures of the ship. I believe everyone in Souda, Chania, and both our Navy and the Hellenic Navy will be watching the TV."

I answered John, "I'm not afraid of giving him an interview. Find out when he wants to do it." John was back the next day with answers.

The anchormen picked a Saturday afternoon to come aboard the ship with a couple of cameramen and several other TV executives and helpers. I assumed these extra people to be the producer, an interpreter, a sound person, and a light man for inside the ship. After I gave them a tour, they placed me in front of the superstructure with the wheelhouse and tank deck blowers in the background.

The interview started with first spelling my name, position, rank, and the name of my home town and state. He asked questions about the LST size, tonnage, and purpose of the ship. The next question was its involvement in WWII, specifically what invasions and battles. I told him Sicily, Salerno, and the big D-Day invasion, also a little known practice operation called 'Exercise Tiger,' during which we lost three LSTs in a naval battle made up entirely of LSTs against German E-Boats. LST 325 also rescued six hundred Australians about to drown in the North Sea after their troop ship had been torpedoed. The ship pulled a damaged LST back to England from Normandy, and eventually made 44 trips across the English Channel carrying needed supplies to the Allies, then returned with wounded soldiers to England for medical care until the Germans surrendered.

He said, "How did such a heroic ship get transferred to my Navy?" After I answered this last question, this newscaster got down and dirty. "How much money are you and your men being paid to bring this ship back for your government? Why do they want it back?"

This was my opportunity to correct a huge misunderstanding and the false information that evidently he and others had been spreading around, maybe to the entire Island of Crete. I was surprised at the question and countered it with, "What are you talking about?"

"Well, are you rich Americans not getting paid by your government to take this ship back to the USA, so your government can make a museum out of it and make more money?"

I spoke emphatically, "NO! First, we are not rich. We are all Navy veterans, and most are veterans of WWII that helped free Greece from the German occupation by taking Sicily, causing the Germans to pull their troops out of here. No one is paying us. Our government is not paying us. We are all volunteers. We have paid our own airfare to get here and all of our expenses while here."

Raising my voice some, "Our government sold or scrapped most of these WWII LSTs. They loaned these ships to our allies, like Greece, to use in their Navies. Over the past fifty years, our government managed to get rid of the WWII LSTs to the point there was not one left in the United States to have for a museum. My crew of veterans just wants one back so that the men who rode and served on LSTs can see one again. No one is paying them to do this."

Appearing quite surprised, the show host paused, stared at me in disbelief, and again uttered, "Am I to understand you and your men are not receiving any money for working in this heat?"

"No, absolutely not one red cent," I firmly answered him back.

He then thanked me and wished me good luck with the project. I thanked him for coming aboard and interjected a thank you to the

Hellenic Navy for their assistance. The interview was over and I hoped I had straightened him out along with a host of others.

After that show was broadcast, things visibly changed, not only with the Greek Navy and their sailors, but also with the local people, merchants, and even the taxi cab drivers.

The Greek Navy escorted us over to the storage building and with some Ouzo bribery, we retrieved a few of the things taken from the 325, plus other goodies like a nice varnished Bos'n deck box full of tools used to splice the mooring lines, canvas grommets and the tools to insert them, a big marlin spike to tighten turn buckles, a few assorted sewing needles, and heavy thread. Boats smiled when the crew handed it to him. Cookie was happy with the return of some of his pots and pans but never got his mixer back that he wanted.

At Quarters, Bruce presented me with a brass anchor (from the local brass shop) engraved, *'To Skipper Jornlin from the Crew.'* They also presented a *Bow Door Key* at the same time. New sailors were often sent around the ship looking for the bow door key which doesn't exist! I had told Boats we should have a key made to put on display just to prove to all LST sailors there was one! Boats also gave me (in a weak moment and probably after a few beers) a key chain; on one side it read, *No One Is Perfect* and on the other side, *Except the Captain.* He later tried to get it back from me - maybe because I was showing it around every chance I had and letting everyone know who gave it to me! Of course I know not everyone agreed with that, but what did they know!

COME ON YOU ENGINEERS, LET'S ROLL

CHAPTER 8

MAIN ENGINES RUMBLE TO LIFE

The engineers made progress in the main engine room. Chief Jim Bartlett had ordered some 30W lube oil for the engines and reduction gears, about five hundred gallons. We hated to order too much until we knew the engines would run. They had changed the oil and filters in both engines, had oil added or removed by an electric pump. Each engine, by the way, held one hundred gallons of oil. They also changed the oil in the generators.

Bartlett had made Warrant Officer in the Navy and had retired from the navy with 21 years total service. For his last duty assignment, he was in charge of the government yachts for President Kennedy. He was not in Dallas when the assassination of President Kennedy took place. He had stayed behind in Bridgeport working on the yachts.

Months before that, he had been asked by the Secret Service to take the President's wife, Jackie, water skiing. She liked to water ski and had no one to drive her speedboat, so she hired a young man to drive and pull her. The Secret Service could not protect her during these water skiing times. They asked Jim if he would pull her with one of the government boats. Jim told them he lacked water skies for her to use. The Service told him to go buy a pair. He had a government credit card and used it on the purchase; after all, this was for the First Lady, not him. I guess a reporter happened to see him and turned him in. The government brought him up on charges for using a government credit card to buy water skies. He got it straightened out after a detailed explanation backed up by the Secret Service, and agreed to refund the money to the government for the skies. I think of all of the government's waste of taxpayer money, millions if not billions, Jim doing as ordered, his job, and it almost cost him a court martial for protecting the First Lady! I wonder if he still has those skies!

After Kennedy's assassination, Jim continued under Vice President Lyndon Johnson during his term as President. When Johnson's Presidential term ended, President Johnson took Jim, now retired, with him back to Johnson City, TX and his ranch to take care of his personal boats. Originally from Maine, Texas was quite a change for him.

Several years later, Jim gave my wife and I a tour of Johnson's ranch with a few nice stories thrown in. He worked for President Johnson until he died and then worked for Ladybird until she passed away. I learned Jim was very competent, as was most of my crew. He knew engines and understood equipment and how things worked.

We started advertising for more engineers on our web page - we were shorthanded in the engine rooms to stand a regular three-section watch underway. We would also take other men with deck skills – "please call us." We put the ship's phone number at the end of the ad. They could also call the National LST Association for more information. We picked up ten volunteers from the ad, but only three stayed to sail her home.

Another very good engineman was Loren Whiting, of Barker, NY. Loren had made first class engineman in four years in WWII. He started a company after he was discharged, named after him - *Whiting Door Co.* He invented and made the overhead 'roll-up' doors for the back of semi-trailers. His business grew to the present time having sixty percent of the overhead door business in the US.

Loren was devoted to his business and never took any time off. One day he strolled out of his office, and out of the clear blue told his secretary that he was leaving for Greece to bring back a WWII LST. She was dumfounded and inquired when he would be back. He told her, "I will be gone AS LONG AS IT TAKES!"

Loren ran the main engine room. Bunked up forward on the port side, he had to come up the ladder to the main deck, go aft back to the Galley, and down below to shower and shave. Some of the crew had put up a punching bag on the main deck listing some of the names of those men who abandoned ship and left us short-handed. I was up on the CONN, way up on top with Carter, and Loren just happened to come out of the forward dog hatch with a towel and his shaving gear in tow. He stopped by the bag, looked all around and did not see anyone, put down his stuff, went over to the bag, and just punched the h-e-l-l out of it. He stopped finally, looked around again, picked up his towel, and proceeded aft. We laughed. Loren was a tall, muscular man, and one of the oldest of the crew (he turned 77 on the way back). Always very quiet and refined, he would have been the last person I would have picked to punch that bag, but almost all of the crew did at one time or another. I tried it out once myself!

The engine oil coolers were just one problem. The boys had to find a starter for the port engine, which turned counter clockwise. What were the odds we would have a spare starboard starter, but not a Port. I believed it was Whiting and Corbin Fowkes, from New Bethlehem, PA, who went over to the 'bone yard' and searched through the LSTs and found two port starters - giving us a spare. The LST 325 was in 'fat city;' we had plenty of starters now!

One other concern, as mentioned before, the DC battery electric controllers that engaged the starters were worn out. The Greeks had lines (ropes) tied to each contact within the controller to disconnect them after the engines started. The carbon, worn off on the contacts to bare metal, actually welded them together when the starter button was pushed to make a circuit which started the engine. This made the starter continue to be engaged after the engine was running instead of stopping when the starter switch was released. Chapman had these controllers on his list to fix if the engines started!

With a good port starter and everything checked out, a Greek engineer, Lieutenant Peter Sarris, came aboard to help us. He poured oil over the valve and ejector racks on top of the engine to help lubricate them until the engine oil pressure came up. This was standard procedure after a long shut down of most engines.

These nine hundred horse power V12-567 GM engines were two cycle – the piston fired every time it came up to the top of the cylinder, unlike 4-cycle engines in most cars that fire every other time up. The chief advantage of a two-cycle engine, it runs slow. These engines idle at a low 340 RPM and wide open, a dismal 720 RPM. Most American cars idle around 800 RPM! This gives the two-cycle engine a long life. It also gives it a lot of power or torque at low speed. It had been said these engines will run forever. They have been running for fifty-eight years with little rest! I hope and pray these 'forever' engines will start! If they do start, I believe they will run until we shut them off. They were great engines. Bartlett had already coached me not to run them over six hundred RPM if in fact we ever start for home. He even warned me with a smile I could call for more 'turns' but I would only get six hundred. I told him I would take it easy; I wanted this ship to make it home, but not under a canvas sail!

TIME TO START THE MAIN ENGINES

Bartlett hit the starter on the starboard engine, causing that old engine to groan as it started to turn. Fuel was already primed to the engine, the blow down petcocks opened and hissed as each cylinder rotated to the top blowing out any water or soot that had formed at the top of the piston or cylinder head. Opening the blow-downs kept the piston from breaking or causing damage to other internal parts because water does not compress. After turning the engines several revolutions these petcocks were shut. Again the engine starter button was compressed and with fully charged new batteries, the engine really began to roll and then that sweet sound was heard of one, then two cylinders firing, then all cylinders. The throttle was checked and the starboard engine rumbled at a nice fast idle running smoothly. Two men on the rope line disengaged the batteries controller contacts with a fast jerk.

One engine had started. Whiting, Bartlett, and the boys moved over to the port engine, and Edwards and Maranto grabbed the other controller's line. We had a crowd watching this operation! The same pre-start sequence was used; the starter button pushed and on the second revolution it, too, sprang to life with a roar, and then brought back to idle. They could not get the controller disengaged at first and a fire in the controller box started. The rope men finally pulled hard and the contacts opened and a CO_2 bottle put out the small fire. Clapping and cheering erupted for the engineers on the main deck; the deck apes were excited hearing the two mains come to life. They knew this had to happen before we continued working or could ever leave beautiful Souda. Please understand that the deck force never offered a well-done applause to engineers or the engineers to the deck forces. Both are generally at odds with each other. Our deck hands could tell by the noise, but also by the blue smoke shooting out of the exhausts on both sides of the ship that both engines were running!

The next day at quarters, everyone was upbeat; we had success. Then that same day, the number one Fire and Flushing motor quit, the only one running. The engineers moved their attention to the generators and found that #3 generator would not produce electricity.

Three more mechanical problems occurred the following day; one we had fixed earlier. That made the next day's quarters downhill for everyone. We continued this up beat day followed closely by a down day. One good thing as September progressed, the daytime temperatures moderated down to the eighties in the daytime and low seventies at night.

The engineers also found the main engines were getting hot after they were running for a short time. Something was wrong with their heat exchangers which cooled the engine oil. Whiting and fellow engineers, Paul Stimpson and Corbin Fowkes, took the ends off the main engine heat exchangers. The copper tubes inside were full of mussels which restricted the flow of the salt water. The salt water pulled from the sea went through the bottom exchangers which cooled the fresh water that flowed up to a second exchanger directly above where the hot engine oil circulated through. The fresh water cooled the oil returned to the engines. Each main engine had its own set of heat exchangers. Reaming these out was a very difficult and tedious job. The enginemen had to run a wire brush on a long rod through the one-inch copper tubes inside about fifteen tubes. These round cylinders were about five feet in length and maybe fifteen inches in diameter. Both the back and front had to come off with about 12-14 nuts on each cover. One had to be careful not to puncture those tubes – there were no spares. When done, one could look right through the now shiny insides of each tube. Whiting and Stimpson made new gaskets and bolted the covers back on and had solved the problem! I told those three guys they did good work. They countered, "But not much of it!"

The XO and I tried to help by checking the steering system. The varnished wooden wheel, worn from so many years of use, turned excessively hard. We could turn the helm and move the rudders, but only by applying real muscle. Something was not right. The steering system on this ship was hydraulic over electric. The hydraulic system energized an electric motor that turned both rudders. Both of us figured the hydraulic system had air in the lines.

Jack and I, working together, drained the oil out of the hydraulic system in hopes of purging any air from the system. Then we turned the wheel from left stop to right stop, forcing any air pockets out of the mechanism. After filled with new hydraulic oil and the system buttoned back up, I let Carter try the steering wheel believing we had fixed it. The system would not work at all! Ok, Jack, maybe we should get the book out! Next, we did everything by the book; when done it worked just as it did before we started to work on it. Still hard to turn but it turned!

We asked for help from the Greeks. They attacked the problem doing what we had done and reported it didn't work at all at the end of the day. I asked if they would like the instruction book. They came back, spent a second day working on it; read right out of the book. When done, it worked just like in the beginning! We concluded that must be normal. If we sail, it will be with a couple of strong men on the helm.

Cookie started taking treats of cookies, donuts, or brownies every other day over to the base. He alternated between the headquarters and the guards at the main gate. We had to come in through that gate every night and were tired of being harassed. One cannot imagine how much those treats helped with the guards.

I made a social visit to the Headquarters and stopped in the office of Captain E. Petrakos in charge of security for the base and for the Greek Guards at the US Base. He had motioned to me a few times when I came to visit Nikoldakis. He seemed very interested in our progress with the LST, was very friendly, and did not talk down to me or demand anything. Each time I told him of our progress, we discussed our navies, our families, and the weather, so we became friends. This time, I wanted to see him and ask him why I had to send names of my crew over to the US Naval Support Base to get each new man on the access list at this base's gate. He explained that was the system, or *modus operandi*, (is that Greek or Latin?) but agreed I could bring my names right to him from now on. Then he said, "Is there anything else I can do?"

I then jumped at the offer, "Since you asked, can you tell your men to ease up a little on us Americans as we come and go? They are very diligent doing their job, but they all know us and we stick out like sore thumbs. We are not a security threat, especially at our age!"

He laughed at that comment and with a grin voiced, "I can do that."

I told him, "Thank you. I appreciate it and so will my crew. Sometime you should come down and see the ship."

He again smiled saying, Yes, I will."

From that day on, we could walk right in as if we owned the place. Only the new men had a hard time. Even though I placed their names on the list at the gate, reading English was not their forte. Several times, I walked all the way to the gate and showed the guards by pointing to the man's name on the list before they would let him in. We finally told the new recruits to find us at Nick's place and walk with us to enter the Base.

The plane from Athens normally arrived at 1800 every evening at the airport and by the time they found their bags and a taxi and rode to Souda, we were in Nick's eating. We then carried their suitcases, positioned the new man in-between us and walked right in. I did have a couple of new arrivals who thought they knew more than anyone else, proceeded right to the gate and tried to walk in. The Greek guards stopped them dead in their tracks and our man ended up hanging around the gate for several hours before I arrived, because I was waiting for them at Nick's place!

A few more breakdowns happened one afternoon at 'Beer Time,' which could be anytime according to Boats. He claimed that the sun had to be over the yardarm somewhere. Boats also claimed he would never drink any beer until it was time, then say, "It's time!"

Chapman and I met in his stateroom and I unlocked the office with my personal key. We had a storekeeper, Don Molzahn, assigned to open the store at certain times for the crew, generally after supper, unless the men caught him in a good mood or he also wanted a beer. Molzahn was not around now, so I grabbed the usual two beers for Don and one for me. I should mention I always marked them down on the charge sheet.

Don stated, "Captain, this has been a hard day. I just can't seem to get the generators, the two that are producing electricity, #1 and #2, switched over to the ship's electric board."

With yet another problem added to all the rest, I decided to question Don on the reparability of the ship. "Tell me the truth. Do you really believe that you and the men can get this ship running?"

He was dead tired and answered quickly, "No, I really don't."

"Don, then just what the devil are we doing here anyway, working our butts off?"

Don came back, "I certainly agree, Captain, this thing was worn out a long time ago and will never run! I can't fix things fast enough."

"We agree," I said. "It will never run, so why don't you tell the crew? We could sightsee for a week, tour Crete, and then go home."

He just laughed, took another large swig of beer, and smashed the can with his big hand saying, "I can't tell these guys this ship will never run. They would throw me right off the fantail! Why don't you tell them? You're the Captain."

I countered that with, "Don, you are bigger than me. I'm sure they would do exactly the same thing to me! Would it help if I promised to throw you a life ring? Maybe we should have another beer." After we both had another cold one, I told Don my decision. "I believe the best course of action is not to tell the crew, but let them continue to work until they are out of money, and so tired and worn out they will go home! What do you think?"

Don quickly said, "Now I know why you are getting the big bucks."

It was time, anyway, to head uptown. We picked up Boats, Dewey, and Bartlett and up to our first stop at the *Sweet 16*. Some newspaper writer, after reading our web page, proclaimed to me, "Your crew, I understand, act like their eighteen years old again."

I answered, "Only when they go on liberty!"

The Odds at the bookie joint went up to twenty to one that we would not get the ship away from the pier! These Bookies were starting to make me mad!

ARE WE HAVING FUN YET?

CHAPTER 9

NORMAL ROUTINE AFTER 1700

A large percentage of the crew knocked off ship's work at around 1700 hour, took a shower, and prepared to leave the ship. It was not necessary to turn on any hot water for a shower since the water in the ship's tanks had warmed up to about the right temperature. They changed clothes, gathered on the main deck, and waited for others to join them for the walk uptown. A few guys rarely left the ship, Edwards was one, except once a week or so or for special events. The Snipes would generally pair up, as did the Deck Apes.

At first, I went with just about anyone heading up to Nick's Place. After a while, it was usually Boats and I and either Bartlett or Dewey (or both) depending if one or the other had the quarterdeck watch. The Captain and XO had another benefit – they did not stand watch, nor did Boats who made out the watch bill!

We wound our way through the shipyard dodging the potholes. We mostly walked on the road so we could have a conversation between us. This made the walk seem faster and we discussed plans for the next day or two as we progressed along. We had a sign-out sheet at the quarterdeck so we knew who was on board and who went ashore. If anyone was looking for us, the watch knew our approximate whereabouts. This helped if someone's wife called asking for him. The phone was right at the quarterdeck near the gangway and against my cabin's outer starboard bulkhead.

I asked Lois to call me at 1600 in the afternoon. It was easier for her to call me, than vice versa, since I had to walk about two city blocks to a public phone and use a credit card. We could receive calls on the ship's phone and make local calls but not long distance. I would try to be around the main deck or in my cabin at the specified time. It was eight hours difference in time from Illinois to Crete, so if she called about 0800 central time, it worked out well for both of us. Our conversations were usually short; just a recap of what had happened at home or on the ship. She always had questions about farm business, but I had a real problem refocusing my thinking from the ship back to the farm. She knew that.

After Dewey and Bruce scouted around, we settled on a few places we liked for various reasons. Normally our first stop was the *Sweet 16*, a juice store/restaurant with several kinds of beer. It had a large blending machine. The operator would throw in whole oranges, a lemon, a peach, maybe a whole apple or two, whatever one wanted. After some ice was added, she turned the machine on to mix away then pour the mixture into a glass like a milkshake. The *Sweet 16* menu offered all kinds of different concoctions to choose or try. They were all good!

We always sat on the veranda in front next to the street. From that elevated spot, we watched the people walk by, maybe saw a ferryboat arrive, and sometimes a cruise ship docked. We watched all the people milling around the area. The owner had German Heineken beer, and it was cold. It helped us relax after a long day. Whiting, Stimpson, Strobel, Meyers, and Fowkes generally joined us, but at a separate table. Rocky Hill and Gary Lyon, who joined the crew later that fall, stopped by from time to time. The proprietor brought out hors d'oeuvres for us to enjoy. That was why we picked that place as one of our favorite stops. *Sweet 16* was close to a pay phone; many a night I made calls to the U.S. from that phone trying to find a dock for the ship. Think about one calling up a stranger in some city or port and start to explain the reason for the call. Tell him about yourself, where you were calling from and why. I am in Crete you know, the big Island of Greece; I need a pier and a home for a WWII LST in a month! One can word it any way he wants to. I wondered what that person really thought as he asked first, where was I, Crete, Greece? Second, what's an LST? Need I say more?

I called Linda Gunjak almost every week keeping her up-to-date on our progress. Linda gave me the credit card I used to make all my calls. I also called Priscilla Roberts Thompson and kept her informed. Both Linda and Priscilla helped me out many times.

Linda sometimes would call my wife after I or others gave her an update. If the reports were good, Lois was glad to hear from her. If a crisis had developed, Lois did not like to have that information dumped in her lap, since she tried to keep all the wives up-to-date on the ship. She would call me and ask for the details. I tried hard not to pass on bad news and so did Jack with the web page updates.

The second place on our nightly tour was three blocks farther away - up to Nick's, and then right, farther west. We found this place by accident. Actually, Bruce found it by noticing the small brass propeller on the doorknob of the entrance door. A true Bos'n Mate, he caught that right away. Through the display window, we observed many brass nautical items like small ships, anchors, ashtrays, numerous gift items, and souvenirs. We passed by the first time, dragging Bruce along with us. Our third stop, the notorious *Sea Wolfe* was another two blocks, located clear on the very edge of town. At first, we just had to see this place because of a report from one individual who claimed it was a bad place. As we entered, I was first - pushed ahead by Boats because I was the Captain! We were not sure what to expect. The place had a female bartender behind the bar on our right but no one else in sight. We went over, sat at a table by the wall to the left, and close to a TV with a news program in Greek turned on. I noticed on the wall next to us were several drawings of immense, black merchant marine ships with each ship's name written on a plaque immediately below. Later, we learned these 'Black Ships' were from time to time anchored in the bay straight out from the LST.

The bartender brought over a dish of peanuts and placed them in the center of the table. She spoke in Greek, asking what we wanted. We said as best we could using hand signals, "beer please."

She then exclaimed in perfect English. "Oh! Americans," then asked what kind of beer and named off three foreign beers. We all decided to try the Greek beer, *Mythos*. She then turned, went to the TV, and changed the channel to CNN in English! Now everyone knows why we made this our third stop almost every night and they always turned on CNN for us. Other people came in and out, and either drank beer or *Ouzo*. All spoke Greek until one time a week later, I overheard English at the bar.

After the peanuts were gone and the beer drank, we headed back to Nick's, but stopped for Boats at the *Brass Shop.* Boats led the way, entered the shop, and observed a young Greek girl, maybe seventeen, and a nice looking woman we learned was the girl's mother. They both said "Hi." Boats searched around the shop for the doorknob propellers, found them, and learned the brass propellers did not come attached to knobs. One must braze the propeller to the knob! The shop had brass ashtrays with a propeller on the outside, small and large model sailing ships, and big and small brass anchors. There were some glass items and many other tourist and old sailor money grabbers. We looked around at the best assortment of nautical knickknacks for a sailor to buy that I have ever witnessed anywhere.

Bruce decided right then he wanted to buy three of the doorknob propellers. They had a price in drachmas of about forty-two thousand for the three. Bruce sat at a table across from the mother and she figured out the price. The mother could only speak and understand a little English, but the daughter was very fluent in our language. All Greek kids were required to take English in school. The daughter interpreted what Bruce said. Bruce was trying to negotiate a discounted price for buying all three at once. The mother put down a price on a plain piece of paper about six by six inches and pushed it over to Bruce. It read 42,000! Bruce crossed that figure off and wrote 41,000 below it, and pushed the paper back to her. She crossed out 41,000 and on the top wrote 43,000 above her price. She then pushed it back again. All this time her low cut dress exposed her very nice breasts. Bruce turned and winked at Dewey and me, rolling his eyes every time she leaned over to push the paper back. She again crossed out Bruce's now 40,000 figures and wrote in 44,000. I told Bruce he had better buy pretty soon while he could still afford all three! He did! That was not the last negotiating Bruce did; he tried buying some things for the ship with about the same results. I never ever let him negotiate for me; neither did Dewey!

We left the *Brass Shop* with Bruce mumbling, "She took advantage of me, I couldn't think."

In later visits, we met her husband who worked at the base with security. He bought us all beers every time we stopped. He would send his daughter next door to buy and bring back the beers. There must not be an age limit in Souda for buying beer. We became good friends with them and we bought an incalculable amount of brass souvenirs from the mother and daughter. I should be careful how I say that! Bruce bought several more brass propellers, but never tried to get a quantity discount again!

Nick's was our next stop for dinner. I grew to like Nick and his family. Nick went out of his way to be friendly and helpful to the crew. The crew had a good time with him, especially Boats as they bantered back and forth over prices and the kinds of meals he offered. Nick made us feel at home. He came up with some American dishes for the crew like the Iowa pork chop and ham and eggs. He soon learned that several of the crew liked beans, no matter what kind, so he always had one meal that included beans at night.

There were no meal order tickets made up. A customer went to Nick's cash register located against the wall in the middle of his restaurant, told him what he ate and drank. We learned that Nick priced his meals about the same – as I recall 12,000 Drachmas or about seven or eight dollars US. Nick's cash register didn't have drawers or dividers for different bill denominations. The register had one big open drawer that he tossed the money in, stirred the pot until he found the correct bills and change, and handed it over. All of the crew exchanged their American money into Greek money at the bank. The exchange was about 1600 to one, so if one changed a 100-dollar bill into Drachmas, your pockets were full. One time when I had to buy lube oil and fuel, I had over a million Drachmas in a brown paper bag walking back from the bank.

After dinner, we went two doors back towards the *Brass Shop* to a place with homemade ice cream in four or five different flavors. This place was mainly a bakery with two-thirds of the store full of pastry delicacies on its shelves. We bought ice cream cones, took turns buying, and then headed back to the ship. We always got back to the ship by 2200 hours. We were all tired and reveille came early.

Most of the crew did not follow along with us for our complete nightly tour of uptown Souda. They might stop at one place and then Nick's, but then ambled straight back to the ship. Everyone lost weight no matter which option they took, about 25 pounds on the average. Belts had to have new holes punched to hold up their pants! Edwards had to buy a complete new wardrobe!

The Mayor of *Lone Oak,* TX, was one of the men who had to rest at first when he walked uptown. He was diabetic and took insulin every day when he first arrived. Mayor Harold Slemmons, a great Texan, helped Cookie at times in the Galley. He had driven truck, farmed, and held several other jobs through the years, but had been elected Mayor twelve or fifteen years ago. He made all of us 'Honorary Citizens' of Lone Oak. Harold lost forty-five pounds and cut his need for insulin down drastically!

I asked Mayor Slemmons what his normal routine in Lone Oak was as Mayor. "Well, Captain, I get up about 0630 every day, have breakfast, and about 0900 I drive down to the office, about four blocks from my home. Lone Oak is not big, you know. I look at the mail and talk to the secretary. I see if there are any pressing matters for me to handle. There generally isn't - we are not a big city, you know! Did I say that already? At 0930, I drive to the coffee shop, about a block away. We have quite a group of citizens, mostly retired, come in for coffee at this time. We discuss our high school sports teams or sometimes national problems, politics, and maybe how a few town citizens are doing that are sick or hurt. You know the general BS of things, and then drive back to the office. About 1100, I drive home to see what the wife has fixed for lunch. I drive back at 1330 to take care of any business, approve a bill or two for the secretary to pay. I drive back home about 1500 and call it a day."

After hearing this, I gave Harold my best advice, "Harold, when you get back, I hope you will leave your car home and walk!" He agreed that he should do exactly that to keep in better shape and keep the weight off.

AMBASSADOR BURNS WANTS TO SEE THE SHIP!

CHAPTER 10

A PARTY FOR THE GREEKS

Dan O'Grady gave me a cell phone to use to call him, or for him to call me. I received one of those calls. Dan said that Ambassador Burns was coming over next week to see the ship and meet all of the crew. In fact, he wanted to bring several of his aides, secretaries, a photographer, and Betsey Anderson, Consul General of the USA. He also invited the Captains from the ODC and several Hellenic Navy Admirals. We were to invite our US Navy Officers from the Souda Base and the Greek Officers from the repair yard. "Just about everyone is interested in your progress. We will have our Navy put up a tent and cook some hamburgers. What do you think?"

I replied, "The crew deserves a break, so let's do it. Dan, really, don't they just want to place some bets with the local Bookies here or see how their bets were holding up?"

Dan ignored my comment, and then enlightened me. Ambassador Burns would be flying back to Washington, DC to talk with Secretary of State Albright very soon. He planned to attend a meeting with the State Department, a couple of Admirals, Priscilla Roberts, and some other Congressmen and Senators. "He needs to talk with you and desires to see the ship first hand to be able to intelligently convey exactly what it looks like and how you are doing. He is pleased with the crew's progress judged by your reports."

I informed the crew at quarters. They were excited about meeting Ambassador Burns. Most of the men, like me, had never even thought of seeing an American Ambassador, let alone meet one in person. We turned to cleaning up the ship to make it look better for an inspection by the Top Brass. We removed things we were never going to use as well as the normal garbage and worn out or broken parts. We formed a ship's work party and hauled those forty plus filthy dirty mattresses back to the parts ship and dumped them into the tank deck; gone finally. I hoped they did not inspect the *Kriti;* we were not improving her (his) looks.

We seemed to have generated considerable attention. All the guests that I knew about boarded the ship, plus a few more! The Admirals were all in whites. The Ambassador dressed causal, white open collar shirt and Navy blue slacks. I had the crew dress in their Chief khaki uniforms; they looked outstanding! Boats, Bartlett, and John Calvin had their campaign ribbons displayed on the left side of their shirts above the pockets. All of them had collected quite a few campaign ribbons. These retired career men looked sharp. The crew spread out on the main deck, shook hands, and talked with most of the visitors. I believe the visitors were more curious about them than my crew of the dignitaries.

Soon the hamburgers were ready and the line formed under the tent. In about thirty-five minutes most everyone had finished eating except for having another beer or glass of lemonade. Dan came over and announced to me the Ambassador would appreciate a tour of the ship. "Would you do the honors of asking the Hellenic Navy Officers to join us?"

I personally announced to the VIPs that I would be giving a tour if they were interested. With Ambassador Burns following right behind and the Greek Admirals next, I showed them the ship from top to bottom and bow to stern. I had avoided the engine rooms, even though the engineers had done a great job removing their oily handprints from the ladders and wiped the oil as best they could off the decks and the engines. With the Hellenic Navy all in white uniforms, the engine rooms were not the place to go. However, when I asked them if they wanted to see the engine rooms, they all enthusiastically said yes. Down the twenty foot ladder I went with my whole tour group following behind. First, we visited the generator room, and then to the main engine room so they could see our successes.

Once in the main engine room, Ambassador Burns popped the question, "How about giving these veterans some help getting this ship going?" The officers of the Hellenic Navy looked at each other, and then at me. I held my breath. They might be thinking they had better say yes for fear of being shut down here!

The Ambassador then added, "Can we count on the Hellenic Navy and especially the Repair Base here to give these guys some help?" They all nodded their heads yes as they turned and looked at each other. The Ambassador then said, "I knew you men would help. Thank You."

Back top side, I rounded up most of the crew and everyone formed up on the main deck. The Ambassador gave a nice speech, talked about our crew and their goal to bring back a historic LST that was at Normandy in June of 1944. He thanked the Hellenic Navy for all of their assistance. He said we were brave veterans and we needed their help as well as the help of our Navy. He then asked me to say a few words, which I was glad to do as the host. I thanked the Hellenic Navy and their Officers, our Navy for their help and the fine lunch they prepared. I then praised Ambassador Burns and Dan O'Grady for all they had done for the ship. I also affirmed that we were going to sail the LST 325 home after a few more repairs. That brought applause! I was not a great speaker, so I kept it short. Our Navy left the tent they had erected for lunch and for the dignitaries for shade. They said we could use it until we sailed. Soon we placed our side boys at the gangway rails and Boats piped everyone of high rank off the ship, including Ambassador Burns.

PLACE THE GENERATORS ON LINE

The Greek electrician came aboard the next morning, and Chapman showed him to the auxiliary engine room. After a long time the Greek electrician finally admitted he didn't know how to get the generator switched over to the ship either, a disappointment to Chapman.

Our Navy called and a US Cruiser had just pulled into the base across the way. The CMC called the cruiser and, after hearing our problem, a Chief Engineer volunteered to send an Electrician Chief over to the "T" to show us how to switch the power to the ship's electrical board. This Chief was an expert with twenty three years of Navy experience. We said great, send him over.

When the Chief arrived, Chapman with Edwards showed him to the auxiliary engine room. They told me the Chief electrician walked around the engine room twice. He looked at the old knife switches on the main board and our very archaic DC generators. He looked at Chapman and Edwards and sheepishly told both, "Guys, I am sorry but I can't help you. I have never seen anything like this system in my entire career in the Navy. I thought you had a computer problem or something I could help you with, but not this!"

I called Don Chapman into my cabin and asked him what he thought we should do with our electric problem. He said he had been giving it some more thought. He was sure the Greeks could have showed us. They had been using this ship right along up until last year.

Don then said, "Let me try again tomorrow, the Greek electrician gave me some ideas." He also informed me that #1 generator and #2 could not be parallel together so the Greek electrician had warned him, because the polarities, positive and negative leads were backwards on #1.

Chapman not only was able to figure out how to put the generators on the board, but he re-charged the field coils in #1 generator, changing the polarity to match the polarity on generator #2! Now they could be paralleled together producing 200 kilowatts DC. I understood that in old cars that had a generator, if the polarity was reversed, all one did was ground the positive wire to the frame, which would change it. That's sort of what Don did to solve the problem. If I said I understood completely, I would be lying.

THE LST 325 GETS A LOVER BOY

George White, our only Marine on board, purchased a pair of pants over town that were excessively long. He asked our restaurant man, Nick, if he knew a good tailor. Nick gave him some directions; he said she was the best in town. George hastily proceeded over to the seamstress's home to have his pants shortened. When he came back to the ship, he told everyone he was madly in love.

He elaborated saying, "She (the tailor) was very tall and thin with dark long hair past her shoulders, the most beautiful woman I have ever laid eyes on!" She had made him try on the pants, measured them, and shortened them right there while he waited and watched. Then she had him try them on again, to see if they were the correct length! Why, she had done 'a perfect job' according to George.

He bragged telling the crew, "I am going to buy another pair of pants too long, and have her shorten them, too!" He explained, "She only works at shortening pants on Fridays since she has another job. I can't wait a whole week." George, with long pants in hand, hurried over to her house for several consecutive Fridays. Then, after pledging the crew to secrecy, he told the crew his plans, "I am going to ask her to marry me next Friday! I love her so much!"

This bit of secret 'Marine' news slipped back to his sons and daughters in Coal Valley, Illinois where George owned a small farm and ran a garden supply and tree nursery business with his family. His sons and a daughter had a reporter who monitored George's switch to being a sailor and wrote updates on the progress of the LST in the local newspaper. In his next article, the headline read: **Local Marine Hero George White Bringing Back a Greek Beauty Queen on the LST!** The article reportedly said, *Mr. White, now a sailor, not only was bringing back an LST, but also a wife! What a man, what a Marine!*

The next Friday George left the ship with several pairs of very long pants. He was clean-shaven, hair combed, and neat as a pin. George had lost his wife of fifty years a few years back. We all waited for the outcome of this love story. A couple of hours later George was spotted coming slowly up the gangway with pants in hand, but down at the mouth. Everyone wanted to hear the news.

"George! George! Did you ask her? Will she marry you? George, come on, what did she say?"

George sadly replied, "Sorry men, it is all off, all over. I won't be going back there again."

"Well – why not?"

George finally broke down, "I got a good look at her husband, that's why – he is the biggest, toughest, looking man I have seen in years! Six feet four at least and was he ever built!" George's love life ended as quickly as it began. Quote from George, *"Quit while you are ahead to love another day."* One of the crew told me George had to find another locker for all of his pants.

LST ADOPTS A MASCOT

A little dog, a mixture of breeds, came around while we were eating at Nick's one night. She certainly looked hungry and begged some scraps of food by sitting up on her hind legs. She kept her distance as Nick yelled at her and her male companion when she got too close. The male companion was a real mutt. He was dirty, skinny and, can I say, just plain homely! We mostly fed the smaller dog throwing bites of meat to her away from the larger companion. When finished with dinner, we left for the ship not giving the little dog another thought.

The small dog and her companion were back at Nick's again the next evening, and again I and a few of the crew threw a few meat pieces their way. On the way back we bought Bruce his strawberry ice cream cone and meandered back to the base and the ship. This small dog followed us, just a short distance back towards the shipyard gate, stopping just short of the gate. I tossed her the butt of my ice cream cone. Bruce and Dewey ate every bit of theirs; I told them they were really selfish.

The next day I walked two miles to the Greek Navy Hospital to see how Frank Conway, one of my engineers was doing. He'd gotten dehydrated and quit taking his meds. The Greek doctor, educated in the US, told me he was doing fine but they would keep him one more night.

The hospital was located to the left of the base gate in the opposite direction from downtown, on a street that paralleled the land side of the base. Residential homes were located on the side away from the base. On the base side sat an impressive Navy Officer's Club sporting tall white pillars on each side of the entrance. Adjacent to it and closer to town was the enlisted men's barracks. A big cement building several stories high boasted a cafeteria and had sailors playing basketball in the side yard. Most of the distance to the hospital had a high chain link fence or a high cement wall enclosing the Navy Base.

On the way back I walked on the residential homes side on a nice sidewalk. I stretched my legs into a fast walk, hurrying to get back aboard ship. I ran into that small white and reddish-brown dog that shared my strawberry ice cream cone the night before. She recognized me, and stood straight up on her hind legs. As dogs sometimes do, she curled her lips and showed off her white teeth 'smiling' at me as she gave out a whine in sheer delight to see a friend or maybe a soft touch. One might believe by showing her teeth she intended to bite, but that would only be if I were Dewey, who ate his whole ice cream cone and did not share!

Of course I said, "Hi" and gave her a pat on the head. She was very excited and continued to walk and run around me all the way to the gate, through it (ducked around the guards) and followed me all the way to the ship. She wanted to join that over the hill crew of mine. Maybe she heard about Cookie Sadlier's desserts! When I came on board, the dog managed to climb about half way up the gangway before the quarterdeck watch, diligent in his duties, told her no. Bruce was the main one that did not want her on the ship. She might make a mess or something on his deck, although I could tell Bruce treasured her as much as anyone did. Someone asked me her name. Carter replied, "Call her Souda, after the town." So Souda it was, and she picked up fast to respond to it. She stayed and slept at the bottom of our gangway. She would not permit another dog, no matter how gigantic, to approach within fifty feet of our ship. The 325 belonged to Souda, as did the entire crew as days passed.

The moment one of the crew left for uptown, she followed along. Souda shadowed them up and back. If she wasn't at the ship when Bruce and I started out on our route at 1700, she would search for us from one stop to the next until she found us. Shortly she knew our route better than we did!

There was a big mangy mean dog that stayed near the Greek guards at the main gate some of the time that gave the crew a hard time. He barked and growled at each of us as we passed through the gate. The guards never called him back or tried to control him. I think they thought it was fun to have him harass the Americans. This dog would not let Souda enter the base with us. I had to carry Souda in my arms past this dog until he finally gave up and returned to the gate.

One night I had enough of this ugly cuss. When we passed through the gate and were in about twenty-five feet, I turned and yelled at the top of my lungs and with arms waving, I ran right at that dog yelling and screaming. I think Strobel and Dewey thought I would be eaten alive. I just hoped my bluff worked! It did! That big dog turned on his heels, put his raggedy tail between his legs, and headed fast towards the gate. I caught him about half way there, and gave him a swift kick in the butt. He turned up his speed and disappeared into the guardhouse looking for protection. The Greek Guards could not believe it and stood staring in complete awe. Ed Strobel, who was along that night, could not believe it either. That dog never bothered me again, and disappeared into the guard shack whenever he saw me.

The entire crew fed Souda tidbits at every meal from the ship. Jack Carter actually bought her dog food and a brush to groom her and I believe gave her a bath. None of us could figure what Cookie did to some very nice steak fillets, but they came out like hockey pucks, way over-cooked. Souda would not eat them either, but took them over where the hill started, and buried them. I believe she thought them to be dead!

Cookie would watch the crew as they brought their plates back. If they had any food still on them, he was not happy! To avoid this, we just scraped what we didn't like in the wardroom's waste container or over the side of the ship, and then took the plate back looking clean and told Cookie how great his meal was. That folks was how one continued to eat well on the 325!

One day Bruce said something unflattering to Cookie about his cooking, probably about the over-cooked fillets. From that time on when Boats and I visited the chow line together, I would always receive a large chunk of tender meat, whatever meat Cookie served, but on Bruce's plate, a tough chunk with gristle would appear, or maybe just a piece half the size he gave me. I believe Cookie had to search and save to find Boats the worst pieces of meat one could ever imagine! Old Navy saying, "Never be on the bad side of the cook!"

I believe Souda was more my dog than anybody else's - maybe because I carried her past that mean dog or gave her more ice cream or scraps under the table. She followed me into most stores and stayed right behind me. At Nick's when it turned cool at night, Souda would wait for Nick to go in the back of his restaurant. She would then quickly slide in under our table on her belly, hiding under our legs.

The proprietor of a general merchandise store where I shopped for writing supplies and other office purchases, noticed Souda one time. He wanted to know if she belonged to me. What could I say but yes. At that moment I believed I would be asked to leave and Souda too. In plain words he told me it was OK for her to be in his store if she was my dog. Souda just wagged her tail!

A pizza place that we patronized some four doors up from Nick's would not let Souda sit by his outside tables when we sat down. All I can say is his pizza business suddenly went downhill! Our Souda became the ship's mascot. My wife said she never got a letter after Souda found us, without mention of the dog and a picture.

THE LST 325 IS NOT EASY

CHAPTER 11

SUCCESS AND TROUBLE

Number #3 generator became a real problem. The engine ran OK, but no voltage came from the generator. It was totally shot, unfixable. We planned on sailing with just two generators, #1 and #2. The generators were numbered from right to left as one faced toward the bow of the ship. The #1 was on the Starboard side, #2 was in the center, and generator #3 on the port side.

An invitation to a 'Change of Command Ceremony' for the LST located behind us was presented to me and Carter by their XO. This invitation came, we believed, because of the help we had extended to them.

The engineers took them over some oil filters found on the parts ship which fit their engines, but not ours. Bruce took over some paint when he learned they were one or two five gallon cans short from finishing their paint job, after he proceeded to show them how to paint! Their Engineering Officer asked Bartlett to teach his men how to operate the fuel purifier. I gave the operations Lieutenant a fuse box he wanted off the *Kriti,* plus some PA speakers.

Carter and I put on our best khaki uniforms and headed over to the Greek Officer's Club. The whole crew had taken my command order seriously, to do everything possible to keep and improve relations with the officers, civilians, and sailors on the base. The invitation to a Greek Naval Officer's Change of Command was a very prestigious honor for us. I wondered if any other US Officers were ever invited to one. It was a very nice affair to say the least with great food, drinks, and everyone dressed in their best. Jack and I only knew a couple of Officers there, but most of the Greek Officers recognized us. Maybe it was our uniforms! Being stared at did not stop us from enjoying the evening, helping ourselves to the food, and saying *Hi* to everyone who came close. Almost everyone would answer us back, smile, or nod their head.

After the ceremony was over, but not the socializing, a couple of curious Officers walked over to us and asked how the work progressed on the *Syros*.

Jack answered saying, "OK, except we have a problem with one of the generators."

Their curiosity peaked, one asked, "Are there plans to fix it?"

I responded, "We will probably sail back with just two generators." Their reaction to my statement told us that we should not even consider or think about doing that. One Officer left and came back with another of higher rank, a Lieutenant Commander, and then another showed up, and the conversation in Greek turned hot and heavy.

Finally, the Officer who first asked the question in English told us we should hire a private contractor to remove the faulty generator and transfer a good one from the *Kriti*.

I asked, "How much would that cost?" More discussion followed and finally a collective answer - about six hundred American dollars.

Jack spoke up, "We could do that, couldn't we, Captain?" I answered in the affirmative then inquired how to get hold of an independent contractor, and did they know a good one? The Officers then had another confab and brought the Commodore into the discussion.

After they talked, they came back over to Jack and me, and surprised us both with, "Captain, it would cost too much. We will do it for you right on the base!" Jack and I together expressed our deep appreciation for the offer to switch generators for us, which is such a big job. We had earned our pay tonight.

I asked them, "How long before you can start?" Their answer was to start next week and have it done in a month!

I then informed them of our plans. "Gentlemen, thanks, but we plan to leave in a week or two at the latest." They were speechless for a second, then with a smile replied they would see that it was done right away. I wondered why I got the reaction every time I mentioned us leaving! Was it so unbelievable to think we had the ship running, or was it because they had money downtown at the bookie joint!

The Greeks changed that generator in three days' time with only two men! This was a particularly remarkable accomplishment since the Greeks usually came in their cars to work at 1000 hours, and were lined up at the gate ready to go home at 1400 hours in the afternoon. Nobody worked weekends, and they generally took the day off before a holiday to get ready for it, and another day off afterwards to recover from it! Because of the country's great and extensive history, Greece celebrates a busload of holidays throughout the year! The two who changed the generator showed up at 0700 and worked until 1900 every day. One worked on our ship making the old generator ready to be removed, the other man worked on the parts ship unhooking its generator to move to the 325. We ran electricity over to the *Kriti* for lights, opened the hatches and Edwards stood by to help in any way he could. We also fed them lunch, and sometimes they ate Cookie's dessert before leaving at night.

The Greeks also came aboard and fixed the AC motor generator. This took several days; it was a repairman's nightmare. Their divers repacked the stern tubes. Francisco got the gyro and radar working. The Greek Lieutenant, the same that helped start the main engines, Peter Sarris, helped set the governors, fixed some of the gauges, the engine order telegraph, and also worked on the steering system.

Bartlett and I changed the oil and flushed out the ring bearings on the drive shafts. I had First Class Don Lockas (with one S) grease all of the grease fittings on the main deck, the elevator, and stern anchor winch. When Don reported back and told me he had greased all the fittings on the stern winch, I went back and checked. I showed him three or four he missed. Most of these had been covered with four or five coats of paint over the last thirty-five years, but I knew where to look for fittings. He came back a second time with the same story; he had greased them all. On my second inspection, I found three more he had missed. I brought him to the front of the men at quarters the next day and gave him a Captains Mast, my first, for lying to me. His punishment was to buy me a beer uptown! I had to set an example with Lockas!

We closed the ramp up forward and the bow doors. We replaced the lids on some of the tanks with new gaskets and bolts. The electricians worked on light switches, replaced a few electric covers, some fuses, and some brushes in motors. They had the ship's main reefers started and cooled down.

The ship's running lights, bow, stern and mast head lit up and shined bright as did the small lights in the rudder angle indicators in the wheelhouse and CONN. The engine order telegraphs for both engines operated flawlessly now. The system was an update and operated from the CONN, a huge improvement over the originals. This newer system operated with lights and a loud buzzer.

The Greeks had fixed the guns (de-milled them) so they would not fire. They cut a hole through the top of the barrels and welded a bead around the inside of the barrels which prevented a shell from being placed in the gun. Firing pins had been removed, and the space left welded shut. With the holes in the barrels, any attempt to fire the gun would cause it to blow up, probably killing someone. It seems John Calvin was curious about how the Greeks were doing with the 40mm guns and went over to the armament shop. John was not a big drinker but on arrival the sailors handed him a sizable glass of 'raki.' This was about 1000 hours and at 1200 the crew saw the Greeks, one under each of John's arms bringing him back to the ship. I asked John on arrival, how the de-milling was going. I only received a groan back. He went straight down to his bunk with his curiosity lessoned considerably!

The bow anchor was lowered to the water and then pulled back up into the hawse pipe. The LST 325 was almost ready for a trial run.

The 'helpful hardware man' in Souda, where we went for bolts and nuts, electric switches, pipe, the flush toilets and many other things, did not have fuel filters for our GM 671 engines. He took me to the travel agent next door to his hardware store to have the woman there interpret for him what I wanted. I told her, she told him, and he smiled at me and answered, "Come back with one of your old filters and I will get you filters!"

I turned around and walked a mile back to the ship to acquire and find a used filter. Then moving fast as I could, returned to his store carrying the oily canister. When I returned with the filter, he directed me across the street to his car and motioned me to climb in. After a mile of driving on an unpaved road, a gigantic warehouse in the middle of nowhere magically appeared. We entered through a garage door, approached the counter, and in Greek the two men started communicating while looking at me once in awhile. The warehouse operator took my old filter and retreated between two long rows of shelves opening boxes, comparing filters with the ship's old one, going to the next until I could barely see him. Soon he returned, placed a new filter on the counter, and positioned my old one next to it. I checked the holes, diameter, and height; both were exactly the same. He had found the filters to fit the 671s! I bought fourteen of them, just guessed at how many we would need for that long trip across the desert. I paid the man in drachmas, and we drove back to Souda. As I got out of his car, I asked the hardware man, "How much do I owe you?"

He stared at me and, somewhat annoyed, said in his broken English, "Friends do not pay friends." He turned and walked back to his business! I hoped I had not lost his friendship. The best part of all, we were considered friends. I visited him before we left and thanked him for all of his help. To cement this relationship, he twisted my arm to drink a shot of Ouzo with him! Does this happen anywhere in the US?

We had become, in many ways, citizens of this little town. We were now almost one of the community. The taxi cab drivers charged me half of what it first cost me for a ride to the Navy base. Jack and I bought Greek plastic flags on a stick and waved them during a parade of the local school kids led by their grade school band. Bruce, Dewey, and I were invited to new business grand openings. It seemed anyone opening a new store would have one shortly after starting up. The *Brass Shop* had one such grand opening, with free pastries and wine! Boats, Dewey, and I would never have missed that and neither did the Greek Orthodox Priest. He showed up at all of them! He later came aboard and blessed our ship and our journey for home! How nice was that?

Nick's son wanted to see the ship. I knew I had to get special permission for that. I went directly to the Captain in charge of the guards at the gate. He gave me a pass for the boy on a certain day. I picked him up and walked him through the gate and down to the ship. I gave him a full tour of the 325. When I told him that was it and said I would walk him back to town, he didn't want to leave. He had never been able to get on the Hellenic Navy base, or see a military ship, yet he lived right by it all of his life. He looked to be about fifteen.

We made friends with several other merchants and one man who said he had been ten years old when the Germans occupied the airfield and the naval base in WWII. He told us he ran out into the streets when the American planes came over dropping bombs. He said he shouted up at our planes to please drop more. He was so happy knowing the days of the Germans in his home town were numbered. America never landed troops on this Island but gave air support to the Allies.

The Germans and Italians never took the mountainous interior of Crete. As told by a German soldier who was there in WWII, then returned on a vacation to see Crete and Souda where he had duty, exclaimed to us, "There was a Greek behind every rock as you went into the mountains. I was shot five times!" The Crete people still have their guns. They fire these guns in the air at weddings! They have refused to give up their weapons, as the 'mainland' people have had to do.

There was a well kept military cemetery in Souda. It was like an oasis, so green and well manicured, with white crosses in perfect rows. I looked to see if any Americans happened to be buried there, but only saw the graves of Australian and Commonwealth soldiers.

Boats had the Starboard side of the ship scraped and painted except for the ship's water line which was black and ran along the entire length of the ship about two feet out of the water. At the stern and bow, we could not reach the side of the ship as it turned away from the pier. We needed a boat to finish the black line. Our man 'Friday,' Jack Carter, came to the rescue as all the rest stood looking at the problem. He walked along the shore and disappeared towards town staying along the bay. He was gone about 45 minutes, when out in the bay and around the pier behind us, he came. He stood up paddling this little skiff of a boat, his image looked close to pictures of George Washington crossing the Delaware!

Strobel and Lockas jumped in the boat and painted the straight black line down to the water around the curve of the stern. After they completed the first area, Lockas grabbed the oar and paddled the boat to move it out from the pier to reposition it farther back. The skiff refused to move no matter how hard he pulled on the oars.

Strobel shouted, "Give me that paddle, Don, I will show you how to row a boat. There must be quite a current holding us here." Strobel really put his back into it but failed to make any progress.

The tide had come in and raised the boat up so the black water of the harbor hid the knot of the line securing the skiff to the pier wall. Boats reached down into the water after watching Ed and Don for a time, untied the line, and said, "Boys, maybe this will help!"

Electrician Bailey Wrinkle kept his tools that he bought, scrounged, or found, in a reed basket with a handle. It looked like an Easter Basket. His basket of tools turned up missing. He asked everyone and looked everywhere. He was beside himself since he couldn't do any electrical work. He was like a lost puppy. I tried to help by asking some of the crew if they had seen his tool basket, but no one had.

Boats Voges, with 20 some years of experience in the Navy, had been through some good years and some bad ones. After serving on several ships, he knew all about practical jokes; send new sailors on an LST to look for the 'Bow Door Key' or have a green recruit on the mail buoy watch, a yellow buoy with green stripes. He had swatted several sailors with a wood paddle when they leaned over to look under the cardboard box to see a live 'Sea Bat.' He had sent young men after green and red running light oil, a left-handed monkey wrench, a skyhook, a cable stretcher, and too many more pranks to mention. He still had not grown up as far as I could tell!

In one conversation, probably over a beer, Bruce told me he had received two Captain's Masts during his time of active duty. For each of these infractions, he was lowered one rate in rank and after each time he worked hard to gain it back. One time it was for not installing the drain plugs in the LCVP, or not checking that they were in, when he lowered the boat into the water. He admitted he was the senior petty officer in charge, but the plugs were the boat engineer's responsibility, not his. The Captain did not buy it. When he retired from the Navy, Voges became a bank president in Ogden, Illinois. He was not your average boson mate.

One morning before Quarters, Boats told me about a cardboard box in the passageway. He claimed it had been there a few days and suggested I take it out to Quarters and see who owned it. I learned to be cautious when Boats suggested something. The box looked harmless so at quarters I asked everyone, holding the box in the air, "Does anyone claim this box? It has been in the officer's passageway for several days." Not having any takers, I opened the box and pulled out its contents - Bailey's Easter basket with a colored Easter egg inside to boot! Bailey, from way in the back line screeched in a Tennessee accent, "You found my basket, you found my basket!"

Bailey downright refused to shell and eat that beautiful blue and red striped egg. He was sure that it probably was not hard-boiled. That was good thinking. The egg became ripe after a few days in eighty degree plus temperatures. Bailey, pressured by the crew, requested a burial at sea. I agreed, going along with this puerile event, and chose the fantail as the most proper setting. I asked Boats to come and say a few words over the egg. He refused of course. To continue this solemn ceremony and bury this egg, I said a few words, "Ashes to ashes, dust-to-dust. Lord, take this fallen egg to a better place and forgive the owner and the maker for they know not what they do. AMEN." Bailey tossed it overboard where the hot September wind out of the north caught it, blew it back towards the side of the ship causing it to be caught in the causeway rail, a 'U' beam on the side of the ship just above the waterline. Evidently the Lord did not want the egg buried in Souda Bay, but kept it in the rail for a long time. Bailey would check on it from time to time as did the Boats!

THE MEN CONTINUED TO PUSH THEMSELVES

CHAPTER 12

HEALTH PROBLEMS SURFACE

If thirty men operated the old washing machine, it surely would fail. Someone would turn the dial the wrong way, overload it, or abuse it in other ways until it broke. Mr. Albert White, who was somewhat limited having only one lung, was assigned to do all the washing of clothes for the crew. Prince Albert, as he was nicknamed, worked hard at the job. The Prince hailed from Roswell, NM.

We were fortunate to have a washing machine, but unlucky not having a clothes dryer. Albert solved the dryer problem by tying several clotheslines across the tank deck and hanging each batch of clothes up with clothespins. He then turned on the tank exhaust blowers. With 80⁻ degree temperatures and above, it didn't take long to dry clothes. The tank deck had become the 'World's largest' clothes dryer as its second purpose!

On those very same clotheslines, I quickly lost all ten pairs of my black *Gold Toe* socks. After complaining to Albert, he just said in disgust, "Really!" He always returned my laundry to my room folded nice and neat. When Albert returned my next batch of clothes, I must have had twenty pairs of black socks!

I needed to send some of the crew home. One man was Mr. John Michaud from Perryville, MO. John was 87 or 88, one of the oldest. When he came aboard, he told me that he didn't take any medicine. I thought this was amazing! After about three weeks, Prince Albert came up to me and asked if I knew John was sitting in a chair in the tank deck looking straight up at the overhead, and had been there for a couple of loads of laundry. He said, "I thought you should know." I asked him to find Doc. When I checked with Jack to see if he had seen Michaud or Doc Jones, he answered no, but tagged along behind me down to the tank deck. Our Corpsman, Norval Jones, from Auburn Hills, MI, had been found and stood there watching John who had not moved, still sitting on a folding chair and still looking up. I asked Doc if he had taken John's vital signs, which he set about doing. Doc listened to his heart with his stethoscope and then backed up. I asked, "What do you think Doc?"

He uttered, "I don't know, his heart doesn't sound good."

I said, "What are his vitals?"

Doc informed me, "John's blood pressure was eighty over fifty, pulse only forty-six and very weak."

I said, "Guess we had better call the ambulance."

The XO waved to me as he started going up to the quarter deck to make the call.

I said to Bruce, "Get hold of him, help me take him up to the quarter deck." John was now looking at me but not saying anything, and then he tried to stand. With Bruce on one side and me on the other, we walked him up two ladders and out to the quarterdeck.

I yelled at Doc, "You go with him to the hospital." He argued it was not his job. I wondered whose job was it! I said, "It is now! You can tell them his vitals and describe what John was doing and the state we found him in." Doc went but was not happy. We had found Michaud's emergency number to call his son and sent it with Doc.

The ambulance came from the Greek Naval Hospital, loaded John and Doc and left. The doctor at the hospital called John's son, found out he had been taking a ton of medicine back home, but had run out or stopped taking the medicine. In three or four days, the Doctor had him fixed up and I paid his entire medical bill - $95.00 American! Right after John's release, and on the Doctor's recommendations, I sent John home. His son said he did not want him to go in the first place; please send him home.

A second good man had a similar situation happen to him. Frank Conway, Blackwood, NJ, who I mentioned visiting earlier, worked for the railroad for forty years and knew the GM engines. I counted on him in the engine room. He quit taking his medicine, became dehydrated. He spent several days in the hospital, and after recovery, went home on his own.

Bill Hart was another man I had to send home. Bill was a quiet polite man with first rate personality. All the crew liked him. He looked to be in perfect health, but I noticed that he could not walk very far without sitting down to rest. He never tried to walk uptown. He tried to be as helpful as his evidently poor condition would let him. He scraped some paint in short intervals, cleaned the Officers Country, and helped some of the crew when they needed an extra hand. He lay down on the deck after trying to do too much one day and the XO called the ambulance and Edwards rode with Bill over to the hospital. At the hospital, the doctors hooked him up with a heart monitor, also an IV to inject some fluids. The doctor called his family and found out he had suffered not one, but three heart attacks in the last five years. The Doctors found his heart out of rhythm. Everyone was supposed to have received a complete CDL (truck driver physical) within five weeks before coming over. Bill had sent the M-man the physical taken FIVE YEARS before! Again, the Doctor explained clearly that Bill should not sail with us. He should be sent home!

Also on the ship was a man who liked his alcohol a little too much, a radioman. The crew told me he was under the influence at 0900 in the morning most every morning. He stood his quarterdeck watch, shot some videos, but most of the time he complained. One night when he returned back to the ship, the Quarter Deck watch, Corbin Fowkes, saw him walking a little unsteady so kept his eye on him. He arrived when the tide was high which elevated the ship at the pier and there was a gusty south wind blowing the ship from the pier. The lines would pull the LST back during short periods when the wind slacked. One had to wait for the wind's recesses letting the ship swing in closer, then time it and hurdle for the ladder. The radioman almost missed the ladder and was lucky to manage to get one knee on the bottom rung. Corbin yelled for help; Ron Maranto was on the deck. They circumnavigated down the ladder as fast as they could and grabbed hold of the man about the time he lost his grip; they hauled him up on the ladder. When told of the incident, I thought this man was an accident waiting to happen. I could also see he was of limited value to the ship. His drunkenness (or close to it most of the time) was a real danger to himself and the ship. As Captain, I could not take the chance to trust him to stand a watch underway. This decision was painfully hard to make being low on numbers for crew.

I came up with the idea of him escorting Bill Hart back to the states to make sure Bill would make it safely. He agreed, eagerly, saying yes, he wanted to go home anyway and take care of some personal jobs. As a result, he and Bill Hart bought plane tickets at the travel agency in town.

Bill tried to convince me to let him stay, arguing, "Captain, I really don't care if I die bringing this ship home; please let me stay."

He was not making my decision easy. I answered him with, "You might not care, but I do. I'm sorry, but I agree with the Doctor at the hospital. You must go home."

As it turned out Bill made it home, but had another heart attack in the airport in New York and did not survive. I felt bad when we heard this news, but knew I had made the right decision.

We had several cuts, some bruises, and many 'dented' heads. Paul Stimpson fell on the main deck caused by wearing some kind of flip-flop shoe that got caught and tripped him. He hit his head on one of the big irons that the deck boys used to tie causeways tight against the ship. He needed several stitches. Jim Young, an engineman and electrician, accidently scraped his leg against one of our running fire pump shafts in the Auxiliary Engine room resulting in a small cut on his anklebone. A butterfly type Band-Aid over it was suggested to save a long trip to the hospital for Jim. Doc disagreed, saying he might get infection. So away he went. They put in a couple of stitches and he returned in less than two hours.

About this time, we had several join us as crew. Electrician Gary Lyon, Roseville MN, had served on a Destroyer not on an LST, and Engineman William 'Rocky' Hill, from Surprise, AZ, both reported aboard as did a man from Michigan, a medium built man who looked somewhat older than he actually was. This man told many a story of being at D-day in June of '44. He was one of the new guys who went right to the gate thinking they would be let in the base, only to have to hang around there until we gave up waiting at Nicks.

When asked of his expertise, he said he could do anything. I inquired as to what he did in civilian life. His comment was, "I have had many jobs." I told him I could use a good man in the galley to relieve 'Lover boy' George White. George had been helping Cookie for three weeks, and requested a change of pace, a new assignment to deck. Why would I keep a Marine on KP (kitchen police)?

He said, "I can handle it, no problem." He turned aft and started walking for the Galley to meet the cook.

I yelled, "Joe is a little hard to get along with! Can you get along with people?" He stopped and walked back a few steps, then assured me he would not give the cook any problem. George was happy at being relieved about 0830 and reported to Boats. I was happy also!

Peace in the galley lasted through lunch to about 1400 hour. Joe stomped up the Officer's passageway to the Wardroom, wiping his hands on his white apron. He was not a 'happy baker.'

"Captain, I want that new man you sent back this morning removed and out of my Galley. He will not do anything I tell him! He can't even peel potatoes right, or wash dishes in hot water, or rinse them off in hot water." On and on Cookie went, his face getting redder and redder.

I interrupted, "Please Cookie, just take it easy and calm down. You surely must have had a girlfriend like that once! I have another first-class man in mind. I will get Ernie Andrus to help you for a while."

Cookie said, "OK, but I like Romeo George."

"Yes, I know you two 'ladies men' get along great. Must be because both of you kiss and tell."

I turned Mr. Michigan over to Boats and he put him scraping and chipping paint. This went on for about two weeks, and then he confronted me in my stateroom saying, "I really need to go home and take care of some business. This was not what I thought it would be; can I have my money back?"

"I quickly explained he could not get his money back. You signed up to help get this ship going and sail it back. There are no refunds. I believe we are about even if I charge you for room and board." He argued for several more minutes and declared this was not over. He packed his bags and left the next morning, after eating another breakfast on the ship. Several men who could not cut it went home asking of course for their money back. I stayed firm – no refunds.

A 'Dock Trial' was organized to perform more crucial tests with the engines, generators, and rudder. We would do everything as if we were going to sea. I didn't want a tug to pull us back when we attempted the bigger 'Sea Trial.' In order to test the vital equipment, a ship holds a dock trial. The ship remains tied to the pier as the rudder, radar, gyro, steering, and engines are operated. To test the main engines, I gave orders for one ahead and one back, then to neutral. Then I reversed the engines and went back to neutral.

The ship rebounded once, after going forward with the help of a stretched line, and some slack in the forward spring line. It came back like a boomerang with added force and a little farther than I had anticipated. It excited some crew before it stopped, made the Greeks in the LCI behind us quite nervous. I had quickly put the engines forward, but it took time for the forward turning propellers to take effect. I decided after that to call the dock trial a success and secured the engines. No sense in pushing my luck since everything worked. We were now ready for the important out to sea trial.

MEN AT THE BOOKIE JOINT WILL NOT SLEEP TONIGHT!

CHAPTER 13

SEA TRIAL

The day finally arrived with all our systems working. The Greek Commander gave me permission to take her for a run. We had a date set - October 16, 2000. I talked to the pilots; they ordered three tugs for 0800 the following day. My crew was excited looking forward to going to sea again. I was more anxious than excited. I didn't sleep wondering if everything the crew fixed would continue to work. A Sea Trial was a test drive, a run for five hours, out of Souda Bay and into the Mediterranean Sea for a short distance. The Greek sailors would box the ship's compass. This is a procedure done to adjust the Cardinal Points of the compass, mostly by adjusting the two black balls situated on both sides of the compass. The two metal balls are about six inches in diameter, generally black in color. These are an item of curiosity. Non sailors or land lubbers generally asked what those two balls are and what do they do. On this ship, one was red; one was green; the same as the ship's running lights on the bow - red for port, and green for starboard.

This reminded me of a fond memory: *A good friend of my wife and I, Mary Sutor, asked me that question as we walked by an actual ship's compass stand or binnacle displayed on the way into a restaurant on the Island of Maui one night. Mary had had a coke, and that was all Mary ever needed to put herself in a happy mood. "Robert," she said, pointing at the black balls. "I have always wanted to know what those things are." I laughed so hard, knowing what my answer would be. She prodded me to stop laughing and tell her.*

"Mary, those are the SHIP'S BALLS!" It took 10 minutes to get her to come up for air!

Mary, now almost crying, continued "Robert, tell me what are they for?" We all started laughing again. Finally I explained that they are also called the Navigator's balls and are used to adjust the compass by sliding them in and out; closer or farther away, to compensate for the ship's steel surrounding the compass so the compass will be as accurate as possible at all points. That was more than she needed to know! She was hysterical.

The balls do nothing for the natural variation, which is the difference between the true north and magnetic north. Deviation influences the compass, which is caused by the steel in the ship, electrical currents, and by some of the electronic equipment on board. The two balls help lessen deviation by moving them in (closer) or out. The variation and deviation combined are referred to as compass error.

The morning broke as most mornings did in Crete with a bright orange sun. A gentle breeze floated through my porthole, no clouds, and temperature at about 75 degrees. A perfect day, I thought, to take a ride on an LST. The crew worked fast and had the electricity switched from shore to the ship, and the electric power cord stored aboard. The pilot and a Greek interpreter climbed aboard. To my surprise it was the pilot who had ignored Jack and me during our visit to the white cylinder building.

The tugs, moored right close to us, first moved the *Kriti* to another pier. Then the tugs hooked onto the 'T' in the famous Greek tug arrangement always used by them for moving a ship. Two tugs positioned at the bow of the ship one pointing aft and the other forward along the port side of the ship and a third positioned at our stern pointing forward. The LST was moored starboard side to the pier, because of the placement of the gangway. Our men secured the tugs to the ship with our mooring lines. This hitch gave the pilot immediate control, allowing him to push forward or back in seconds.

Our main engines ran smoothly having warmed up the past 30 minutes. Generator #2 hummed with that distinguished cackled exhaust sound of a Detroit 671 that all enginemen recognize. We tested the rudder by turning the ship's wheel hard to the right and hard left. The engine order telegraph was tested as I called for forward and back on both main engines, then all stop. The LST 325's old mooring lines creaked as the ship moved a little with each engine order, but with a counter order, she steadied herself at the pier.

Gyro and radar worked fine. With old radars, one used a hood placed over the top of the radar face. The hood made the display dark enough to find contacts in bright sunlight. Generally, a lookout saw the contact and then one looked on the radar to see if it was there! At night, when dark, the OOD (officer of the deck) removed the hood.

I asked if the pilot was ready and for permission to take in our mooring lines. These lines were big and heavy – actually the old WWII hemp lines or similar ones. The men strained to pull them aboard especially after the bitter end hit the water and instantly soaked up some of the bay water, adding more weight. The Boson used three or four men to a line and then he helped too.

Boats passed the word to the CONN on his radio, "All lines on board." The pilot talked to the Greek interpreter, who asked me permission to get underway. I gave the OK.

I prayed the old girl would run and nothing would break down in the bay. I wanted the 325 to come back safely under her own power. I was confident and wanted to show the Greeks a successful sea trial. Most important, I was not paying any attention to the odds makers over town!

The forward tug pulled on the port bow as a large plume of black smoke shot up out of its exhaust stack. The bow of the LST started to turn left. The pilot had the stern tug also pulling which brought the stern out some, and then he stopped it. The LST slowly turned almost fifty degrees out from the pier. The pilot called for ahead on the starboard engine and back on the port. The two mighty GM's twisted the LST which helped the tugs bring this big girl around and close to ninety degrees out from the pier. The bow was soon aimed at the center of the Bay. The pilot stopped the forward tug and asked to have all three tugs released from the ship. Boats' men unhooked the lines in swift time as the pilot called for all stop on the ship's engines. When the tugs were free and clear, he said, "Both engines ahead one-third."

The interpreter, with a smile on his face, told me that I had the controls. I asked for all ahead two-thirds, then ahead standard. I told the wheelhouse to steer 080 degrees. The men cheered as I went up to standard on both engines and out into the bay. The 325 plunged ahead, smoke billowing out of both engines. The exhausts, placed port and starboard on LSTs, exited out on the sides of the ship five feet down from the main deck. Both are located forward of the stern about one-third the length of the ship, almost directly opposite of the CONN, where I stood. Sighting ahead on the gyro repeater, I made sure my course was correct. The gray lady gained speed hitting nine knots. The dark green water of the bay pushed out in big waves by the bow and behind us the wake was just a-boiling, being churned by the seven foot diameter wheels. I wondered what the bookies were doing in Souda at this moment! I smiled at the thought of their sheer panic.

Some of the men had not been on a moving LST since the end of the War on August 15, 1945. The Korean War vets had not been on one since 1953. I had not been underway on one since April 2, 1965. None of us had expected to be on an LST ever again. Here we were, sailing again on a ship we loved, and many said we could never make her move! My crew had worked hard to get this ride and if it all ended here, it would be a great accomplishment and worth all of our time, heartache, sweat, and money spent! These men could hold their heads high at home and keep their pride. They would have a story for the younger and older members of their family. This was the greatest crew to ever sail an LST by far, but I was very aware that the crews of the other one thousand and fifty LSTs that were made in WWII would argue - not so. Where else could one find a crew, most with three years of experience on an LST, had traveled the Atlantic and Pacific Oceans, and had thousands of miles under their belts? Certainly not in WWII when boys were drafted or enlisted right out of high school, trained for a few weeks, and sent off to war on an LST. Even the Captains had little or no sea experience.

Some Captains received political appointments to ships like John F. Kennedy. For the record and a bit of trivia – what kind of a ship did Kennedy ride on out to his PT 109 boat in the Pacific? Why, he was given a first class ride on an LST! One other huge difference with WWII crews, the LSTs were new!

An Admiral once said he would rather have a good crew and a poor ship than a good ship and a poor crew. I felt lucky – I had a GREAT CREW AND A GOOD SHIP to boot.

I pulled out my Greek cell phone and turned the CONN and controls over to a smiling and happy Jack Carter. I knew that Jack would want to be at the helm of an LST again, one more time for old time sake. Jack wanted to be the OOD (Officer of the Deck) of LST 325 as bad as I did. He would have similar memories flooding back. He might be reliving a time in his life when at a young age, he suddenly had loads of authority and responsibilities as a Navy Line Officer. After leaving the Navy, it took years before I had that same amount of responsibility.

My first call was to the Command Master Chief at the US Naval Station as we sailed right by the Naval Base. It was off to my left high on the bluff overlooking Souda Bay. The 'T' ran smoothly and zipped along. As we've jokingly said, 10 knots was water skiing speed on an LST!

The Chief answered "Captain Bob, what's up?"

I told him, "Why don't you get off your butt, go outside, and have a look in the Bay. You might see something that's sort of gray and making waves!"

There was a short pause, and then he screamed into my phone, "Do you have that ship underway?"

"You better believe we do."

All I heard was, "Hey you guys" as the CMC must have called to the men in the office and then, "I have to go. I'll get the Captain and the rest of the men and have a look! I don't believe you Bob, but everyone here will want to see this!" The cell phone went dead.

This was 'the shot heard around the world' or at least to Washington, D.C. I could imagine the discussion that took place at our State Department with Madam Albright. It may have gone something like this; *"Have you heard Madam Secretary?* **Those old guys** *in Greece have that LST running. Now what in Heaven's name do we do?* (I would guess they might have used the other popular place's name!) *They are going to ask to bring it back across the Atlantic!"*

I also called, Mr. O'Grady so Ambassador Burns would not be surprised when his phone rang! Dan must have been in the Ambassador's office as he said, "Captain, here is the Ambassador."

He congratulated me and said, "Tell the crew *Bravo Zulu* for me."

All of us on the CONN looked down at the crew. Those not on watches were all on the main deck giving each other 'High Fives' and waving at Maranto who was in the diver's boat following alongside. He was making a video of this once in a lifetime event. Their heads were over the sides of the ship watching the water slip along as this fifty-eight year old lady cut a proud path through the green waters of Souda Bay.

I felt sorry for one of our crewmembers – Ron Maranto. He had volunteered to take still and video pictures of our progress or lack of. Then along came the Sea Trial and he naturally wanted to ride the ship! I said, "Ron, a video of a sea trial from a small boat that runs alongside would be the proof the crew needed that they sailed the LST." The Greek divers agreed to take Ron in their little boat. So there he was in the boat, shooting a great video and watching the rest of the crew as they waved and jumped around in sheer delight riding on the LST once again. His disappointment showed in his face as he looked up at me - *if looks could kill*!

Maranto had signed on as an Electrician's helper and worked with Jim Edwards and Don Chapman. Ron was a volunteer at the *D-Day Museum* in New Orleans and assisted in the building of the LCVP (Landing Craft Vehicle Personnel) they have on display now. They had built it new from the ground up and it was a fine boat! When they decided to build a new one because they could not find an LCVP that qualified, they asked the Greek plywood manufacturer who actually made the marine plywood for the LCVPs (AKA Higgins boats) in WWII if he would make the plywood for their proposed new boat? He re-tooled his factory, since the length and width of the plywood for an LCVP had slightly different specs than the standard sized sheets of plywood. He did this and then donated the plywood. Ron had a plaque of appreciation to deliver in person when he arrived in Athens.

Out at the end of the Bay, it was time to adjust the magnetic compass. The Greeks did this procedure for us as I turned the ship, and they did a great job as our compass was right on. Compass accuracy might prove to be a good thing later if or when we cross the Mediterranean Sea and the Atlantic Ocean. Standard procedure when setting a course was to always make note of the compass reading in case the gyro was lost. The Lionel Company that makes toy trains manufactured the 325's compass during the war. They changed their operations from trains to compasses and telegraph keys for the Navy.

After the Greeks had calibrated the compass, it was time for a shakedown of LST 325. I knew I was not going to do anything to cause a breakdown; after all she would be two years short of sixty in twelve more days. She had come out of the Philadelphia shipyard in Pennsylvania on October 27, 1942. That shipyard only made thirteen LSTs. Once the Midwest shipyards on the Illinois and Ohio rivers were constructed and started producing ships, the Philadelphia Navy Yard returned to building other military ships. Philadelphia made the luckiest LST of all, the 325! It went through all of WWII with no one killed and now, if God permits, it will have a new life that I hope will last forever, its fourth life!

A 'Sea Trial' mainly tested the engines, propulsion and steering systems. Finally, I started the tests - Starboard Engine back full, Port engine ahead full, right full rudder, left full rudder, all back full. With only blue smoke when the speed of the engine changed, everything worked as it should. Even the 8-second delays between forward to back engine orders, worked as designed. The clutches are actually referred to as 'tires' because, when off the reduction gear, they look like tires. They are filled with air to grip and engage the engine, and deflated to disengage.

Now about four hours into the *Sea Trial*, we turned the ship towards the Greek Naval Repair base and our dock. I had requested to dock port side to the dock so Boats and crew could paint the other side of the ship, the port side. He had the starboard side scraped and painted. Sort of painted yes, but not scraped very well. He had purchased some long extensions for the paint rollers. The freeboard (distance from the water to the main deck) on the LSTs was eighteen feet. Subtract the pier height, approximately three feet; one had a long reach up to paint the whole side. However, with roller extensions, and paint from the US Navy (from different ships that came in over at the Naval base) he made quick work of it with his seven or eight old salts.

The Greeks had started painting their LST by putting men over the side on Boson chairs, sort of a rope with a flat board similar to a kid's swing and used to support a *young* man while working over the side. This Greek LST moored close behind us, had started several days earlier and had made very little progress as their sailors only had two hands and were hanging on with both of them! It only took a day with the Boats giving commands and keeping the paint in front of his crew to cover a big part of the side of LST 325. The Greeks noticed it almost instantly – especially, I imagine, by those hanging on the side. Guess what – the next day the rollers and long handles were in the hands of the Greek sailors, and paint flowed as those long rollers went up and down. Yes, the race was on.

The Greeks ran out of paint, and again the Americans came to the rescue; Boats was more than happy to loan them a five gallon can or two to finish up as I mentioned before.

THE BIG BLACK SHIPS ARE IN OUR WAY!

On our way back, those *big Black Ships* were anchored out in the Bay. These Black Ships, as I called them since they were big and black except for the superstructure which was white, were military ships run by Merchant Marine crews - Captains/Masters/Mates. The crews worked for our government and the ships belonged to our military. They were full of military equipment and carried a lot of fresh water and fuel. All of this equipment belongs to our Army - trucks, tanks, Humvees, guns, ammunition. These ships carry army/navy personnel on board to keep the batteries charged and everything in a ready state. These ships can go anywhere and be there fast and first, thus referred to as Prepositioning Ships. Deployed around the world they supplied water, electricity, equipment, and logistical supplies wherever they were needed. The inside of these ships appeared similar to parking ramps; equipment could be driven up from the very bottom, deck to deck right up to the main (top) deck, then off - loaded by cranes onto big airboats or smaller landing craft. We met the Captain/Master, Engineering Officer, and some of the crew in the *Sea Wolf* bar. We talked to them often, but they only stayed in Souda a few days, .and then sailed for an undetermined length of time. Their routine varied so our enemies never knew where they were.

Not surprising, the crews on the *Black Ships* had heard about the crazy Americans putting an old ship back in commission and with plans to sail it unescorted across the Atlantic. They were surprised to run into us. The Engineering Officer helped us with some questions on DC motors, our fire and flushing pump for one. We also told him we had a limited amount of fuel but the Command Master Chief had promised us Jet fuel, K-5. Chief Rabb had mentioned they had a million gallons of kerosene or obsolete Jet Fuel. They now used K-4 or something similar (I may have it backwards.) I didn't think we could use the jet fuel. The engineer quickly explained that I could by adding one gallon of lube oil with fifty gallons of Kerosene for lubrication.

The Master of one of those ships asked me what kind of a license I had. He said if you do not have all of the paperwork to sail the ship, they would take my license when I got back to the USA. I said, "I will hate that, it will take at least two weeks to get my Illinois drivers license renewed at home."

The Captain exclaimed, "You mean all you have is a plain automobile driver's license!"

I said, "You got it."

The LST had one of the loudest air horns I had ever heard. It may be short on some things but NOT on the volume of its horn or whistle as the Navy called them. I asked the interpreter to ask the pilot if we could sail in between the black ships and blow our whistle. The conversation between the interpreter and pilot went on for some time in Greek. They pointed at the Black Ships, glanced up at the whistle handle located in the CONN. I whispered to the XO, "The whistle blowing is not going to happen."

The interpreter turned to me and smiled, uttering, "Captain, your pilot, (and said his name which I'm sorry I can't recall) told me he has been a pilot here for 20 years. He has never in all that time ever deviated from the course into the Repair Base or out of the base to the Mediterranean Sea. It would be fun to shake up those Americans a little, and yes, you may go between them and blow that whistle all you want!"

I told Jack to hang on and shouted down the voice tube, "Right twenty degrees rudder, steady as you go. Someone man the whistle handle, and let's have some fun!" I called down to the engine room to be sure I had air to the horn. I had the 'T' pointed exactly between the two ships. I then slowed down to one-third ahead. The anchor watch sauntered out of the Black Ship's wheel house up on top of the Black ship on our port side.

Jack seized the handle on the whistle and gave it a big jerk. At first a little air hissed out. Then a low deep roar squawked to a deafening sound. I have compared this to a freight train trying to warn a car on the crossing, only much louder.

Jack eased up only to blow it again, longer this time. Crews on both of these ships scampered to the rails from every deck. They came, we believed, to watch a big collision that obviously was going to happen. When they saw us, they waved and blew their own whistles – not nearly as loud as ours, but still loud. I think the Navy headquarters believed an enemy attack was eminent. "What are those crazies on the LST doing now?" The pilot enjoyed our antics, as did the Greek interpreter. Our crew waved their hats back at the men on the black ships. They would have to get used to hearing this ship's whistle!

Greek tugs called out by the noise started towards us. I gave the CONN back to the pilot and he had us hook up the tugs, now to our starboard side. With the tugs fastened solidly to us, the pilot did a marvelous job of placing the 325 along the pier. We tied up, and pulled the electric shore power cord over the side to the pier. The Greeks hooked us up to shore power; we shut down the mains and generator, secured steering, pilothouse, and engine rooms.

We were now ready to travel, but we soon found out the State Department had come out of their initial shock of the crew's success with the LST running. They had more up their sleeves. Our underway plans for the LST 325 to head for home were far from a certainty. We had the old girl running but soon found out the paperwork was not forthcoming.

WE COULD NOT LEAVE SOUDA

CHAPTER 14

STATE DEPARTMENT STALL

When we returned from our very successful Sea Trial, we had everyone talking. The bookies uptown lowered their odds from 27 to 1, down to even odds or 1 to 1! No more bets on the old guys! All of the crew and our supporters back home only had one question, "When are you coming home?" Edwards was not the only one wanted in Texas. In all seventeen states, the families were waiting and wanted their men home!

The port side of the ship had to be scraped down and painted; Boats wasted no time going right to work.

Jack and I climbed the stairs up to the Headquarters to see the Commander. He was all smiles, probably at the mere thought of us leaving and finally getting rid of us, and his life back to normal. As we entered his office, I simply asked, "What are the procedures to finalize the paperwork releasing the ship so we can sail for home?" Since this was a first, he freely admitted he was not sure. The CDR volunteered to talk to the Commodore, who he hoped could find out some answers from our State Department. He asked me if I wanted to take the ship out some more and make sure everything was ready for an ocean crossing. I told him no! There was no reason to wear the old girl (or him) out! I referred to the ship as *him* as the Greeks do.

The CDR laughed and said, "Well, if you do want to sail it some more, I can arrange it."

After that discussion, the CDR told us he had received a lot of heat from our State Department and the 'big boys' in Greece. Our State Department wanted to know who authorized letting us take the ship out on a Sea Trial. "Your US Navy was also upset. I told them all, Captain Jornlin requested a Sea Trial and I said OK. They wanted to know who gave me the authority to do that." The CDR continued, "I was placed in charge to supervise the project to get the LST restored and running. What were these veterans doing over here working their fool heads off to get the LST running? Then when they do, I am not supposed to let them take it on a Sea Trial? I also told your Navy that you were not in the Navy anymore and that I know they have zero control over you. I should not have had to explain to anyone in your government or mine. An operational underway test is what you do after you recover a ship out of mothballs and place it in running condition. Taking the ship on a Sea Trial was the next step."

CDR Nikoldakis added that he told them about the Hellenic Navy's LST that was brought out of mothballs and that it had been on <u>THREE</u> Sea Trial runs. All three ended with troubles. He went on in some detail, "On the first of three trial runs, our LST had engine problems out in the Bay and we had to send a tug to pull her back. On the second test run, the Captain made a practice beach landing, backed over the stern anchor cable, wrapping the cable in the screws. We had to tow it back again! It took our divers two days to unwind the stern cable from around the screws. The third trial went smoothly until the ship's Captain was along the pier and the ship lost electricity. With these newer LSTs, they have variable pitch propellers. These are nice, since the Captain never has to slow the engines down, or use a clutch to change from forward to reverse. Electric hydraulics turn the screw blades forward to reverse. One little problem happened when the electricity was lost as our new Captain learned; the screws went into reverse automatically, so the ship departed right back out into Souda Bay. We were happy a Ferryboat was not going by at that time! Fortunately, the crew restored the electric power, the screws turned back to forward pitch, and the ship returned to the pier."

The CDR then said to Jack and I, "The two of you took an older ship, a ship we thought was dead and not restorable, out for five hours. You scare half the town and all of us with your whistle blowing and you come back under your own power to your pier. You add to this by declaring the ship is ready to cross the Atlantic Ocean! In short, you and your men have shamed the Hellenic Navy! I will get back to you as soon as I hear something. Enjoy the rest of the day."

I set about trying to purchase fuel so we could go home. I walked to the Greek fuel-purchasing department. It was right across the square from the *Sweet Sixteen*. A very polite woman asked me what she could do for me. I told her who I was and that I wanted to buy tax-exempt diesel fuel. When leaving Greece, I believed no Greek fuel tax had to be paid. She took me over to another office right in the Ferry dock area. After a half hour wait, we went in to speak with the man who could exempt us from fuel tax. He asked me questions about the LST. Since it was not a Navy ship now, did it come under a yacht designation? I supposed that it could. He wanted assurance we would not carry cargo, only the crew. He had a Russian name and was not particularly friendly. He said come back tomorrow.

As instructed, the next morning I picked up the fuel lady and we returned to the man's office and waited again. He finally called us in. He simply said that the ship did not qualify for tax-exempt fuel. The lady argued with him speaking Greek and answered why not, but got nowhere. He said, "*No.*" Sorry was not in his vocabulary. He did mention the undertaking by our crew reminded him of the movie, *Space Cowboys*.

I said, "One big difference; this is not a movie."

When I told the CDR at the Base, he replied, "Those Russians are that way. I have found it hard to deal with them!"

I knew we needed and should have approved life rafts, so Voges and I visited the Marine equipment store. It was located about half way between *Nick's* and the *Brass Shop*.

I asked, "Do you have canister life rafts?"

They said, "Not on hand. We can order them." They searched through a catalogue. After looking at the pictures, we pointed to a 20-man life raft. We needed two of them. At this point, Bruce tried his negotiating skills one more time – with about the same result. They quoted us a price of $1,500 each.

Bruce asked, "How long will it take for delivery?"

They answered, "We will give you a 1,000% guarantee we will have them in a week."

I said, "That will be OK, we expect to leave at the end of next week." We paid half down on the rafts. We had two Eperbs on board, brought from the USA. Eperbs are emergence distress beacons that send out a radio signal pinpointing your location. These are still in use today.

As we started walking back to the ship, Bruce asked, "Do you think a 1,000% guarantee is as good as 100%?"

I laughed, "Bruce, it has to be 10 times better!" Souda followed along right beside us as we entered the Greek gate. This was one more item marked off my list of things we had to do before we sailed.

The Greeks let us go over to a warehouse and pick up 30 lifejackets. These fit around your neck. We had about 35 old dirty ones left on board, the 'May West' type worn like a jacket, and they tied in the front. We also bought some flares and a flare gun from the life raft people.

Back aboard the ship, we heard several of the crew laughing. Bruce asked, "What is so damn funny?"

Dewey explained through his laughter, "Well, John Calvin got up this morning and made the statement that he had an erection last night, his first one in three years!"

Dick Meyers passed by at that time and said to John, "Did anyone see it?"

John said, "Of course not!"

Dick said, "Well then, it doesn't count!" He kept right on walking.

John Calvin from Dunnelon, FL was also a 20-year man with our Navy. He made Chief Engineman and was in WWII. John had a bad accident only a few months before coming to Crete. He was in a parking lot placing groceries in the trunk of his car when an older lady backed out opposite him. She accidently hit the accelerator instead of the brake, rammed her car's rear bumper into John's car smashing his legs at his knees. After many surgeries, he could walk but could not maneuver the twenty-foot ladders down to the engine rooms. We made a bos'n out of him or deck ape. John did a great job as a helmsman and watch stander. When we eventually became very short of engineers, I threatened to rig up a block and tackle to drop him into the main engine room!

The Boats stopped at my stateroom, motioned for me to follow him to the front of the cargo hatch. Piled on top of Boat's cargo hatch were some round disks of solid lead about one-third of an inch thick and twelve inches in diameter, about eight of them. (Everything on deck belonged to Boats or so he thought!) I knew Strobel had cut them out of some canvas code bags. These bags were used to stuff the ship's secret files and codebooks in if the enemy boarded the ship in a time of war or if abandon ship was ordered. At that point, these weighted bags were dropped overboard. Strobel had a use for the white canvas but not the lead, at least not at this time.

Boats, with a little help from me carried the heavy disks into Strobel's stateroom located on the port side opposite the head in Officer's Country. He picked up Ed's mattress and stuck these lead disks under the center of it, one on top of the other. He then situated the mattress and Ed's covers back down on top. He made this bunk look as good as he could with that swelling in the middle!

The next day Boats, with me in tow, found Strobel working with his canvas bags. Boats kept me ahead of him just in case Ed had figured out who the bad boy had been. Boats then asked him how his mattress felt. "Do you think we should buy some new ones?"

Ed replied, "Yes, mine has developed a big lump and my back hurts."

Boats eventually asked Ed to take us to his stateroom to see his lump-filled mattress. Of course I tagged along. Boats lifted Ed's mattress and showed Ed the lead disks, and said, "No wonder you have a lump in your bed!"

Ed just said, "Well I'll be." Boats and I left without comment.

We purchased thirty-five new mattresses, and with our Greek-American friend, John, we were able to arrive at a good price on some three-quarter-inch plywood to brace up some of the bunk bottoms. That crew of mine was in heaven! I secured two of the new mattresses and filled the deep hole in my bunk for an easier in and out!

Carter and I waited several days, then returned to see CDR Nikoldakis and asked him about the paperwork. It was a long walk up that hill and back. Nikoldakis asked us if we knew our State Department demanded that the Hellenic Navy allow the 325 to sail back under the Greek flag. "Our Admirals told them, 'No way.' We would be liable if you sank or maybe hit another ship in the ocean on your way home. Besides, we have this treaty with the other Mediterranean nations that we will only have a certain number of ships under our flag. If we let you take the L-144 out, we will be over our treaty limits. So, it is back in your state Department's corner."

The XO and I made an about-face and unhappily started down the long stairs, up our gangway to my anxiously waiting crew for our answer.

While we waited for the paperwork, the CMC and his wife transported the entire crew to the big city of Chania one Saturday afternoon for some R&R. A Navy bus picked us up in front of the ship and in twenty minutes via the winding road, we arrived. The bus let us out at the Crete Museum, a three-story building with very interesting architecture that featured several huge rooms loaded with different artifacts separated by millenniums. The History of Crete began 4,000 years BC, or when someone started keeping records. Chania was a walled city built by the Phoenicians back thousands of years ago. We learned from the CMC's wife, who gave us this history lesson, that Turkey had ruled Crete for some 300 years back in the 10-12th century. The Crete people hated the Turks. Legend has it the Greeks could not father their own children; a Turk had to do it!

We walked around the town. It had narrow streets with shops featuring crafts, antiques, and jewelry stores selling silver, jade, and other precious stones. We also found clothing stores, bakeries, nice restaurants, and taverns. Chania attracted tourists as well as the locals. Some of the streets were only five feet wide, and led back to small living quarters like the pictures I have seen showing biblical times. There was a modern part of Chania farther to the land side. This walled city was nestled right on the Mediterranean Sea in a semi-circle, which made for a sound sheltered harbor. A discreet restaurant was featured in the lower level of the light house at the entrance, maybe once a small fortress guarding the way in.

We ended up at one of these outdoor dining places, which featured beer in a glass shaped cowboy boot! Ever tried to drink beer or anything out of a boot? The crew tried it and seemed to get along OK. The CMC and his wife bought lunch, but then came up with an average price for each man in the group to pay. Guess it was 'Dutch Treat' after all. We paid it out of the slop fund. Everyone seemed to have a great time and we appreciated what the CMC and his wife had done for us.

The CMC then told me he would buy us some ball caps with 325 stenciled on them, and estimated the price. In a week, the CMC brought the hats to the ship. I quickly realized the hats were not made well and the 'one size fits all' was too small to fit any of the crew. I had considerable expertise in ball caps. As a District Sales Manager for several seed companies, I easily gave away ten thousand hats in my thirty years and I knew what people liked. We made the Chief return them.

The CMC had more made which were better, but this raised the price even higher! He asked me to help with the cost of the first caps since the manufacturer would not take them back. I refused to do that. I said. "You ordered them; you are stuck." Later, we decided to pay for half of them and keep some peace between us.

THE M-MAN WANTS TO COME BACK!

After hearing of our sea trial success, the M-man wrote a letter to the Greek Navy. He did this without any approval from the board members, the National LST Association, or anyone else. Several sources in the Hellenic Navy vowed they would never turn the 325 over to the M-man for obvious reasons. His letter stated that Congressman Ralph Hall, because of his full schedule in the House of Representatives, could not attend the Transfer Ceremony of the LST. Therefore, he (Melcher) was the only one who could sign for the ship. He would need fourteen days notice to arrange for transportation and travel time. Melcher also told Linda Gunjak, Secretary of the National LST Association, that she was not to send any of the Voyage Fund money to us. The Gunjaks had been collecting the donations (given mostly by LST veterans) to the Memorial to help us bring this LST home. The M-Man's letter went to the Hellenic Navy, the ODC, and the Ambassador declaring he (Melcher) was also the only one qualified to bring the ship home. (This was sort of a laugh considering he only made second class engineman in the navy!) He told them, among a bunch of other nonsense, he had only given me authority to get the ship operational. He would now bring a competent crew to sail it home! He sent a signup sheet to the ship to post on the galley bulkhead for our crew to sign up and be on his crew. I wish all could have witnessed the names that went on that list, such as: Barefoot Bill, Jimmy Carter XI, Slippery Sam, Al Capone, and many I should not put into print. I knew it was close to impossible for him to raise a crew in a month of Sundays and not from my crew.

After talking it over with Strobel, Carter, Voges, Bartlett, and Edwards, we decided to hold an emergency meeting of the *USS LST Ship Memorial* Board of Directors. If the board members present could vote some new members on the board, we could also vote to remove the M-Man! Mr. Gunjak had an argument back in June with the M-man and resigned as President of the Memorial. We had voted Congressman Hall on the Board as President. The directors were Edwards, Ballard in Louisiana, Jornlin as Secretary, Linda Gunjak as the Voyage Fund keeper, and Melcher as Technical Director. I called Hall and Ballard, explained what the M-Man had done and the fact that the Greeks were not going to turn the ship over to him.

Congressman Hall said he would do whatever the majority wanted, stated as a true politician. Ballard said he needed an invitation and date to the (supposed) big *Transfer Ceremony* for him to vote to remove Melcher from the board. I had to promise we would invite Ballard to the ceremony if one was ever held. I had heard months ago that a ceremony transferring the ship was to happen, but under the circumstances, it was probably a fantasy. I had no direct knowledge as it was never mentioned. None of the crew wanted to wait one more day to sail, once we received the go-ahead and paperwork. They certainly would not wait for fourteen days for someone to arrange transportation and fly to Greece!

I had Edwards write a letter to the M-Man, stating because of his actions he had jeopardized the return of LST 325. Therefore, by a vote from the majority of the board he was no longer a board member. He was to refrain from any further correspondence with the Greek Navy, our Navy, or the State Department. He no longer had any authority to represent the USS LST MEMORIAL and was not a spokesperson for the Memorial.

I also sent the following letter to Congressman Hall, Ballard, and Ambassador Nick Burns, Peter Leasca (Boston), and Mike Gunjak, representing all US LST Association Members. This letter was from the crew of LST 325, Crete, Greece. It stated:

We the undersigned crew of LST 325, in Souda, Crete, do proclaim our support to the Officers of this ship and to Robert Jornlin, our Captain. We also proclaim Ambassador Burns, the ODC, our US Navy, and especially the Hellenic Navy have supported us in our quest to bring back LST 325.

The crew signatures were on the letter. Only one member did not sign: Mr. Dave Williams.

HOW DO WE GET OUR PAPERWORK?

CHAPTER 15

THE 325 BECOMES A PIRATE SHIP

I went into the Greek Coast Guard Office to learn what I needed to qualify for a SOLAS certificate that I hoped they would issue to the 325. They looked at me like I was talking Russian or some other foreign language! The Greeks said I didn't need one. SOLAS stands for *Safety of Life at Sea.* I had two problems. I couldn't obtain a SOLAS certificate in Greece and the ship couldn't make the grade to be registered as a U.S. vessel.

About this same time, a gentleman called me. He told me that he had met a Maritime Lawyer by the name of Sean Connaughton who said he could get the LST registered, and to have the Captain call him. The man gave me the lawyer's phone number and also expressed his services would be offered 'Pro Bono!'

I called Mr. Connaughton as soon as I could. He informed me he thought he could have us registered in three days! As directed, I called him back in three days. Sean told me he was sorry, but after talking with the Coast Guard, there was no way to do it without dry docking the ship, running all the equipment, obtaining a tonnage and load line certificate, a title and more. I asked if Navy ships have titles. Sean laughed and said not that he was aware of! "Frankly, Captain, you could spend a year and a lot of money and it still would not pass."

I was now desperate and said, "What can I do?" Sean flat out said we could bring it back unregistered. I asked him if that was legal? When we arrive back in the states, will they arrest me?

Sean told me, "A non-registered ship is really a *Pirate Ship*. A *Pirate Ship* does not have a Country. If one doesn't have a Country, then one doesn't have any laws. If one doesn't have any laws, well one cannot break any! I will defend you 'Pro-Bono' in any Maritime Court with that argument and win!"

Sean added one more important detail: Pirate ships couldn't enter any port anywhere in the world. The U.S. and the other countries had agreements on this and all were very strict.

Sean then said, "Consequently, Captain, do you think the LST 325 can be sailed from Greece all the way back to the United States without stopping anywhere?"

I answered, "Mr. Connaughton, in all my experiences with LSTs, it would be next to impossible. However, I have a crew determined to try it."

He said, "Captain, you have my number. If I can be of any help, please call me!"

Sean added, "Oh! One other thing, Captain, You cannot fly an American Flag!"

After the Sea Trial, I had several men who decided they had their ride on an LST and that was enough. Ed Whitman left without saying a word. He bought a plane ticket, I guess with my dinner money! He had lost his job with the RR. His girlfriend had found another boyfriend. He went home. I learned later that he actually lived with the M-man and his wife in Brady, NE. Jim Bartlett had to go home to take care of some business. He never said what that business was. I never asked him, believing it was none of my business. I knew his brother was sick and lived alone and Jim took care of him. He also was the proud owner of two Corgi dogs that needed care. I was not sure who was watching after them. He had sold his home he built in Marble Falls, TX and maybe had to go to the closing on the sale. I knew we were going to miss him; the whole ship would miss him, as he was our 'fuel and water king.' He purified fuel, filled the main engine day tanks (fuel) and could fill and empty ballast tanks, run the generators and the main engines. He knew a lot about the Engineering systems on the ship.

Dave Williams, billeted as quartermaster and radioman, started preparations to leave for home according to some of the crew. I had quite a discussion with him up at Nick's where he went to use WI-FI for access to the internet. He told me he was leaving because the ship was unsafe. In order to get him to stay, I asked him to point out what he deemed hazards and safety issues and we would fix them. In addition, I let him move into Bartlett's former stateroom in Officer's Country.

When Williams came to Quarters the next morning, I knew I would have some problems with certain crewmembers. They had told me he was critical of the ship. He had said the ship was not safe and it would never sail.

Simply stated, for anyone to tell the crew the ship would never sail and that they all should go home, was the quickest way to find out the temperature of the Souda Bay water and how deep! After a couple of the crew asked me why I was letting Dave have an Officer's stateroom, I told them the truth. I needed every man to sail the ship. We stood too close to the breaking point, with too few men to operate the ship safely. That explanation was not enough. One had some very direct and harsh things to say about Dave to his face. Dave was standing there to hear them – at least at first. When the crew stopped pointing out the reasons why Dave should not stay, I looked back for him to give a rebuttal. Dave was long gone. He half packed his bags, leaving most of his clothes behind. Dave had told me he was leaving and I had delayed that decision with an offer of a better stateroom and a promise to fix the safety issues he pointed out. I believe my actions were only a short stopgap before he would have left anyway. Maybe it was better for the ship and him to leave now instead of later.

One almost had to be on board to understand this was a close-knit group for the most part. They were tired, not only physically, but also mentally from negative assaults from their friends and strangers, our state department, Coast Guard, and the bookies over town. Maybe I gave them too much information at certain times. We were all willing to fix safety issues, but none of us figured out how to be younger. Old age was a big factor against this crew accomplishing this task, and many had pointed this out. Dave Williams was a Vietnam veteran and considerably younger than most, even younger than I was. As a radioman and quartermaster, he was limited in his knowledge of machinery and Damage Control. For him to say the ship was unsafe was largely made up I thought, and perhaps a result of his many conversations with the M-man. He seemed a loner for the most part and did not see eye to eye with

Nickerson. I thought he was intimidated some by Nickerson as both were vowing to be the Chief Navigator, a position that was not going to exist on the 325!

AMBASSADOR BURNS GOES TO WASHINGTON

A high-level meeting was held at the State Department in Washington D. C. that included Ambassador Burns, Congressman Ralph Hall, Priscilla Roberts, several Senators, several other Congressman, a couple of Navy Admirals, and I believe, the Secretary of State, Madam Albright, along with her Washington D.C. team that had refused us a working LST.

Priscilla and I had talked many times since my arrival in Souda with reports from both sides of the pond. She told me this meeting started out with the State Department telling everyone these Navy Vets had this LST running and now wanted to bring her home. This was an old ship, had been through the whole Second World War and then the Greeks sailed her for the last thirty-five years. Department officials were worried about the men's safety crossing the Atlantic in the wintertime. Their gloom and doom tale of woe had us reach the middle of the Atlantic and the dilapidated old ship broke down, or developed a leak. Well, we (State Department) would have to send the Navy at a great cost to our government to rescue everyone. Then these old sailors would have to watch as the Navy sank their beloved ship, an LST they searched everywhere for and put so much work into making it run. Their hearts would be broken. The Navy could not leave it in the ocean as a Navigation hazard.

Priscilla said the State Department almost brought her to tears with their sad story. They asked Ambassador Burns for his opinion. He said the crew had the ship running well from the reports of the Navy on Souda. He had been to the ship, found it cleaned up, and the crew seemed competent and exceptionally determined to bring the ship home.

An Admiral stood up and looked around at the State Department officials who, for the most part, were uninformed about any aspect of sailing a ship, and didn't know an LST from a rowboat. Priscilla indicated he was disgusted with all of them.

The Admiral said, "Gentlemen and Ladies, I have heard enough. Here we have some very dedicated Navy veterans, the majority of them WWII, trying to bring back a ship from Greece they all served on. In the war they dodged bombs, torpedoes, mines, aircraft scrapings, and mortar shells launched from the beaches they landed their ships on. You have thrown roadblock after roadblock to stop them without any success. You have forgotten you are dealing with real men. You do not say why you want to stop them, except for some concerns about their safety, health and, I can't believe, their hurt feelings if the ship sinks! They haven't even asked for our help, but worked and accomplished the impossible. If I were retired, I would be over there helping them. We all should be thinking of ways to assist these men. If you can't do that, please get out of their way and maybe give them a prayer that they will be successful."

Priscilla said, "The meeting changed from eminent failure to positive suggestions to help!"

I said to Priscilla, "Please thank that Admiral!"

OTHER EVENTS CAUSED DOUBT

I had problems dealing with the Embassy to allow us to sail with such a small crew. Fortunately, I had sailed an LST with twenty-five men and five officers for more than a year in and out of Little Creek, VA. Then NEW HEADLINES! Terrorists in Yemen blew up the USS COLE! What a tragedy! Because of that, many more questions about the dangers of sea travel and, did I believe it was wise to sail the ship at this time?

We attempted to put out the word: if the *USS COLE* came through the Suez Canal, could the LST 325 escort her back home? This request was quickly denied; the *COLE* went south around the horn of Africa and then across the Atlantic to Pascagoula, Mississippi.

The next incident, which really put pressure on us not to sail, was the terrible tragedy of a Greek Ferryboat out of Souda that ran aground near an Island on a windy cool night dead center on the marker light. Some 150 or more passengers lost their lives.

As reported in several Greek newspapers, the most plausible cause of this accident centered on a championship Greek Soccer game. It definitely had to be pilot error to run a boat aground directly on the light, placed there as a warning to keep ships from hitting this land mass. I assume having set the Ferryboat on automatic pilot, all of the Officers had gone down below to watch that game, or even worse had a TV on the bridge to see their good Greek team playing that night. An automatic pilot would hold a course, but someone on the Ferry had not allowed for a strong wind off the beam of the ship that had pushed the ship off course.

This same ill wind, after the Ferry ran aground a distance from shore, caused the canister life rafts when deployed to blow away. The Ferryboat crew quickly, it was said, climbed into several lifeboats and disappeared. This left most of the passengers stranded on a sinking boat absent now of life rafts. Many more would have died, but some Greek Army soldiers on board saved many of the passengers.

Again I was asked if I should make this dangerous crossing in that old ship. "You saw what happened to a highly trained and qualified crew on the ferry," they interjected!

I told Mr. O'Grady, "For one thing, there was no TV on our Bridge or the ship for that matter. Secondly, since it was our very first and only trip, we would be paying attention and navigating all the way." That did not change their thinking, but I had neutralized some of their ridiculous, if not stupid, reasoning.

Jack Carter and I made another trip up the hill to the Headquarters. Again, the Commander said, "No paperwork yet. The last proposal was to let the LST be under the Greek flag out past the twelve mile limit into international waters. We turned that idea down for the same reasons as before."

Jack said to the Commander, "Sir, what are you having for Christmas Dinner?"

The Commander, surprised, leaned back in his chair and asked, "Why do you want to know that?"

Jack very seriously answered, "Well Sir, the Captain and I are going to be the only ones left on the ship pretty soon, and Christmas is coming. He and I will need a place to eat Christmas dinner!"

The Commander looked at us for a second, maybe thought about his wife's dinner plans, then quickly leaned ahead saying, "We better go upstairs and talk to the Commandant!"

Jack and I followed Nikoldakis upstairs to the Commandant's Office, where the CDR told the Commandant what Jack had asked him.

The Commandant just laughed and asked Nikoldakis, "Well, what are you having?" The Commandant told us that he would personally ask his bosses in Athens to speed this process up. Jack and I again strolled back down the steep stairs to the ship.

On the way down, I told Jack, "I've got some news for you about the need for a place to eat Christmas Dinner. Just find a place for you; I will not be here, OK?" Jack laughed and said he would not be there either! Our long faces gave the crew the answer to what we had learned, but they couldn't understand our laughter!

I had also talked to First Secretary Dan O'Grady about our problem with the loss of crew. I had informed him that a few more were tired of the delays, frankly had lost hope, and I believe were thinking of leaving. He replied, "Captain, you have to keep them on board. I know the paper work will be coming soon." Promises, promises...... I thought.

MY NEWT ROCKNE SPEECH AT QUARTERS

Jack Carter had put out the word on the web page that the State Department was holding up the paper work. In a couple days, I received a call from a person in our State Department. He begged me to stop the phone calls and e-mails. He said they were jamming up their systems and they could not get anything done. He went on to say that the State Department was not the problem, the Greeks were! I told him, "I sat directly across the desk from our Greek Commander in charge, and looked him square in his eyes as he said the U.S. State Department was the one holding up the transfer paperwork. Sorry, but I believe him! When the paperwork arrives, I will stop the e-mails and phone calls." He had a few more words, but I hung up.

Mr. Richard Meyers wrote a letter to Madam Albright and I faxed it to Dan O'Grady to please pass it to her. A synopsis of his letter follows:

When I was 17 years old, I was in the Navy on an LST in the South Pacific. My ship from time to time was under heavy fire from Jap airplanes. We were called to make several landings and suffered damage from mortars, but NO ONE worried about my health and

*wellbeing in the State Dept. – no one! Now I am 74 years old, know
what I am doing, and I want to bring back an LST from Greece. Now
you are worried about my health! Please stop it and give us our
paperwork. We want to bring this ship home. I thank you.*

   *Signed: Richard Meyers, United States Navy veteran, Lincoln, NE
in Souda.*

I believe this letter may have done some good with Madam
Albright, along with what the Navy Admiral expressed at the high-level
meeting. I first read Dick's letter to the crew at Quarters. I learned the
day before there were four crewmembers looking into the prices and
availability of plane tickets. These men hung around together and
thought alike. I knew they were not die-hards like most of the crew. I
could not afford to lose four more crew; I just couldn't. We were down
to a bare minimum crew of thirty men. We could sail with a couple less,
but not with four less.

After reading Meyer's letter at quarters, I flat out told the crew,
"Ok, I know a few of this group are planning to jump ship and go home
because you have evidently lost faith in us receiving the necessary
paperwork. I have warned First Secretary O'Grady that more delay by
the State Department may cause the loss of more crew, and if more of
my crew leaves, I will have no choice but to abandon the project. If that
happens the rest of us will fly home and will work hard to elect
Republicans, which may remove him and the Ambassador from further
government service."

Dan informed me that his job was not political; he would stay no
matter who became president. He said he and the Ambassador were
working hard to obtain the paperwork. They were behind the project,
and for us, all the way. He said, "Captain you must keep the remainder
of your crew. The Ambassador is working hard to get the transfer done."

In as stern and positive a voice as I could muster, "Men, all of you
have worked hard to get this ship running; I know this better than
anyone. We are so close to accomplishing this impossible task I can
taste it. Even the bookies have drastically dropped the odds now to even
money. You must be aware that at one time those odds reached a high of
twenty-seven to one that we were simply not good enough to get this
ship away from this pier. Isn't this enough proof? You have showed the
Greeks and the world what we are made of and have confirmed over and

over your commitment to this ship. Stay a little longer and show the Doubting Thomas's at home. Look to your left and then to your right. You will cause these crewmembers to fail, stopping them from accomplishing their dream of sailing an LST home."

"Guys," as Knute Rockne said, *"Give me one more win for the Gipper! I am asking for you to give me one more week to get this job done; how about it?"* I heard several say OK, one more week. A few clapped their hands.

The Boats and I set out for uptown and checked on our canister life rafts with our dog Souda right behind. The 1000% guarantee had not been enough! The life rafts had not come in, but the owners assured us again with a 1000% guarantee, in fact they would now give us a 10,000% guarantee that the rafts would be here next Monday! He explained that with the Ferryboat crashing into the island, life rafts were in big demand and that had slowed our order.

The XO and I set off up to the Headquarters again after three more days had dragged by. We had the same results as before. I wrote a letter to the Commandant and the Hellenic Navy, saying, "We will take the ship just as it is and where it is. We, the USS LST MEMORIAL, will not hold the Greek Government, Hellenic Navy, Souda Repair Base, or its officers responsible for any loss of life, injuries, or the loss of the ship in our Trans - Atlantic crossing to America. We take full and complete responsibility for our actions to sail this ship back home. I, as the Captain, will sign any release of similar words produced by your attorneys."

A bunch of us traveled back to Chania Friday morning, included as best I remember - Voges, Taylor, Strobel, Chapman, Edwards and myself. After walking around the town, shopping, and acquiring the price of plane tickets home, we stopped for lunch at a neat looking restaurant with an outside dining area. It was not busy at this time of day or this late in the fall. We had a couple of beers. We talked about what to do; my week was ending. Nobody had any startling suggestions. We had a couple more beers and ate lunch. We talked more on how we were going to save the ship. We had to show some progress or the four (and possibly more) crewmembers were sure to leave. I was worried if some left, then more would also give up with half of the crew going home!

Someone wondered if any of us had any brainy ideas. Surely, in our collective repertoire there must be something. I stated, "I am fresh out of ideas." Then out of the clear blue, after pondering our situation and eliminating all other possibilities, I realized there was only one move left. I spoke up, "Hey, how about taking the ship without the paperwork?" There was dead silence for a long time. All of us were law abiding citizens and this was definitely against our moral code, but I was desperate to do something before we had too few crew to sail the old girl. Someone ordered another round of beer.

Questions came fast. How are we going to do that? What would they do to us? I summed it up, "Gentlemen, we have absolutely nothing to lose. We are in the 11th hour of the last day. Our government gave us the LST 325 by an act of Congress, signed by the President; why do we need paperwork in the first place? What can they do to us? We have worked too hard to lose this ship now. She may well be a Pirate Ship, but she belongs to us. How do you all feel about sailing Sunday morning?"

I cannot remember if I made this decision right at the time or waited until after I got back to the base.

CAPTAIN, YOU ARE CRAZY. LET'S GET BACK TO THE 'T'

CHAPTER 16

SWASH BUCKLING CREW TAKES THE

PIRATE SHIP

What say mates?

When I arrived back on the Base, I hurried to the Headquarters and told the assistant duty officer, a Lieutenant, "I am leaving with the ship Sunday morning at 0800. I need a pilot and a tug."

He said, "Yes Sir!" I turned on my heel and started out the door. Then just as I reached the outside steps, he ran after me and asked, "Do you want two tugs?"

I said, "Yes, that would be fine." Whatever the pilot wanted was OK with me. I went back to the ship, and told the rest of the crew and the XO that I had informed the Greeks we were leaving Sunday morning at 0800. This, I believe, made the few crewmembers contemplating going home perk up. Either the possibility of sailing or just waiting to see what kind of trouble I would be in, made them want to stay.

Dick Meyers uttered loudly, "Well, it was about time we told them where to get off. We will take names and kick some butt come Sunday."

There appeared some e-mails and posts on our web page from some individuals who said the ship needed a new Captain to move this job along and bring her home. One alluded to even having the M-man return, saying he could evaluate the situation, then make things happen and move the Greeks off dead center! The ship must sail soon, they are losing crew fast. A good Captain would not run the ship like a committee. He would make decisions and give orders! Evidently this man knew nothing about commanding a crew of volunteers in their seventies. If I had the seven weeks back the M-man wasted last August, the XO and I would not need a place to eat Christmas dinner, we would be home! This bothered me some, but I had a good idea who the culprit was and considered the source. I felt damn unappreciated at this point. My son, Kirk, perked me up by answering in my defense, writing a post saying his dad could get it done if anyone could.

Saturday morning arrived, but nothing happened on the base. No calls, no one showed up at the ship or even on the dock, not even a stray dog for Souda to chase a quarter mile back towards the gate. Boats, Dewey, and I left for town Saturday night as usual. I told all the crew I wanted them back aboard by 2000. We would be leaving in the morning and I wanted everyone wide-awake and fully rested.

We stopped at the *Brass Shop* to tell our friends we were leaving. They were sorry to hear that, and we collected a big hug from both the mother and daughter. The daughter wrote out the address of her folks for me. Boats bought a snow-covered (white cotton) reindeer that sang *Jingle Bells* in Greek! We had it playing, when two guys off the Black Ships passed by the door. One exclaimed to the other, "That is Jingle Bells in Greek!"

The other one said, "You are really officer material, you know!"

The BP OIL CO had given us fifty thousand gallons of #2 diesel fuel. However, we had to steam to Athens in order to claim it. BP did not have any facilities on Crete. My hastily put together plan to take the Pirate Ship would take us away from Souda but not Greece. We had to sail right back into a Greek Naval Base at Piraeus to pick up our fuel and our four LCVPs. I had five thousand gallons of diesel delivered to the ship by truck last week making it possible for the short voyage, some one hundred-seventy miles to Athens. The LST would use between seven to eight gallons a mile depending on sea conditions and direction of the wind. Athens yes, but our escape would halt there without the BP fuel.

How and who found us the BP diesel was still very much in dispute. A real friend of the ship who lived near Toledo, Ohio, Mr. George

Katakis, had gone to the BP refinery located close to him and talked to a Mr. Dan Waterfield. Mr. Waterfield was in the BP advertising and promotions department. He became very interested in our project, but wanted to know more about our Corporation and our non-profit status. He also needed to know how many gallons of fuel we needed to cross the Atlantic.

George, to find answers, visited President Mike and Secretary Linda Gunjak of the National LST Association, also headquartered in Toledo. They of course, knew all about us and had the 501(C) (3) tax-exempt number, and could answer the questions such as, how many retired Navy were on board, how much fuel would we need, how soon we needed it and so forth. They went to see Mr. Waterfield, and answered all of his questions.

Dan then called Houston, TX to BP North American Headquarters and told them our story and our plight.

Another coincidence happened; the President of BP (North America) had worked as an aid for Congressman Ralph Hall while attending College. Priscilla Roberts, with much determination, told the BP President about us and our need, convinced him, and pushed BP over the hump to donate the fuel and to do so in just two weeks!

In the midst of all the problems, I received this phone call from a very nice young woman. She said she had some good news for me. I said, "I could certainly use some of that!" She informed me she represented BP OIL, in Houston, TX, and BP wanted to donate the diesel fuel for our trip home, some thirty thousand gallons.

I answered, "That's so great. The crew and I have been pooling all of our money, gathering our credit cards, checking our balances in hopes of having enough to buy the fuel to get home. However, we have a small problem, the thirty thousand gallons is short of what we need. We really need fifty thousand gallons to get us all the way home."

She hesitated and then said, "Let me check with my boss as I am only authorized to give you thirty thousand gallons." When I asked her for her name and phone number, she said she would call me back.

The word spread to the media; newspapers, the internet, TV and to our many LST fans, the news that BP was providing the Veterans all the diesel fuel necessary to bring the LST 325 back to the USA from Greece.

When she called back she said, "BP is supplying the entire amount of diesel to get you home." Then added, "At least that is what we have been seeing on TV, hearing and reading. Consequently, you have your 50,000 gallons Captain. You will have to go to Athens and pick it up, because we do not have any facilities on the Island of Crete. Good luck and if you need anything or have any problems give me a call."

I excitedly said, "Thank you, thank you, and please thank your boss. We can now put our money and credit cards away! You have answered our prayers."

Many deserve credit for the fuel donated, but I personally think Mr. Katakis deserves most of the credit as he initiated the request. Mr. Katakis on the other hand credits Bob Busch, the man who started the National LST Association because he is the one who asked him to help the guys in Souda obtain some fuel to bring the LST home! It certainly was a lifesaver for us. With fuel in the ship's tanks, this crew would be hard to stop. All of a sudden America was closer!

Sunday morning showed up right on time, we had early reveille at 0530, breakfast at 0630. The engineers warmed up trusty old generator #2 and began the process to switch to ship's power. Chapman and Edwards, at almost the same time, cut off the shore power to the ship then threw the circuit breaker, placing us on ship's power. They unhooked the shore power cable on the pier, and with a lot of crew helping, managed to pull the big cable onto the ship.

The Greeks had not put the parts ship back alongside after the sea trial, so that was not in the way. Boats had scraped and painted the port side now positioned next to the pier, scraping off only the peeling paint. We just hoped it would last until we reached the USA. The ship looked good at this point.

All was dreadfully quiet on shore as I looked for some kind of activity from the Greeks. All Sunday mornings on the Base were quiet, only Souda shifted around and wished she could come aboard. She had several times climbed the gangway almost to the top only to be told no, "Souda you can't come aboard, you are not going."

We had a problem with the big gangway. The ship didn't have an accommodation ladder on the port side. When we turned the ship around after the sea trial the Greeks had furnished this gangway and put it up with a big forklift. We did not have a lift of any kind and the Greek forklift was not in sight. Made out of iron the gangway stretched a good forty feet, and a good three feet wide with side rails up at least three and one-half feet. It weighed at least a ton. It was positioned close to our ship's port boat davit, which we had raised all the way up, out of the way. We had Boats lower the davit arms, which came down by gravity, putting the arms out over the side of the ship. A tall person off the dock could reach up now and grab the cable end. We tied a line onto the hook that fit into the LCVP lift cable, and four of us tried to pull the cable out and down to make it stretch enough to reach the gangway, but no such luck. Failing, we cranked it down more by hand. When we reached the gangway, we tied it on, then ran the davit winch, and hoisted up the cable, which lifted the gangway. The top of the gangway slid at first along the ship and then swung aft towards the davit. Once it left the ship, we pulled on a second line fastened to the gangway and swung the gangway out away from the ship. At the same time, we lowered the davit back down. The heavy weight pulled the davit's steel cable down until the gangway landed on the dock parallel to the ship.

Action stirred on the Greek Base; the Officer of the Deck, not a lowly Lieutenant but a full Commander, came down the cement stairs from Headquarters almost on a run. Seeing him transit the stairs, I told Boats to find our aluminum ladder that hooked on the side of the life rail and install it. We needed it to climb up and down to the dock since we'd removed the gangway. I knew the Snipes worked on starting the main engines; once started we only had to untie the lines and we would be free to leave Souda!

The Commander hurried up the ladder, spotted me, came right to me, gasping for air. He blurted out, "Captain, you need to call your people."

I said, "I am leaving, Sir, and I am not calling anyone."

He said again, "Please Captain, come up to the Headquarters and call your people." I assumed he meant the Ambassador.

I answered, "Sir, my people are the ones holding up the paperwork so we can't leave. I am not calling them!" At this very moment, the starboard engine turned over; the Commander heard this rumbling deep within the ship. He was pale already and hearing the main roll over did not help. He turned and with all haste scurried down the ladder. Running was now out of the question for him so he walked, made a beeline straight up to the Headquarters via the seventy-five steps or more. I assumed that I, or maybe we, were sort of in trouble at this point. We had reached the point in our departure like an airplane's takeoff, where the plane must fly or crash, whichever came first!

The starboard main engine gasped and started with the usual blast of blue smoke out of its exhaust with that deep throb of a V12 coming to life. Boats wanted to know if he could take off some of the lines in preparation to get underway. I told him, "Not yet Boats, I have this feeling after that Commander departed that the Greeks will stop us from leaving."

Then Boats wanted to know what the Greek Officer said, "He didn't look happy with you!"

I fired back, "I told him you were now in charge Boats, and you were taking the ship home!" He gave me the bos'n mate's look, and with a shrug of his shoulders, turned and walked away.

I could hear and see this blue car making all kinds of dust, coming down the base road from town. It pulled right up to the ship and out leaped Commander Nikoldakis – in his bathrobe and slippers. He did have his Commander's hat on. He motioned for me to come down on the dock, so down I went. I thought we had become good friends over the past couple of months, but at this moment, I think maybe not!

Most of the crew watched at full attention now, looking over the port deck rail. They wanted to see if the Commander might shoot or hang me right away, or wait till after he got through chewing me out. No matter, my crew was not going to miss it. Boats and Dewey told me later they thought maybe I would have a short trial first before the hanging. Meyers and Lockas explained to me their money was on a hanging from the ship's mast over at the Headquarters. They quickly added, apparently to not hurt my feelings, they only made that remark because they had never seen a hanging! At least my crew enjoyed this. I asked Carter to join me on the pier. I undoubtedly needed him for moral support or maybe to run interference to make an escape! He muttered thanks, while saying, "Captain, I really want to hear you explain this anyway."

The Commander, with a little stubble of a beard, a somewhat red face, and a little uncombed hair sticking out from under his hat, told us we could not leave. If we left, he would go to jail, be placed in a Greek prison and the key thrown away. He then inquired, "Have you had a chance to see a Greek jail? Our prisons are not nice!" Silence on my and Carter's end! He continued describing our situation, "The Commodore is really mad. I think he may put all of you off the base and into a hotel somewhere."

Regaining courage and my voice, I spoke out in our defense. "Commander, I have no choice. I have to get the ship underway now since most of my crew intended to leave the project. If I lose many more, I will have to abandon the project after all of our work."

He then accused me, "You are stealing the ship."

I countered, "No, I am not stealing the ship. Our government gave us this ship so how do you steal something that one already owns? Besides, if I was going to steal the ship, I would not have come over and told your Duty Officer that we were leaving this morning at 0800. I would have taken the ship at midnight on a dark night without telling anyone!"

Right as the conversation with the Commander slowed to an end, the Commodore himself arrived in a black shiny limo with Greek white and blue striped flags flying on both front fenders. I turned slightly to the XO saying softly, "You can speak up anytime!"

The XO answered, "Sir, you are doing fine."

The Commodore climbed out wearing his sparkling white uniform with all of his medals hanging on the left front pocket. He looked as if he might be on his way to a fancy formal affair somewhere. I braced for a verbal attack or whatever came my way. He came right up to my side, put his arm around me and gave me a big squeeze. As he held me in his grip, he said, "Captain we can't let you leave, my government will put me and him (pointing at Nikoldakis) in jail for who knows how long! What do I have to do to keep you from leaving? Do I have to put a tug next to the ship to keep you here?"

I replied, "No, just give us our paperwork so we can legally leave, Sir!"

He immediately responded, "If I give you my word I will attain the paperwork, will you give me your word you will not leave?"

I happily answered. "Yes, Commodore, you have my word."

He then replied, as he released me from the bear grip, "You will have the transfer papers very soon, in ten days at the most."

At that exact time, my engineers, not knowing about the negotiations on the pier, started the engine next to us, the port main engine. Black soot and blue smoke rolled out along with the sound of the roar of a 12-cylinder engine picking up RPMs and proclaiming it was ready for business.

The Commodore looked at us for just a second then quickly shouted over the engine noise, "Captain, you are not leaving?"

I quickly replied, "Commodore, I gave you my word, and I have yours; I am not leaving."

I turned and drew my hand across my neck below my chin, the signal to shut down. Edwards, who had probably come up to tell me the engines were running and would soon be ready, now ran down and told the engine room to shut them off! In a few seconds, the port engine came to an abrupt, silent halt and shortly the starboard too. I was glad we were standing far enough away from the LST so no soot got on the man's white uniform! The Commodore shook my hand and Jack's, then walked to the limo where a sailor, also in a white uniform, opened the rear door, and away they went.

Commander Nikoldakis looked at Carter and I, shook his head as one does in total disgust and disapproval, turned, went to his blue sedan, crawled in, backed it up and pulled away retracing his way back towards the main gate. Carter still had not said anything. I finally let my breath out and asked him, "What are the odds that we will get the paper work?"

He replied, "I believe he will do what he says if he can move our paperwork past the higher command. We have convinced him that we could leave, and Captain, he doesn't want to be in the same cell as the Commander!" With his hand, Jack slapped my back and laughed at his own joke. We managed to scale up the ladder and board the ship, with Jack at my side smiling, we held quarters; it was now about 0900. I told the men, "We have the Commodore's word, he promised to get us our paperwork, and I promised him that you guys would not leave with the ship!"

The XO stepped up and informed them, "The Commodore told us he believed we will have the paperwork at the end of the week. We scared them big time, and he told us the truth. They do not want a national incident any more than I believe our State Department does."

I gave everyone liberty except the ones on duty. Bruce and I, Bartlett, and the XO drove East in the opposite direction from Chania and Souda. I heard there were some very old ruins that had been uncovered of a very progressive culture some 4,000 years BC. These people had running water, heated baths, inside toilets, and some of their art, when uncovered, looked almost like fresh paint. Our friend John Pounarakis let us borrow his car; he had two. John had come down to see the fun, but had stayed away from view until the Commodore and Commander had left.

We headed out for *Iraklion* about 80 miles east of Souda. I always drove the car generally until noon and then let our designated driver, Carter, take over. Over the past months riding with Pournarakis or in taxies I noticed a funny sign once in awhile. It was solid red with a white 'T' in the middle. On this trip I learned what that road sign meant. They mark the end of a one-way road, not the beginning!

John's car was not much. I had to reach out of the driver's window to open my door. When one went around a corner with the turn signals on, the headlights of the car came on and stayed on. Not knowing the headlights were on, when we stopped at several places for a half hour or so to look at old castles or other interesting sights, the battery died. Fortunately, I had some friends that could push. Since his car was a stick shift, with my crew pushing, I put it in high, let the clutch out, and it started.

Iraklion was not large by our standards, but very charming. It reminded me of Chania, with many neat shops to explore. We visited the ruins, which were impressive, found a place to have lunch and a few Mythos Greek beers. We had to push the car again to start it, then proceeded back to Souda and returned the car to John.

This trip was our second passage into the wonders of Crete. The earlier excursion took us straight south, then across the mountains to the other side. We must have missed the main road, which we thought we had turned on in Chania. This road turned into a very small goat trail. We went through a small village where we received some looks as we sped by. We stopped for several herds of goats to cross in front of us, turned 90 degrees in places, and vaulted up some steep grades. At the time we were about ready to give up and return in the direction we came from, we arrived at the summit of this mountain that traverses Crete. We crossed a ridge and started our descent. I slammed on the brakes as the big blue Mediterranean Sea covered the whole horizon ahead of us. Looking down from this high elevation was one of the most beautiful sights I have ever witnessed, so impressive we all vacated the car for a better look.

We progressed down to see if by chance a small café happened to be located in the small village below. *Khora,* the town we believed we had found, was snuggled up to the water's edge with a big sandy beach. It had a small café with a veranda looking over the beach and the Mediterranean Sea. The owners, a husband and wife, made us feel welcome and pointed at a small round table in front for us to sit and enjoy the view. We drank a couple of beers and ate what the owners recommended that looked like a Mexican taco. It tasted good.

Out on the beach several couples ventured out and yes, the girls became topless. I had heard from Boats that he thought Greece had some nude beaches, or was it Dewey? This late in October the temperature settled cool, maybe low 70's. Bartlett thought we should have come over earlier in the season. I quickly asked, "Why Jim?" He just smiled. With Jack driving, we returned to our home on the 325 after stopping at Nick's first. We had left our troubles behind for a day and had witnessed some beautiful country none of us would have seen, except for the LST 325.

We had orders; we had to remove the Greek numbers L-144, which were in four places, two on each side of the bow and two on the stern. I started the act of painting over the numbers on the port bow. Some of the crew thought this was a good time to see the Captain working and a photo-op came about for their scrapbooks. Someone even gave me a picture he had taken of me painting. Everyone was in good spirits. Boats and Strobel painted two signs, one for each side of the ship with LST 325 on them. They used a couple of four by eight foot sheets of three-quarter inch plywood. Strobel had acquired the plywood from the Greeks. These were bunk bottom plywood sheets left over now because of a smaller crew. These signs looked small on this big ship, but were the best we could do. Meyers and Calvin tied them outboard to the lifelines, port and starboard, about sixty feet aft of the bow where the deck leveled out.

Several times I tried to help with the work going on around the ship. However, every time I tried, they told me NO. Some of the crew told me Captain's should not do physical work as it didn't look right and they didn't want their Captain working. This old crowd served in our Navy at another time. I thought if they only could see me at times on the farm! Carter and I still snuck in some manual labor from time to time.

ELEVENTH HOUR OF THE LAST DAY

OH! The thought of going to sea again, warm salty air blowing so gentle on my face, feeling that ever-so-slow roll of an LST. Dolphins playing along side, flying fish from wave to wave glide with the mighty purr of the main engines pushing the ship along, sort of like a bulldozer pushing snow. The smell of fresh coffee and the cook's apple pies in the oven. To see the bright stars at night again, looking so close one could almost reach up and touch them and the beautiful full rainbows in the misty rain. Our Helmsmen all staying on so steady to the course. Our bow cutting so smoothly through the Atlantic's high waves . . . . .

Captain wake up; you have the watch!

CHAPTER 17

DRY-DOCK AND TRANSFER PAPERS

ARRIVE

The week crept by. I had another Captain's Mast; Mr. Dewey Taylor came back late the Saturday night before we tried to leave on Sunday. He was only fifteen minutes late but the crew made a big deal out of it. I called him out at quarters in front of the crew and told him it was a major infraction of my orders. He said, "Yes sir, it was."

I went on, "I can't have this kind of insubordination, so I have to make an example of you and throw the entire book of *Navy Uniform Military Justice* at you. Your punishment for being AWOL was confinement on the LST 325 for a total of five days commencing the day we leave the Greek Navy base at Athens. You understand that we will be at sea."

Dewey shouted, "Yes Sir, and it won't happen again!"

Carter and I went out and bought a Satellite Telephone. We thought it might just come in handy installed up in the spy shack. In order for the phone to be connected with a phone number and billing address, it took a lot of negotiating with a company in Texas. Linda, secretary of the National LST Association, helped immensely with this.

We had our maritime radios to cover all the channels necessary. When asked what channels we had, I passed on the answer from Jack. He said we could talk to anyone who could talk to us. Our call sign was WW2 LST.

Along about Nov. 9, 2000, a Thursday, I received a phone call from the Greek Headquarters to come up to the Commander Nikoldakis's office. I headed up the steep stairs with a little spring in my step. The spring was the result of walking up that long stairway a couple of thousand times and up to the town square at least once a day. Mostly it was my hope that our paperwork had finally arrived. I had to wait outside at the CDR's office. I sat down in the outer office and could not miss hearing the conversation going on next door. The discussion was with the Commodore, and I imagined it was just about setting a date, and a time to sign the papers handing over the ship to us. Soon the CDR beckoned me into his office.

He asked me to please sit down. He disclosed the reason for the delay in the paperwork; it was obtaining the ship's latest hull report from the last dry-docking of the ship. He dropped the shipyard report down flat on his desk, explaining, "The Greek High Command wanted you to know the condition of L-144 before we took ownership. They felt it would relieve them of any liability just in case something would happen on our way home."

I asked, "Did they have the report translated into English?

He held it up and studied the first page. He leaned back in his chair as he did when asked an unusual question. A big grin developed on his face and said, "NO!"

He asked me to come around on his side of the desk and he would translate and go over it with me. Around the table, I went, and page by page, the CDR explained things necessary or what he believed pertinent to the ship's safety. When he finished going through all the pages, he stated, "You know that ship is not in that bad of shape. The bottom, in particular, is very good on studying the thickness readings."

The major point in selecting which LST to sail home was the one with the best hull.

He then told me next Tuesday was the date for the signing of the transfer papers. The signing would be upstairs in the Commandants Office. "Does this meet with your approval?"

What a silly question. I could hardly hold myself back, but managed to answer, "Yes Sir, it certainly does!" He wanted us to find someone from the U.S. Naval Base to witness the signing, which would be no problem.

He then reached back and brought out a very nice knife in a scabbard with an eight-inch long blade, with a white bone handle. It had an inscription in Greek imprinted on it. CDR Nikoldakis explained that it was an old Greek saying, giving a traveler good luck and good hunting. He said these knives were hand crafted on Crete. I thanked him and said, "I have a small gift for you in appreciation of all your help."

I had bought several brass propeller ashtrays from guess where! Inscribed on the bottom of each:

Thank you for your help getting LST 325 operational.
Capt. Bob Jornlin and crew.

The gifts were in individual boxes, and I had them wrapped.

I handed CDR Nikoldakis one of the gifts. He opened his present and I told him to turn it over. He seemed very pleased. I am not sure the CDR smoked, but almost every Greek sailor did.

I thanked him, shook his hand, and not looking back went out the door, down that long steep stairs for the first time with a smile on my face, and visions bouncing in my head of sailing for home.

The crew, every one of them topside right by the gangway, all had smiles on hearing the good news with a few high fives thrown around. Telling Lois was the first order of business. She had been waiting and asking almost every day for the past month for those words. It created big news back home and such a relief to all - it looked as if we would leave the town of Souda behind and start developing sea legs on the decks of LST 325. I continued my rounds, and gave out my brass propeller ashtrays. I gave one to the Captain in charge of the repair yard. He allowed his men to help us. He thanked me several times, placed it right on his desk. I had one for the Commodore, and planned to give it to him Tuesday. All of us said many good-byes and thanked so many who had helped us.

Boats called John Pournarakis to procure us a Navy truck, as our life rafts had finally arrived. Thank God for that 10,000% guarantee! I called the CMC and asked if he could find us a man for the transfer paper signing to be our witness. He indicated he would have someone at the Greek naval Headquarters on Tuesday.

Dan O'Grady passed a letter to the ship sent by a government attorney, saying we should not be allowed to sail a Military Ship or own a working LST as it was a significant piece of military equipment. The letter went on to say that we might take the LST, sail it to South America, and sell it to some terrorist group that could use it to shoot up an American city! I told Dan to please to give that SOB a good slap behind the head, and tell him, "We are all United States Navy Veterans. We are not going to sell this ship to anyone, and we would not shoot up an American City!" (Well, maybe if that lawyer was in it!) "We have not been over here spending our own money and away from our families, to take this ship to South America or anywhere but home. We intend to make this LST a traveling museum on the lakes and rivers of America." I added that his remarks were humiliating and demeaning to the men who have served their country with distinction. I bet he had never been on a ship or out of an air-conditioned office in his entire career.

I never heard anything more from him. I hope Dan gave him my message! Congress had given us the ship and there was nothing he or anyone could do about it.

WHAT WILL THE GIRLS IN WASHINGTON DO NEXT?

**** Cincinnati Enquirer 12/7/2000
Veterans plan to cross sea in old warship

PART II

THE VOYAGE

CHAPTER 18

THE DAY THAT WILL LIVE IN INFAMY

November 14, 2000

We were busy most of the weekend and on Monday. We tested all the equipment and started the main engines again. The old GM's came to life, like expecting something was going to happen. We loaded enough supplies to take us the entire 6500 miles, all the way home. The Navy exchange let us purchase most of our food from them and this was a big help. The XO talked the Navy into furnishing a truck and driver to help haul the food. Chapman ran the generators and went to ship's power at 1700 hours Monday night. I checked with the pilots in order to make sure one would be available about 1100 tomorrow. They happily replied it was all set.

I climbed the stairs to the Headquarters to receive instructions from Commander Nikoldakis about where to go near Athens to meet the pilot to take us into the Salamis Island Greek Naval Base near the city of Piraeus, and found out the radio channel the pilot used. I asked if he could have someone notify BP we were planning to be in there Wednesday morning to pick up our fuel and more lube oil. He replied he would be happy to take care of everything.

That evening Boats, Dewey, and I made our final rounds uptown; our dog Souda was right with us as if she knew something was about to change in her life. We had a lengthy discussion about her. We had discovered that she was pregnant and expecting within a couple of weeks. The woman who told us seemed to know Souda; in fact, she disclosed *our* dog had her last batch of pups right under her front porch and she had six! It was too late to have them aborted and her spayed. I wanted very much to take her aboard ship and bring her along on the voyage. I asked all the crew if they would please consider adopting Souda or a puppy or all of them when we arrived home. No, I am sorry, was the unanimous comeback. Boats Voges was a big help; he suggested she could go in my stateroom and have her pups on the couch in my office. I replied, "If I allow her on the couch, would you clean up her messes on the deck?" His answer was a stern no! I felt terrible about leaving her, so I built Souda a doghouse on the pier alongside the ship with some old scrap left there by the shipyard workers. Maybe the doghouse would provide a place for her to have her pups.

Leaving Souda behind was a gut wrenching decision for me. I had really grown attached to that little dog and she with the ship and the crew. Fortunately, I had seen the tugboat crew ahead of us playing with her, calling her over and feeding her treats. I knew they would take care of her and most likely let her come aboard the tug! Later, thinking what I would have done differently on this whole ordeal - I would have brought Souda back, pups and all!

We all received a second hug from the mother and daughter at the *Brass Shop,* the three of us said good bye for the second time! They said, "Sorry to see you men leave." I would guess a few other merchants were also sorry. It is not true, however, that two bars closed up and one café when we sailed away. There may have been one less bookie joint though!

At exactly 0900, Jack and I started up the monster hill. We had put on clean khakis to look our best for the pictures, as we both had our cameras. The Chief from the U.S. base was already at the entrance of the headquarters, Chief Charles T. Roland, SWKS. Jack and I introduced ourselves and proceeded up to the second floor to the Commodore's office. In the office was the Commodore, our CDR Nikoldakis and Captain (HN) E. Petrakis, the Captain I had talked to in charge of Security, Jack Carter, the Navy Chief, and me. We were invited right in and received handshakes all around. I wondered if they were as happy to see us leave as we were to leave!

They gave me the transfer papers to read and approve. I whispered to CDR Nikoldakis, "Commander, these papers are in English." He just smiled a little and waved. The transfer papers consisted of two pages that I read and examined thoroughly. I was a little concerned that it read,

The USS LST Memorial, Inc. (hereinafter called the LST Association).
This made it legal enough and I certainly was not going to make them
re-write it! Then I signed several copies, passed them to the
Commodore, who signed, then the witnesses, the Captain for the
Hellenic Navy, and the Chief for the LST Memorial. Jack and I took a
few pictures after the signing, and then gave our cameras to Commander
Nikoldakis to take pictures of us. I took several of the CDR and the
Greek Officers. Then it was time for several Ouzos. Jack and I shook
hands with our friends the Greeks, then announced we had a date in
Athens and my crew was ready to sail.

Jack and I went down those stairs again. I told him I would not miss
the stairs. He uttered, "Nor I!"

The crew stood at the rail, I would not say patiently. We had a
group picture with Edwards and me holding the Certificate of
Ownership. Then I gave the order to prepare to get underway. I had
some big plans on how to leave the dock, make a full turn out in front of
the Greek base, and down from the Headquarters. We would blow our
horn and then proceed in a cloud of blue smoke out towards the
Mediterranean Sea and on to Athens. The pilot came aboard and the one
tug came alongside. I guess the ship was our responsibility so one tug
was plenty! The Boats had all lines untied from the pier and had started
pulling them by hand on board. I went ahead on the starboard engine
with left rudder putting the starboard stern out, then came back with
both engines, then ahead on the port. The tug was on the starboard bow;
I asked the Greek interpreter to ask the pilot to have the tug pull back.
He did and the starboard bow came right out as I shifted to right rudder
and went one-third back on the starboard engine, twisting the ship until
we were headed straight out into Souda Bay.

At this point in my grandeur departure finally from Souda, I was
ready to turn the ship a full 360 degrees. At this exact time, the Boats
energized the bow anchor windless to pull in the forward spring line, a
big, long, heavy line. This maneuver killed the #2 generator and that
lost the engine clutches, the gyro, all lighting, radar, and our marine
radios except for hand held ones, and the steering! I believe this may
have been deliberate on the part of the Boats. We knew he liked to play
jokes and I had confessed to him my show-off plans. The engineers
should have had two generators on the line, which was standard

procedure for leaving and entering port. Then we would have had enough electric power to run the anchor windless. Maybe Boats just wanted to go back to the dock and receive another hug from the *Brass shop* women! I blame myself for not making sure we had two generators on the line. Yes, I am really looking good! Did I mention we had a sizable crowd out on the pier!

The pilot asked if I wanted him to push us with the tug back to the pier. I quickly shouted, "No!" We have left Souda and we are not going back. I had him order the tug to push some on the starboard bow to straighten us up so we pointed out into the Bay and towards the Mediterranean Sea.

In about five agonizing minutes, I heard #2 generator start up again. Lights came on, the air compressors pumped up the engine clutches, and the motor generator came back for AC. We started the radar, we had steering, no gyro - that would have to be reset. I asked the wheelhouse for all ahead standard speed and the main engines generated my blue smoke I anticipated leaving behind to blow in the wind. Carter leaned into the whistle, as we headed out for the other end of Souda Bay and the blue Mediterranean Sea.

This was not even close to the departure I wanted. In fact, it was truly an embarrassment, but I was happy, finally starting for home. I wanted it to be perfect and show the Greeks what a bunch of old US Navy Vets could do. However, history we were making. We had done the impossible – we left the pier at Souda. My crew had proved so many people wrong, made them in fact eat their words. Those who believed in us would simply say - I knew they could do it! Some had to lose a measure of money at the bookie joint, maybe one was the CMC!

PIRAEUS AHEAD

On reaching the entrance of the Mediterranean Sea where we would leave Souda Bay, I asked the pilot if he would like to stay on board and help us sail the LST all the way back to the U.S. I told him he would have a good time, and I would buy him a first class airplane ticket to fly back to Greece. The interpreter told him and in fair English, he said, "No! I jump off first!" Again, this was the pilot who didn't talk to Jack and me on our first visit. We both had made several visits over the last month to the *Tower of Pisa.*

We then stopped and let the pilot off on the tug following along on the port side. Jack and I waved good-bye as I gave an order to come up to standard speed, and shouted down to the wheelhouse a course to steer almost due north. In a few minutes I talked to Jack by radio in the gyro room and gave him the degrees we were steering by GPS. With a flip of the switch, he had reset the gyro. We now had all systems working again.

I turned the ship slightly to three hundred forty-five degrees true towards Athens and our destination of Piraeus, where the Greek Naval Base was located. We had to pick up four LCVPs, of which not one, I was told, would run. Commander Nikoldakis just leaned back in his chair when he informed me saying, "Captain your crew can fix anything; you do not need these boats to run."

I countered, "That may be true, but not while underway and certainly not fast enough when the ship is sinking under them. I would like one that runs just for safety."

He shook his head no and emphatically stated, "None of the LCVPs would run." We also were going to pump fifty thousand gallons of #2 diesel fuel from BP into the ship's coffers and another eight hundred gallons of 30W lube oil.

We were making a surprising nine knots - even ten at times. Just for those who may not know, a knot is equal to about 1.2 miles per hour. We had one hundred-eighty miles to go and our itinerary was set to be there in the morning. I had to tell the Greeks about what time to schedule a pilot and tug to come out and guide us in. The sun was bright and the sea was calm helping us along with the wind to our backs. Sort of surprising, all systems were running fine. We steamed without seeing one single ship all the rest of the day. It was perfect. The report from the Snipes below was good. The old engines hummed along in perfect harmony with each other. One can tell in the engine room by the sound and feel when standing between them when they are in harmony. They were just like a perfectly matched team of Clydesdales! The blue exhaust smoke had diminished as the engines warmed up and burned off the carbon deposits that had built up from idling.

CHAPTER 19

THE LST TRIES TO BECOME A

SUBMARINE

Boats relieved me at 1600, a few minutes early actually. He had the 1600 to 2000 watch (4:00 to 8:00 PM). He came up all smiles looking forward to being an OOD and very excited about us getting underway. I went down to my stateroom, kicked off my shoes, jumped in my bunk right on my back, and looked up at the overhead. For the first time in several months, the pressure was gone, at least for the moment. We were underway and going home, so great a feeling to finally get the paperwork and get underway from the Naval Repair Base. We certainly had our troubles there. I stayed in my stateroom until Cookie served up dinner, and then went up into the wheelhouse to check on Boats and the wheelhouse watch. He was on course and doing a good job. Everyone on watch was happy and diligently attending to business. I went back to bed after eating, mind and body completely exhausted, and fell asleep instantly after saying a few prayers of thanks!

At about 2100, I got out of my bunk and walked into the Wardroom looking for someone to talk to about how we had accomplished this feat. Nobody was there, so I started making my rounds again. The night sky had a beautiful moon that lit up and shimmered off the blue water. All of the stars were out nice and bright, and a gentle breeze from the south was still helping our speed; it was a very nice 75 degrees. Jack had the CONN and I certainly did not have to worry about him, so returned to my stateroom to lie down again. I had watch again at midnight. I was soon in a deep sleep.

Perruso, our roving security watch, showed up yelling at me and turned on my stateroom lights. As we all know, the LST 325 has never been easy. I saw by the paleness of his face that something was definitely wrong and his high pitched voice as he yelled sent a chill down my back.

He shouted excitingly, "Captain, wake up! We have a good twelve inches of seawater in the aft end of the tank deck, and sir, it looks to be coming out of a hole on the port side right above the auxiliary engine room, and the water is rising fast!"

I choked out an answer to him, "It can't be."

He shouted again thinking maybe I was still asleep, "Captain, should we wake the crew up? Are we going to sink?"

To calm him down, I quietly answered him, "We are not going to let this old girl sink, Dom. Please take it easy and show me where the water is coming in and let me take a look." My mind was racing. The auxiliary engine room was below that spot, not the Sea. We have a ballast tank to the port side of that engine room. I was thinking about where the water could be coming from. As fast as I dared run with Dom following me, I headed for the tank deck two ladders below. Going down the ladder on the starboard side into the dark tank deck, I stepped into some eight or ten inches of water in the aft end of that huge hole that could hold twenty large Sherman tanks! The tank deck runs two hundred thirty feet long, thirty feet wide, and fourteen feet high; I realized that eight inches of water was a lot of water!

Not ballasted down much, the bow was up slightly higher than the stern, so the water was running back towards the stern. I found the place where the water was coming out over the auxiliary engine room, as Perruso indicated. On closer examination, I could see it was coming out of one of the deck drains. These drains are to pump water out of the tank deck, or at least that was the intention of the designer! The tank deck had six of these drains; two forward and two aft, and one on each side of the auxiliary engine room about in the middle. I thought at first someone must be pumping ballast into the port ballast tank, but no one had permission to do that!

With Dominick following, I had to go back up into the crew's mess, then go outboard and forward about one hundred thirty feet, then down a twenty foot ladder to the auxiliary engine room. No one was pumping ballast and the engine room was bone dry. I thought hard for a minute, and then realized the pipe that sucked the water out of the tank deck drain, must have a hole rusted through it. No surprise the pipe might be gone completely inside the ballast tank! These pipes went to an eductor located on the fire main piping down in the very bottom of the bilges in the auxiliary engine room. Their original purpose was to drain the tank deck of any water possibly coming through the bow doors or rain falling from the cargo hatch, exhaust vents, or elevator. The Greeks had removed most of this eductor pump system from the ship. That old system or something must be forcing water into the ballast tank in order to fill the tank to the top pushing water up into the tank deck.

I knew the tank deck was above sea level on the ship. I shut off the fire main and flushing pump, which had an overboard discharge pipe going through the ballast tank, to regulate the pressure on the system; it might have a hole in it and therefore the culprit in this mystery. I went back up to the tank deck and waded again over to the drain. The flow of water had not slowed up or stopped as I hoped. Water still poured out of the drain at the same rapid rate. I hurried back down to the auxiliary engine room, and restarted the fire and flushing pump, as this supplied the water to the reefer cooling system as well as to our fire main distribution system.

Next idea was to lower the water in the ballast tank by pumping water out through the ballast system and overboard. This would lower the pressure in the tank and should stop the water from continuing to be forced out of a full tank. I had Jim Edwards, who had the generator watch, and Dominick help open the valves that I pointed to. With the right valves open to discharge water out of that tank and into the sea, I hit the button that started the big one thousand five hundred gallon per minute pump. Again I went up above to check if I had accomplished anything. To my relief the water had stopped coming out and had started running back into the drain.

We pumped all eighteen thousand gallons of seawater out of that tank plus most of it out of the tank deck. I had Dominick take the inspection cover off the top of the tank, an oval cover about two feet in circumference. Using a flashlight, we entered the tank and found water pouring out of a two-inch pipe that I traced out of that tank into the

Auxiliary Engine room! The end had rusted clean off! This was the cooling water discharge pipe from #2 generator, designed to carry the 671's cooling water overboard, not run it into the ballast tank.

Since we didn't have any spare welders or plumbers, a fix would wait until we reached the Navy base in the morning. I gave orders to have the ballast pump turned on every hour, leaving all the valves open to pump that tank and keep the water level down. It was easy to tell when the tank was empty; the suction gauge needle on the pump would jump as it sucked air. Problem solved for now. This did remind me of another experience I had in the US Navy:

One night in 1964 on the Hickman County LST 825 at 0100 hour, dead asleep, the security watch awakened me with a very similar situation only it was the main engine room flooding. We were in port and tied up to a pier. I put on my pants and headed down to the main engine room only to find two inches of water over the deck plates, but rising!(Deck plates are two and one-half feet above the bottom of the ship and used to walk on in engine spaces.) I knew I had to open the eductor valve to start pumping water. Finding that valve already open, I checked the overboard discharge valve and found it closed. We were pumping sea water right into the main engine room through the fire main! I opened the discharge valve and the water immediately started to go down. What a way to wake up, but all I suffered was wet feet that time. My experience learning as much as I could how equipment worked on the LST had paid off back then, and certainly did now!

Just before my watch on the CONN at midnight, a report came of water again pouring into the tank deck. Someone had not gotten the word! I told the security watch to go down and tell the generator watch, Ron Maranto, to push the start button on the port ballast pump and explain to him it was set up with valves all open to pump out the port tank. Then make a sign and put it on the ballast pump that reads: 'Every hour start this pump and drain the ballast tank until it sucks air.' Report back to me after you have posted the sign. I wanted to be sure it was done! The next morning one of my engineers told me he could switch the generator cooling water discharge to the Starboard side of the ship and he thought the pipe through that ballast tank was OK. I told him to do it, but have someone look in the tank and make sure the pipe didn't have a leak. That made a permanent easy fix for now! I should have known that navy ships always have double systems.

The XO came to me to approve his e-mail posts going out to our web site. I refused, letting him take control of this responsibility. This is like Cookie wanting me to approve his menu every day. Come on men - do your jobs based on the best interest of the ship. I had told Cookie we were on a budget of sorts. I told Jack that he had to keep his reports positive, not give out bad news that would make the wives worry, or the State Department, or our Navy.

We arrived in nineteen hours at the entrance channel to the Greek Naval Base; it was right at 0835. Jack had radioed the pilot and tugs on channel eight several miles back. It was one of those beautiful Greek days, sunny, warm, with very little wind. I believed it to be a prettier day than maybe it really was, because we were still underway and made an uneventful crossing – as far as people were ever going to know! The pilot, very friendly, took us directly into the Naval Base. He placed us in the harbor across from the Greek Naval ships, at a long pier all by our lonesome. Mooring away from their ships was a safety move and gave the BP fuel barge room to get alongside of us.

We took on fuel and 800 gallons of 30W lube oil in good time. The BP Greek fuel barge Captain came aboard after we had secured fueling, with his bill for the oil. I forgot the exact amount but somewhere in the thousands of dollars. I asked him if he would take American cash or Greek cash. He said, "I can't take money of any kind."

I replied, "Can you take a credit card, Visa or Master?"

He again shook his head no, explaining, "I do not have a credit card machine."

I started to worry. How would I pay this man? I just asked him, "How do we pay you, Sir?"

He answered, "Don't you have a company check?"

I answered, "No, we don't have a checking account in a bank back home yet, but I believe I have a man with his checkbook on board."

Somewhat relieved, he happily told me, "That would be fine."

Cashing a check in Greece from back home had to be almost impossible, therefore, why take your checkbook to Greece? No one will take a personal check in a foreign country, or will they? I called for my man Strobel, asking our treasurer Jim Edwards, to find him. Have him bring his checkbook and come to the Captain's cabin. With no questions, Ed wrote out a check for the exact amount from his personal account in Decatur, Illinois. He handed it to me and I gave it to the BP Captain. He signed our bill paid and off he went as quickly as possible.

Next order of business, load aboard the four LCVPs or *Landing Craft Vehicle Personnel* boats that the Greeks were towing over to the ship. My first thought was at least they float! We hoisted them aboard one at a time and Boats placed a belly line around them making all four boats fast to the ship. Now if the ship rolls they will stay tight to the davit stops, and won't be swinging out and banging back with every roll of the ship.

That night Ambassador Burns came aboard, his visit nicely narrated by Jack in his report to the web skipper. Carter's post on 16 Nov. 2000: Ahoy Pamela, here is the latest news for the web site. Cheers, Jack.

We left Souda, Crete around noon on Tuesday, with the title to the ship in the Captain's hands. After a beautiful moonlight cruise on flat seas with the moonlight glistening on the water, we arrived in Athens, met our Greek Navy Pilot and tugs, and went into the Naval Base at Salamais. No time for tourist activities, as last night Ambassador Burns and his entourage came aboard. He gave a fine speech, congratulating us on our success and presented us with a very large framed group photo. More importantly, he gave a signed and sealed letter documenting the fact that the ship is ours and requesting that any authority seeing it give us their cooperation. This is very important as we are sailing as an unregistered ship and do not have the usual documents. We had a film crew on board all day preparing a documentary. BP pumped 50,000 gallons of diesel into the ship. We are now flying BP flags port and starboard. Early tomorrow we will sail for Gibraltar. We are still at sea level, but flyin' high.

Jack left out that Ms. Betsy Anderson, the Consul General of the United States of America, accompanied Mr. Burns, and was the one who signed the actual document. As the Ambassador told me, "What the letter says will not do much, but the red wax seal will impress everyone."

As the famous saying goes - *We shall sail on the high tide in the morning!* It was the morning of the sixteenth of November, the pilot was aboard and a tug was standing by alongside. As we backed from the pier, we quickly found out that the shifting switch for the forward and back clutches on the port engine was not operating. The night before, the floodwater from the tank deck drained down on the port reduction gear and the clutch switch shorted out. Chapman said, "Go ahead Captain, we can fix it on the way." Don probably could have!

I gave a quick thought to leaving, but decided on the safer route and had the pilot put us back to the pier. We had help here if we needed it and the Greeks had parts. We reviewed our parts room first hoping we had a spare, but no such luck. Chapman and Edwards went over to the Greek side and inquired if they had a spare switch.

They looked in their parts inventory records, but came up with a big fat zero in the column of total number of spares on hand. Having none, the Greeks quickly decided to take one off a mothballed LST (they had two there.) One was the X-391 our first choice in 1995, which had been stripped and flooded. It was not a big job to remove a switch located ahead of the reduction gear and just aft of the flywheel on the main engine. Around noon, they returned with the part. One of the Greek sailors came back with Chapman and Edwards and helped fix the switch. For that deed, I gave him my last bottle of Bartlett's scotch for his efforts of finding, removing and helping install it. We made another friend! The clutch was completely fixed and tested by 1600 hours, but a pilot and tug were not available until morning causing us to stay another night in Greece. I stayed on the ship, as did most of the crew. A few went over on the base and made phone calls from the pay phone right by the main security gate.

The next morning we were excited to get underway and away from Greece. At exactly 0800, the same pilot and tug showed up again. The engineers had problems this morning with the fuel primer pump. They could not get it to push fuel into the engines. This was a hand pump and caused several men to wear themselves out, completely exhausted from turning the handle. It seemed forever with no sound of a main engine starting, so I went down to see what the problem was. I remembered having to blow in the gas tank on some vapor locked old cars to move fuel into a carburetor. As I entered the main engine room, I picked up a plastic tube, something Bartlett had jury-rigged as a sight glass to monitor the amount of fuel main engine fuel day tank and with all my might blew into the tube. They had an air lock in the main suction line. Chief Whiting loosened a nut and turned the priming pump and a large gust of air and fuel shot out of the line. He retightened it, and the engine was primed and started. All I probably accomplished was getting myself completed winded, since Whiting, I believe, really solved the problem.

This took some time so the pilot was a little nervous when I reached the CONN. He had another ship to escort out. Some fifty-eight feet up the ladders from the engine room and still trying to catch my breath from blowing in the tank and climbing ladders, I asked to take the ship out and the pilot said OK. I took it away from the pier, turned it around, headed for the channel and out of the narrow inlet exiting the Naval Base. I then gave it back to the pilot, since it had suddenly turned very foggy. How foggy? You could not see the bow of the ship! At about halfway out to a place where we had a straight shot out of the inlet, the pilot gave it back to me and said he had to leave to pilot another ship. With that, he turned, left the CONN, went down the three flights of steep stairs, and off the ship to his pilot boat.

Jack was with me and I told him to get the hood on the radar and look for incoming ships. We already had a lookout posted in the forward twin 40 mm gun tub. I called him on his hand held radio and told him to keep a sharp lookout. Let us know if you see or hear anything ahead of the ship. We also were blowing a prolonged whistle every two minutes. We were going just 1/3 ahead, but I went to stop on the starboard engine. When we came into this channel, there were about twenty-five old freighters anchored right outside the channel to our left, but now to our right as we came out! We eased along; Jack picked up some of the freighters on the radar and said it all looked good ahead. When those ships were behind us, I came right to move out farther into the Curnoic Gulf, which leads west to the *Corinth Canal*.

We had free passage given to us by the Greek Navy through the famous and historic *Corinth Canal*, a canal built through solid rock in the late 1800's, finished in 1893. It was only seventy feet wide and almost four miles long but they pull the ship through with small towboats. It was cut through solid rock with walls on both sides some three hundred feet high! Nickerson wondered why we would make that sort of dangerous transit. I explained it would save us about seventy-five miles and seven and one-half hours; it was a short cut through Greece instead of going around the south end. We also have a film crew coming out to film us for the documentary of our trip back home. It was a chance of a lifetime to pass through it on a WWII LST. It would be another adventure to tell those grandkids as they sit on your lap. Nickerson was not impressed.

We sailed to the Canal in good time. The fog lifted when we were a few miles out of the harbor. Jack could not raise anyone at the canal on the radio. After the XO called the operating authorities for twenty minutes or so, a merchant ship finally answered up and reported, "Sorry LST, but the canal has been closed because of high winds that are predicted for the next five days.

"Unbelievable," Jack said! I had already turned the ship away starting back in the direction we came. A strong east wind blew us towards the canal and the high cliffs that came straight down on both sides. What if we lost the engines or electricity? I wanted plenty of room and time to fix the problem before the ship smashed into the rocks. Someone might have told us! I believe this was yet another test by our State Department or whoever was still dead set against us sailing the ship back. I put the ship up to standard speed.

As the helicopter circled us, the people doing the documentary called asking why we were leaving the canal. I explained, so they took several pictures from the helicopter of us sailing away. We arrived back close to where we started this morning at 1600. We turned almost ninety degrees to the right in order to go south and around Greece through the Mirtoon Sea. At least one person was happy – Nickerson!

THE GREEKS HAD TREATED US WELL, BUT WE DIDN'T WANT TO WEAR OUT OUR WELCOME!

CHAPTER 20

CROSSING THE MEDITERRANEAN SEA

The next morning, now November 18th, we turned and went through an area between mainland Greece and the Kithira Island. The day dawned with sun and warm temperature, so clear and pleasant. One could see forever, and the sea was the darkest blue and so smooth. A flat calm sea was always the way I wanted it on an LST, but devoted LST sailors liked some 'Rock and Roll' occasionally! Just wait. Sort of like the weather in Illinois – if one doesn't like it, just wait a day. It will change!

We could now set our most favorite course, that being 270 degrees, or straight west young man; it is where America lies they tell me. It took a good part of two days from our turn around to reach the Island of Sicily, but finally there she was on the starboard bow.

I could not help but fade back in time and dream about a little history - the invasion of Sicily on July 10, 1943. The LST 325 got her baptism under fire in that the first invasion in the European theater using this new kind of ship. That, friends, was some fifty-seven years ago! The LST 325 was in the landing group designated *KOOL FORCE* during that invasion, code named *Operation Husky*. Some eighty LSTs took part in this invasion and history says it was a very hard fought invasion as the Germans and Italians had tanks and big 88 mm guns. The LST 325 had several shells hit within one hundred yards and it had bombs fall all around it, several LSTs sustained damage to the right and left of her. The German bombers and fighter planes attacked the LSTs for several weeks. The 325, after unloading its men and equipment (some of the men were General Patton's Officers,) was reloaded with Italian prisoners to haul back to Tunisia. LST 325 was right behind the cruiser *USS Boise,* called in to blast the German tanks approaching Gela in a counter attack. Gela was just one of the invasion beaches these ships were going to slide up on and unload their cargo. This ship operated for over thirty days in and around Sicily. German planes sank two LSTs during this time.

Back to the present, the island of Sicily was off our starboard bow. We saw a huge dark cloudbank dead ahead. I could see lightning flashing within its blackness. First the gusty winds, then the pounding rain hit us from out of the Southwest. We were soon in a storm with gale force winds. I wondered what kind of a fluke was this as this very ship had hit a big storm some fifty-seven years ago in this exact same area - right before the invasion of Sicily! The winds in 1943 came out of the Southwest and rolled the LSTs around for several days.

Huge waves started to pound our port bow. The helmsmen were fighting to keep us on course with that belligerent steering system. When a wave and big gust of wind would hit the bow at the same time, it would turn the ship some fifteen degrees to the right of our course. Things got worse when my main engine room Chief Engineer Whiting came up to the CONN and told me he had to shut down the starboard engine. We had blown a two-inch hole in the #12 piston as water had gotten into the cylinder somehow.

CARTER'S 21 November 2000 web page report:

We have been sailing along the south side of Sicily since midnight. It has been slow going because of engine and steering problems. Don't worry because the US Navy is watching over us like a 'Mother Hen!' The weather has dealt us another bad hand. We are back in the rock and roll days again. All remember those six-second rolls and jarring shudder when the bow dives into a big one. Life is now long watches at the various duty stations. It is also hurried meals quickly eaten so you can relieve the watch on time. It is also finding your way around a ship in the blackest night imaginable, hanging on to something, anything, with the ship rocking and pitching and you are alive, and you can take anything that's thrown at you.

The loss of the starboard engine now made it very difficult for the helmsmen to keep her on course. They were still, should I say, a little rusty on steering the ship. If one did not apply enough left rudder to move her back on course before the next wave or gust of wind, the ship would be blown maybe twenty-five degrees off course. In this situation, with the wind flat on most of the port side, it was almost impossible to bring her back at all, even with full rudder! We had to throw the rudder the other way. So instead of left full rudder, you went to full right and made the ship turn a full three hundred-sixty degrees in a right turn using the wind instead of fighting it, a full circle. The problem was *meeting* that turn before the head of the ship came to its intended course. If the helmsman did not take off the right rudder and apply considerable left rudder, the ship would go right on past our course again sometimes twenty-five or thirty degrees! We would have to make another three-sixty!

The Navy had indicated to me that they would watch us all the way across the Mediterranean Sea. At this point on the second three hundred-sixty turn, I prayed to God that they were not watching! The Island of Sicily stayed out there on the starboard side for a long time. With the storm raging against us and with just the port engine, we only made fifty-two miles in the next 24 hours. The helmsmen soon learned to keep almost five degrees left rudder on at a minimum to keep the LST going somewhat straight.

Carter and quartermaster Nickerson both thought that we should go into Catania, Sicily and fix the engine. I asked them what facilities Sicily had to fix a ship. Jack knew Sicily had an American Air Force Base there. It was inland a few miles, but they could fly us back to Greece for parts. I thought about it for about ten seconds and then made one of those Captain's decisions, which was *No*. We are going to continue on a westerly course because that was where home lies. We could be in Sicily for weeks if we stop there.

Carter replied, "Captain, what if the port engine dies also?"

I then turned and jokingly said to Nickerson, "Don't you think if that happens that Mr. Carter would make a great Captain?"

The storm had let up before I could call the Ambassador. The rolling of the ship, sometimes up to twenty-three degrees, would break the satellite connection and drop calls. We were down to the normal ten to twelve degree rolls and making about five knots. I told Ambassador Burns of our little problem, we needed to get into a port somewhere.

He said, "What place do you have in mind?"

I told him we had met several Navy Chiefs from Rota, Spain. I understood it to be a big US Navy Base where our aircraft carriers docked and I believed had everything we needed. I felt sure we could get the starboard engine fixed there.

He said, "OK, I will call Spain and see what I can do." In an hour the Ambassador called back and gave me the bad news, the answer from Spain - negative! We were not a registered ship so we could not come into Rota. "Where would you like to go next?" the Ambassador asked.

I answered, "How about Gibraltar, they speak English and they have a big shipyard." He countered saying that the US has no diplomats there or Navy.

"Ambassador, with due respect, those are two things we don't need. WE NEED A SHIPYARD."

The Ambassador called London next since that was where all of the government people that could give us permission were located. Gibraltar printed their own money good only in Gibraltar, had a Governor, a big rock, and a huge shipyard facility. In a very short time, the Ambassador called me back. He revealed that the English did not even put the phone down when he called to discuss this. I told them you and the crew were all US Navy veterans, with eighteen being WWII! They emphatically said all WWII American Navy veterans were welcome in any English port in the world and they didn't care how they managed to arrive, by submarine, a parachute, or an old LST! Furthermore, we will have our Governor welcome them on arrival. The Ambassador then indicated he asked them about the international Coast Guard laws that were in place. They answered that by simply saying, "Have your Coast Guard come and visit us. We could explain what these men did in WWII, and we do not remember having laws then as to registered or unregistered ships!"

The Ambassador asked me when I was expecting to get to Gibraltar. He said he would have Dan call and schedule our visit to the shipyard and have a tug to assist. I told him it would be on Nov. 29th, a Wednesday, if the old girl held together. The Ambassador replied that he had faith. He would have Dan schedule us for 0900.

This reminds me of another story:

A veteran of WWII was arriving on vacation in France. Upon going through customs, he was very slow finding his passport buried in his luggage. The customs agent, impatient with him, said, "Sir you should have had your passport out. You know you need a passport when coming into France!"

The veteran answered back, "Sir, I have only been here once before, and that Sir was on June 6, 1944 and I didn't have a passport. In fact there were no Frenchmen around to check one either!"

The Mediterranean Sea was a very busy place as the oil tankers and canister ships take about the same route and most travel the full length traveling east or west. One night Boats was on the CONN and called me. He had twelve contacts. Some five ships were passing us, several coming extremely close. I called each ship and explained, for their safety and ours, they should set off giving us more room as we were a fifty-eight year-old LST and from time to time our steering went out. These ships were just curious as to what we were and moved away giving us some space. Our running lights were located way up on the bow indicating to everyone with any maritime experience - we were old! Running lights on newer ships were placed back on the superstructure. For one thing it was easier to check if they were lit or not.

We still had seven ships coming at us having us blocked from turning in either direction. One was dead on, had a steady bearing and a shrinking range, four miles away and closing fast. I called him and asked if a port-to-port passing would be OK for him. He answered back yes. I confirmed my intentions, indicated to him that I was turning my rudder ten degrees to the right to safely pass him to port.

He then responded, "If you are moving over with a ten degree rudder; then I will just stay on course."

I quickly rebutted his decision, "Sir, we are a fifty-eight year old LST and we lose steering about every two hours and one hour and fifty minutes has passed since the last time!"

He answered back, "I hear you loud and clear. My rudder is over ten degrees!" That was life in the Mediterranean Sea.

Boats corrected me, "Captain we haven't lost steering all night."

"The chances of a failure have just gone way up. It was past time," I answered him.

CARTER'S 23 November 2000 web page report:

Well, here we are sailing along the coast of Tunisia on a bright sunny morning. The temperature is 18 C; the wet bulb temperature is 15 C. You can convert that into humidity if you wish. The sea still has a few white caps, but was moderated from yesterday. The wind is on our port beam today instead of on the bow. We are chugging along at five and one-half knots. At present, we are 20 NM north of Bizerte. At 1000 we will line the port rail and render a traditional passing salute to 'Dirty Gerty from Berzerte,' a nearly forgotten WWII creation. We had very smooth seas last night with little wind. The sky was very clear on the mid watch, an astronomer's dream and a nature lover's delight. The Big Dipper and Cassiopeia were circling Polaris on opposite sides and Orion and his dog walked across the southern sky. We are now more than half way from Athens to Gibraltar. Our cook is down in the tank deck chasing the turkeys around. If he can catch enough of them, we'll all have turkey dinner today. The Chief Bos'n is hoping the cook will catch them all, because those birds sure mess up the tank deck and he is about out of feed. And I am about out of B. S. Yesterday we were honored by a US Navy P3. I hope they send us copies of the photos. Our 0830 position was N37-34.6, E010-13.4 See you tomorrow!

With our fast five and one-half knot speed, we were passed by every one of the big ships. However, Doc Jones, my lookout, pointed off to the starboard side. There appeared this forty-foot sailboat behind us and a good distance away but you could see him coming on plain enough. I thought to myself, this mighty warship under my command would soon be overtaken and passed by a sailboat! What a horrible thought! The sailboat slowly crawled abreast of us, and dogged us more as he changed his tack moving closer. He stayed abreast all night and in the morning about the second day of this race for the *America's Cup*, the weather changed, the wind turned more to the west. Then the air become so still. To my joy his sails slackened from no visible breeze and he slowed way down almost to a stop. We jumped out in the lead, passed on by him as he disappeared out of my sight! My reputation was intact! This was the only ship we passed since leaving Souda and most likely the last one! I shouted down the voice tube to Lockas with one S, "Are we having fun yet?"

Another day went by and the weather held. No storms and the sea calm. I called Dewey up on the CONN and told him his five-day confinement had ended; he could leave the ship whenever he wanted!

He spoke up laughing, "Thank you Sir! I have learned my lesson and you, Sir, sure showed the crew. You are not one to disobey."

A Navy plane, a P3, buzzed us again and came up on channel sixteen and asked how we were doing. I answered we were doing fine, just plugging along. A German freighter came up on the channel and gave me hell for talking on Channel sixteen, which was a NO-NO. Sixteen was used to call or hail someone and then one should change to another channel to talk. The Navy plane said good-bye and I thanked him for checking on us. The German was back up telling me to get off the channel again. I just answered back and told him he was talking to a WWII LST that was at Normandy on the morning of June 6, 1944, made the landing with equipment that helped push the Krauts back to your Homeland. I further stated, "I have half a notion to come over where you are and do it again!"

The German just said, "I hear you," and that was that! I have always wondered what the Navy Pilot thought as he flew out of sight. My patience was running thin after having to put up with all of the problems trying to get underway, not to mention the everyday ones that were cropping up now.

The LST could not just keep sailing along - LST 325 was never easy. Whiting had told me that he shut down generator #1 and #2, both with oil leaks. We lost the gyro and we were steering by reading the magnetic compass. We checked the course with the GPS and then asked what the magnetic compass read. The steering system was really giving us fits. It would work for minutes or sometimes hours, and then go out. The OOD would blow the whistle when the steering quit. If not on duty at the time of failure, I would replace Boats who went back to aft steering to hook up the manual operation.

Chapman would run down to aft steering with his hammer (he used the wood handle) to push on the contacts and reset them. In the steering controller, there were three separate contacts. The center one would go in and supply current, then the left or right contact would go in to turn the rudder in that direction depending on how the ship's wheel was being turned. Somehow, it would stick in neutral. Don Chapman had to push on the center contact and it would take off again. The LST had two big wheels in aft steering which, when turned by hand in an emergency, could steer the ship. One had to disconnect the electric steering motor, and then hook up a double roller chain to activate the two wheels. It took only a few minutes with a little practice and we were practiced! Trust me! The wheels turned easy, but it took several turns to get one degree of rudder movement. The OOD had to be careful and considerate to keep the rudder movement as slight as possible to keep the ship on course or he would soon wear out the poor guy turning the hand wheels. The OOD was actually now steering the ship. The sound power phones worked but we had handheld battery operated radios we carried with us and used them to communicate. Not having a cord to limit ones movement made the radios a better choice. The rudder angle indicators still operated so the OOD knew where the rudder was, right or left, and how much.

November twenty-sixth, about three days or four hundred nautical miles from Gibraltar, the steering system quit completely. So now, we were on one main engine, only one generator out of three, manual steering, with no gyro. In this mess, I now have a contact crossing from right to left. He has the right of way, but moving slow.

I came up on Channel sixteen and we moved down to Channel twelve to keep everyone (Germans) happy. He explained he was a 'hydrographic ship' and they were towing a sled five miles back with all kinds of instruments attached. A big six-inch cable that included all of the wires that feed information to the ship was actually pulling the sled. They were taking pictures of the bottom of the Mediterranean Sea among other things. They were on a more southerly course at about a thirty degree angle to us. The Hydro ship's Captain thought our speed was fast enough to cross safely in front of him. He must have been kidding me!

Behind us, a merchant ship doing about twenty knots came up on my starboard side fast, but way back and maybe north (starboard side) of us three miles. The hydrographic ship commenced calling him every five minutes. His course direction and speed put him dead on to cross their cable, so I started to call the merchant ship for the hydro ship in hopes he might hear me, with no luck. When only a distance of seven or eight miles away, the hydro ship began sending up distress flares, one about every minute with calls on Channel sixteen and fourteen. The hydro ship was now calling and telling me what an idiot this person seemed to be. All ships must monitor sixteen and have someone who speaks English listening to it, as stated in the maritime laws for all ships. Question, did it apply to a *Pirate Ship*?

The merchant ship at a distance of only four miles, still traveling at twenty knots, finally reacted asking, "What is the problem?" The Hydrographic ship's Captain pointed out the dangerous situation developing to the Merchant Captain. He was about to run over and cut the Hydro ship's cable. "Immediately turn your ship right ninety degrees," he shouted at the merchant Captain. "Then wait for me to advise when it will be safe to turn back west again." The Hydro ship Captain, still in his excited state, advised me I had better turn right also and he would tell me when I was clear of their sled and could turn back to our course.

He added "And you have a good night, Sir!" I turned north or right ninety degrees, and then turned right again ninety degrees to fall in behind the Merchant Ship. In about thirty minutes, the hydro ship gave us permission to come back to our original course. This did make my watch go by faster!

We limped into Gibraltar at 0200 hour in the morning on November 29, about seven hours early but better early than late. Carter tried for a half-hour to raise the Harbor Master with no luck. He used the radio channel listed in the book with info on all the ports in the Mediterranean Sea, and he tried channel sixteen with no response.

Finally, a sleepy person came on the radio and asked, "What you want?"

Jack told him we would like to check in as required. He gave Jack another Channel to call - high on the marine radio frequencies. Jack turned his radio to that channel but received no response at first. Someone finally answered. Jack asked the same question and heard the same response. This person instructed Jack to go back to the first person! When Jack called the first person again, who now was not happy being awakened a second time, Jack said, "We would like to anchor here in the harbor. We have an appointment with the shipyard at 0900 today."

The port authority said back, "No, you can't anchor. Come back at your appointed time!"

We set out into the dark night in the Mediterranean Sea loaded with traffic going and coming through the Straits of Gibraltar. I told Jack, who now relieved me of the watch, "Sail up along the coast of Spain for three hours, and then turn around and come back. This will eat up a total of six hours, positioning us at the shipyard at our appointed time. I'm turning in for the night."

He said, "Sleep well, Captain."

Leaving the CONN I asked Carter, "Is it just me or does it seem like the harder we try to play by the rules, the more we get into trouble?"

We had entered Gibraltar Harbor when it was dark. It had the usual harbor lights, some flashing red, some green, most white, and the anchor lights of several ships moored along the right side. The shore on the English side had hundreds of lights, the Spanish side only a few. Some of the anchored ships were lit up like Christmas trees, making it a little confusing the first time one entered a new port.

I set my alarm for 0700. When I woke up, I looked out and there she was, the Rock of Gibraltar. It looked huge and was very black. I saw what looked like a solar panel on its south side. Actually, it was a water collection area from WWII, catching rainwater for those taking shelter inside the 'Rock.' I hurried up on the CONN and found Jack, still there on watch with Boats. It was about 0730 and I was scheduled for the 8 to 12 watch anyway. I reduced speed to almost nothing since I still had an hour to kill and had a short distance left to enter into the harbor. This offered everyone time to take some pictures of a very impressive, historic structure going back into Biblical times.

At 0900, we were in the harbor, which appeared larger than last night. A tug came out and a pilot climbed aboard, and sauntered up to the CONN escorted by Boats. He looked at the Greek markings in the CONN and asked me what the Greek name of this ship was. I told him it was the *Syros L144*. With a smile, he announced that he sailed on this ship when in the Greek Navy as a young officer! He asked if we were ready to go into the yard. I decided I had better inform him we only had one engine, one generator, and we are on manual steering, but yes, we were so ready.

He calmly said to me, "I believe we need another tug." He called on his radio and another tug arrived in a few minutes. With two tugs at his disposal, he did a great job of moving the 'Iron Marvel' into the shipyard with little help from the 'T' herself, and moored us starboard side to the pier. He positioned us very close, but aft of a British Navy Oiler, the *Brambleleaf.* Its placement was actually in the English Navy Base; we were in the *Cammell-Laird* Shipyard, with our bow twenty-five feet away from the stern of the British ship.

I HOPE REPAIRS WILL START SOON

CHAPTER 21

A BIG WELCOME TO GIBRALTAR

We were still tying the ship up when the Governor of Gibraltar, David R. C. Durie, arrived. We waited for the shipyard men to place the gangway in position. They were fully aware the Governor wanted to come aboard. Just as the English hierarchy in London had promised, the Governor walked up the gangway and onto the main deck. He was accompanied by US Navy Captain Chris Melhuish, the only US Navy Officer in Gibraltar. Captain Melhuish was a liaison person for Navy ships and US citizens visiting Gibraltar. He could solve a lost passport problem or help with any issues Americans might encounter with the English or maybe even the famous Gibraltar monkeys! His last duty was Captain of the *USS Constitution*, (Old Ironsides) in Boston Harbor. Dressed in whites, he looked very impressive.

I had sent orders down to the main engine room and wheelhouse to secure the engines and the wheelhouse. The electricians were hard at work hooking up the power cord to an AC- DC converter placed on the pier by the shipyard. I never believed we would get DC electrical current. DC was common back when I was in the Navy, but now most ships are AC. The yard must have resurrected it from a back corner of some warehouse. I met the Governor, a medium-sized man that seemed pleased to be aboard a WWII ship. He was standing on the helicopter circle as I approached and extended his hand out towards me. I grabbed it and shook it as firmly as I could. I first saluted, then shook hands with

Captain Melhuish and welcomed them aboard. "Would you like to see the LST?"

The Governor replied, "Yes, I certainly would, Captain Bob, and welcome to Gibraltar." I took both on the nickel tour, something I was getting very used to doing. I had the history of the ship down pat and knew her dimensions, every compartment, all of the equipment, its purpose, and how it worked. The ship was not very clean having been underway for thirteen days, and short on crew to do anything but operate the ship. After the tour, I offered them a cup of coffee. Governor Durie asked if he could say a few words, and I quote, "to your great and very brave crew." We walked out to the main deck.

I had Carter and Edwards gather up the crew. A few were still working doubling up the lines and securing the gangway, but all stopped and came to hear and meet the Governor and the Captain. I introduced both men to the crew.

The Governor happily addressed the crew, "It is a real honor to welcome this historic ship and its veteran crew to Gibraltar. We at Gibraltar consider what you men have done as admirable, working so hard and long to restore this Hero ship, then sail it from Crete to Athens, across the Mediterranean Sea into Gibraltar."

The Governor boasted, "Men, Gibraltar has good shopping and great restaurants. We have this Rock to look at and tour, and there are one hundred and sixty-seven pubs to explore. Please enjoy yourselves. We in Gibraltar will be watching and praying for a safe Atlantic crossing for the ship and each and every one aboard. If you need anything, just let me know. Oh! Be careful of the monkeys - they can bite!"

There is a saying: *If the monkeys disappear from the Rock of Gibraltar, so will the English!*

Captain Melhuish told everyone welcome and he was there to help in any way he could. He did make our short stay enjoyable and helped in several situations.

I asked the Governor and the Captain if my cook's helper, Ernie Andrus, could see a doctor. I explained he had a swollen ankle, maybe infected.

The next day an English Army Doctor made a house call to the LST and examined Ernie's ankle. He bandaged his ankle up and prescribed some pills for him to take; he hoped the medicine would help the swelling. The Dr. told Ernie, "Please come and see me before the ship departs for the US." Who says Doctors don't make house calls? This was a first for LST 325. I hoped Ernie's ankle would heal up and fast.

I had to meet with the Harbor Master who asked several questions and wanted to see the ship's documentation, insurance, etc. As a *Pirate Ship,* we lacked all of these. The only documentation I had was a list of my crew, which I turned over to him! He was pleased with the crew list, shook my hand, and said, "Welcome to Gibraltar." He then departed the ship.

The yard supervisor came aboard. Whiting and I showed him the broken down engine, then Loren explained the problem. The supervisor said a crew would be aboard in the morning to examine the problem and fix that piston.

Whiting told me that he and the engineers could fix the generators. Chapman said he would fix the steering, by-passing the hydraulic system. He planned to run electric wires directly to the controller in aft steering from a switch he was making for the wheelhouse. Then all our helmsmen needed to do to steer, was slide the lever left or right and hold it until the amount of rudder necessary was reached, then let go. The XO was going to try to fix the gyro as he had ordered a tube and it was waiting at customs down close to the airport. Fifty American flags were waiting for pickup there also, donated by Whiting and family to fly over the ship during our trip home. Each of the crew was to receive one for a souvenir. The airport was built in the neutral zone between Spain and England at the beginning of WWII.

Having things somewhat under control, I was about to leave the ship when to my pleasant surprise appeared my engineman, CWO James Bartlett, climbing the gangway with luggage in both hands. Carter had advertised for several days for Jim to come back. He had put it on our web page saying:

Jim Bartlett come back, Jim Bartlett come back. We need you.

Jim called me on the satellite phone and asked if he was to come back, would the ship pay his airfare? His reasoning was he had paid airfare once and paid his money to go on the trip. I thought he had a sound argument and we needed him. I said yes, come on back. I would make sure Edwards reimbursed him. Jim was an asset in the Engineering department and we needed more engineers for crew. He had worked for two and one half months in Souda before he had to go home. He also had become a good friend, but this had nothing to do with my decision to pay him back for airfare. It was solely for the good of LST 325 and the success of our venture.

I had put Loren Whiting in his stateroom when he replaced Jim as the head man in the main engine room. I bunked Jim down on the port side. He liked to be close to the engine rooms anyway. He put his bags down by his new sleeping accommodations, but did not have time to unpack. It was time to tour Gibraltar and find one of those English Pubs the Governor was so proud of and recommended! While wandering around uptown on a very narrow street, we ducked into a place called the *Cannon* when a sudden heavy rain storm developed. It was a small pub, as most of the pubs were in Gibraltar. The patrons were friendly and acted as if they knew each other, indicating to me they were regular customers. They asked an endless array of questions about the ship.

We found out yesterday the *Gibraltar newspaper* had a big article in it with a picture of the ship. It told of the upcoming visit of LST 325, with a crew of veterans - average age seventy-two.

The article went on to say, *"When a US Navy ship comes into Gibraltar, we usually tell the Mothers to lock up their Daughters. In this case, we are telling the Daughters to lock up their Mothers!"*

After a short while, the rain stopped and we moved down the street, jumping over puddles of water, to a famous old pub called *The Clipper*. This tavern dates back to the sailing days of tall ships called *Clipper Ships*, thus the name. It was larger inside than the *Cannon*, and very busy. It had a big wooden bar with two large wood pillars made of teak and heavily engraved, and a huge model of a Clipper ship hanging in the center. It had four rows of different bottles of *grog* that nearly spanned the total width of the bar. All around were pictures of beautiful old sailing ships. Several of our crew had already found this place and were sitting at a table with grins like those a kid has when his Mother loans him the family car for a big date. With the crew sat a somewhat shorter man, handsome, with dark hair and stocky build. I wondered who he was and where he came from. He was quick to tell me he was assigned by the Navy to bring a GPS satellite tracking system and install it on the mast of the ship if it was OK with me!

I asked him, "Who do you work for?"

He quickly replied, "Sorry, I can't tell anyone."

I told him, "Your answer gives me a fair idea." He just smiled and sipped his beer.

The next day he installed the tracker up very high on the mast. The tracker did not weigh much and was easy to carry up the ladder, where he fastened it to the mast, but the twelve-volt battery was another story. In order for the feed wires to reach the battery, he needed help getting it to the first platform on the mast ten feet up from the 03 deck. With Carter and Edwards using a line wrapped twice securely around the battery, they pushed and he lifted; it was soon in position. They then taped the lead wires to the mast and ran them up to the tracker. He announced to us with some pride, "With this tracker activated the Navy will know the ship's location at all times!" He said, "The LST can't hide anymore!" He stayed in one of the better hotels in Gibraltar and went out to eat with us several times right up until we sailed. I wish I had written down his name. I also was glad it tracked the ship - not the Boats and Dewey on liberty!

The US Coast Guard called and asked if they could give us a complimentary inspection, voluntary on my part. I told them sure, come on aboard. I figured a little cooperation with the Coast Guard would help when we reached the USA. The inspector was from Rotterdam, Netherlands, and arrived the second day we were in Gibraltar. I thought he would be aboard for three or four hours, give us a list of the discrepancies he recommended for us to fix, and maybe hold a fire drill and a man overboard drill. To my surprise he spent three days on board going through every tank and compartment, from bow to stern. He also held a fire drill and abandon ship drill. He suggested we throw all of the Greek Life jackets off the ship, explaining they were worse than not having one if we fell in the water! I never tried one to see if that was true! Some of the crew kept a few to use on the deck for padding when they had to kneel down to fix something.

I must admit, our first fire drill looked like the *Keystone Cops* in action, or should I say *McHale's Navy?* Have you ever heard of a *Chinese Fire Drill?* However, we did have a fire team and had assigned men to life rafts in case we had to abandon ship. The fire drill would have been fine but for one man, not assigned to the fire team at all.

Knowing we had CG on board, he thought he would help. He was in the Coast Guard Auxiliary in Miami. If he had only mustered on the main deck like the rest of the crew as instructed, I believe the fire team would have done just fine. Mr. Nickerson, after hearing the broadcast over our PA system of a fire drill and the location of the fire, ran aft to the location at the stern winch. He grabbed the nozzle end of the hose and dragged it straight out of the holder towards the ship's side rail, not waiting for help. This does not work as someone must guide the folds of the hose out of the rack. The hose kinked on him and he kept yanking, creating a bigger knot. When the fire team arrived, he would not quit tugging on the hose. Finally, the hose was free, but he had pulled the hose away from the hydrant making it impossible to connect the hose end to the fittings on the fire main. I was on the 01 level with the inspector looking down on this catastrophe. Any other time, I would have laughed, but I was getting a serious look from the inspector.

We had a second fire drill and the team did a good job. In most drills or a real fire, those men not actually involved reported to the main deck where a roll call was taken to determine if anyone was missing. Before we left Souda, a 'Buddy' System was in place. Everyone picked a fellow crew member to keep track of. If your 'buddy' did not show up for muster, was not on watch or not on the fire team, you reported him missing. We immediately would look for him to see if he could be hurt, trapped, or overcome with smoke.

I assigned Ron Maranto to take the CG Inspector around the ship. Ron was not happy with me since the inspector made him work opening tanks and voids, which in my opinion was not necessary. I believe they were trying to find something terribly wrong, maybe to keep us from sailing. Their opening and checking all the tanks, ballast, fuel, and voids were unnecessary as we sounded these tanks for leaks and kept a log. Taking off the covers broke the seals around the hatch covers which hurt the ship's watertight integrity. The same old theme - we have to save these old people by not letting them go sailing.

The inspector came up with twenty-three violations that he said we should fix before we sail. At the top of the list was fixing the broken window in the CONN! I asked him to point out the window. When he did, I lifted and unhooked the window, which was fastened up against the roof, sort of out of sight and let it swing down in place. I said, "You can cross that deficiency off your list!" There were two windows in the CONN, one on each side and we referred to them as our two air conditioners! The inspector was not as cocky any more.

I received a letter shortly from Admiral John E. Shkor, Coast Guard Atlantic Area Commander. He first commended the crew and me, and then listed the deficiencies that needed corrected. The following are just a few of those deficiencies as best I can remember:

1. Inadequate lifesaving equipment – CG not partial to the canister life rafts Boats purchased from the Greeks. I am sure they had a 10,000 percent guarantee that they would inflate!

2. Questionable condition of the main engines and steering system - both in the process of repair as the inspector was inspecting and he knew that.

3. The apparent lack of an Emergency Generator - I liked the apparent part. We were not a passenger ship, therefore not required to have an emergency generator! Had anyone told the Admiral the LST had three generators on board and needed only one to sail the ship, which actually gave us two emergency generators.

4. Uncertainty as to the crew handling emergencies - This was, I believe, from the poor fire drill. I had confidence that we could handle fire, man overboard and abandon ship. I could always take over fighting a fire since I received training by the best at Treasure Island. As Damage Control Officer on the *Jerome County,* I conducted fire drills, trained, and lectured the ship's personnel on proper procedures. I may have looked old but at sixty-one still very capable. No one in the Navy or Coast Guard had bothered to check my credentials and training to my knowledge.

The Admiral, maybe directed by our State Department, advised me not to sail in December across the North Atlantic. He must have known we had little choice in this matter. We could not leave the ship for six months in Gibraltar. Everything of value would have disappeared off the LST. The dockage charge would have been greater than our meager bank account! This gave the Coast Guard an out - if we had trouble, they could say they had warned us.

Nothing would have been left of this ship if left idle for six months. Our government's delays caused this winter crossing. The Admiral's other suggestion was to have the ship towed as a dead ship back to the U.S. We had asked the Navy to tow us as a drill or a practice exercise; their answer was a flat out no. They could not help a private organization. Does anyone wonder how our Navy can go to the aid of other countries all over the world, but can't help some navy veterans bring back a navy ship? At the end of the letter, the CG Admiral admitted they had no jurisdiction over us. After all, we were a *Pirate ship*! He actually said, "An unregistered ship not under US Flag."

Our maritime attorney had said since the LST was not a U.S. registered ship; we could NOT fly an American flag. I did not fly one, I flew two, one on the mast, and one on the stern! No one had said we could not fly two! We also flew the *Don't Tread on Me Flag* on the bow jack staff even when underway, located right beside the Greek good luck symbol. We were Americans; the ship was a hero from WWII. One had better bring a big ship with guns to stop us from flying the American flag!

Carter and I were invited over to the *Brambleleaf* for dinner by one of their Officers. We accepted. It would be great to eat aboard an English ship and make some new friends. Our problem – it was in the British Naval Base and it was a long way (maybe 2 miles around) to get to their gate, yet we were only twenty feet from their ship. The British had erected a security fence between the shipyard and the English Base separating the two. It stuck out about five feet into the harbor and was ten feet high with barbed wire on the top! Jack and I went over to the fence, with the British crew watching from high above on their ship. He thought he could get around the end of the fence.

I said, "If you can do it Jack, so can I." He stepped out to the end of the fence with only dark black water under him. He placed his right foot at the end and as smooth as could be, swung around to the other side and stepped into the British Naval Base! Jack had longer arms and legs, and I had some doubt if that maneuver would work for me, but I placed my foot where he had and landed on the other side.

The British ships have an open, fully stocked bar; we don't! I had never witnessed Carter having a beer or any alcoholic drink, but the English insisted Jack have one for the toast. Me? I had one for the toast.

(Sort of like drinking Greek Coffee; I wanted to be polite!) They initiated a toast to the crew of the 325 and I gave one back, "To the continued good relations with the English, the best Allies a country could have." We had a great dinner and were asked back several more times after that. I think they liked to see us go around the fence, because the crowd was always bigger watching us go back! The XO was a real American; never tell him he can't do something! The crew was invited over for a dinner with the English Oiler's crew also.

The Captain of the *Brambleleaf* showed me a British e-mail joke, first asking if I had a sense of humor. I told him I thought so. With that, he handed me this e-mail. I have to set the stage for this. It was right after our Presidential election in 2000. The election was in a stalemate between George W. and Al Gore. The English Captain's E-mail read like this:

NOTICE OF REVOCATION OF INDEPENDENCE

To the citizens of the United States of America, in light of your failure to elect a President, and thus to govern yourselves, we (The British) hereby give notice of the revocation of your independence, effective today. (17 Nov. 2000 16:56)

Her Sovereign Majesty Queen Elizabeth II will resume monarchial duties over all states, commonwealths and other territories. Except Utah, which she does not fancy. Your new prime minister (the rt. Hon. Tony Blair, for the 97.85% of you who have until now been unaware that there is a world outside your borders) will appoint a minister for America without the need for further elections. Congress and the Senate will be disbanded. A questionnaire will be circulated next year to determine if any of you noticed. The following rules are introduced to help the transition, effective immediately:

1. Look up revocation in the oxford English dictionary. Then look up 'aluminum.' Check the pronunciation. You will be amazed at just how wrong you have been pronouncing it. Raise your vocabulary to acceptable levels. Forget filler noises such as "like" and "you know." They are not acceptable and are inefficient forms of communication.

2. There is no such thing as US English. We will let Microsoft know on your behalf.

3. Hollywood will be required occasionally to cast English actors as the good guys.

4. You will have to relearn your National Anthem, 'God Save The Queen' but only after carrying out task No. 1.

5. You should stop playing American football. There is only one kind of football. What you refer to as football is not a very good game. The 2.15% of you who are aware there is a world outside your borders may have noticed that no one else plays "American football." You will instead play proper football. We suggest initially it would be best to play with the girls. Those of you brave enough will, in time, be allowed to play rugby. This sport does not stop every 20 seconds for a rest or wearing full Kevlar body armour like nancies. We hope to get a US team together by 2005!

6. You should declare war on Quebec and France using nuclear weapons, if they give you any merde. Merde stands for "sh*t."

7. July 4th will no longer be a holiday. Nov. 8th will be, but only in England, "indecisive day."

8. All American cars are now banned. They are crap and it is for your own good. We will show you German cars so you will understand.

9. Please, tell us who killed JFK. It has been driving us crazy. Thank you for your cooperation!

I thought this email was funny; the Brits do have a sense of humor!

I received a nice letter from the Governor thanking the whole crew for allowing him to visit and tour the ship. He said he hoped to visit the ship again, when next in the USA.

The Destroyer, *USS Arleigh Burke,* sailed into town and moored in the yard but on the opposite pier. The Commanding Officer and XO came right over to see us and toured the LST. They had a couple of sailors bring a number of brooms, mops, cleaning materials and laundry soap. Later they sent over several sailors to replace inspection covers over the main and auxiliary engine rooms, after the yard workers were done. The *Arleigh Burke*'s mission or assignment was to replace the *USS Cole.*

The *Arleigh Burke*'s crew decided to throw a party for our crew; the invite included dinner so Cookie could go, too. He would never be invited back the Captain told me later. I guess he had too much to drink or his true colors came out. He apparently got out of hand with the woman sailors at the dance. I saw them laughing at him mostly, but only observed him after the party moved off the destroyer and spread out into the shipyard. I could see Cookie was showing off a little too much.

We were invited by the British Army to see firsthand the old tunnels and caves of the Rock - tunnels dug out in the eighteenth century and the WWII tunnels dug out before 1940 for the defense of the Mediterranean and Gibraltar. The old tunnels face the Spanish and are higher up in the North end of the rock, where the famous Gibraltar monkeys are located. Jack knew the monkeys liked dry uncooked pasta and brought a bag along safely tucked in his jacket. He shared some giving us the experience and fun of feeding them. The monkeys soon learned who had the bag of pasta. One jumped on the XO's back and was able to reach into his jacket pocket, snatched the bag out, and just as quickly scampered away. He left with the majority of monkeys following behind him. Most of us had pictures taken with one or two on our shoulders and no one received a love bite!

The British Army Lieutenant led us to another opening at the south end of the *Rock,* gave us flashlights, and took us inside to the WWII tunnels. The tunnels were wide and large with rooms leading off to the sides, some running into a parallel tunnel or to a ramp leading up or down to another level. One could drive a semi-truck and trailer right down through the main tunnels. They showed us the room where General Eisenhower had his headquarters and planned the invasion of North Africa, called *Operation Torch.* This invasion plan started the downfall of the German machine. We walked for miles, a total of three hours time and went to several levels. The Rock had its own generators for electric power. I was able to stand alongside one of the engines, ten times bigger than the 325's. They had a Hospital and berthing rooms for ten thousand men and large storage rooms for food, ammunition, and supplies. Nothing much was there now, only the big engines that would take more fixing than we gave the engines on LST! At the end of the tour, the Lieutenant led us out of the maze.

I asked, "How many miles are in this Rock?"

Our army guide said, "Forty-three miles!"

"How many miles did you show us today?" I asked.

He smiled answering, "Only about three miles!" The *Rock* was one thousand four hundred feet high and covered two square miles. It was not bad walking all that distance; we had practice making our rounds in Souda! I did think we had walked the whole 43 miles however!

WEATHER REPORT ON ATLANTIC COMING

CHAPTER 22

THE CNO ORDERS MORE DIESEL FUEL

Captain Melhuish sent a message over to the LST inviting Mr. Carter and I over to his office in the British Navy and Army Headquarters for a critique on the winter weather the LST would face once outside of the Straights of Gibraltar. The British Headquarters were located inside the Naval Base just ahead of the LST. Jack and I took the shortcut around the security fence. The headquarters was a white, two-story building with a courtyard in the center and appeared to cover a square city block. All the offices faced into the courtyard. On arrival, they asked us to wait. We later found out the Captain was talking to the CNO, Chief of Naval Operations in Norfolk, VA. Jack and I were able to watch the British Officers choir singing Christmas Carols in the courtyard while we waited. They were practicing and singing the old favorites. I thought this had to be early. It couldn't be Christmas already? "Jack," I asked, "what is the date today?"

He answered, "December 7, 2000."

Two British Officers grabbed Carter's old beat up ball cap right off of his head, then quickly replaced it with a new flat British Army Beret while we watched the singing. They evidently thought an Executive Officer on a prestigious ship should have a better-looking hat. I certainly could not argue with them! I only wished I had worn a dirty old hat!

Captain Melhuish had sent for a team of weather experts from our Naval Base at Rota, Spain, to brief us on what to expect when we sailed into the North Atlantic. I had decided not to sail the original planned route to France, England, and Boston. I was going straight across the Atlantic with my favorite course of 270 degrees. I had watched and studied the weather for weeks showing severe, brutal storm after storm hitting England. I wanted none of that!

Captain Melhuish came out of his lofty Office on the second floor and motioned for us to come up. Jack and I maneuvered up the stairs and introduced ourselves to the weather guys. The Navy experts told us the weather appeared good for the first one thousand miles west out of the Straits of Gibraltar for the next two weeks. We were not going to sail for five or six days since the Yard had not finished fixing the exhaust manifold, and then had to install it. We were ready to travel at first light or whenever we could button everything up on the "T."

Captain Melhuish told us the Admiral wanted me to go South past the Canary Islands, then turn west at twenty-five degrees north latitude headed towards the Bahamas. He also wanted us to buy another twenty thousand gallons of diesel fuel. He felt we were a little short for the trip across.

We had spent thirteen days instead of nine as planned getting to Gibraltar, so I had used a little more fuel. Also by going south farther, I would be traveling more miles across or around the thicker part of the earth. We calculated the distance to be four thousand, three hundred miles into Mobile. It was easy for him to say to buy another twenty thousand gallons of fuel. He did not have to find it and pay for it! In this ship, with its big tanks and the two-inch gap at the bottom of the suction line, I could not plan on retrieving every gallon on board. We filled only the eighteen thousand gallon fuel tanks keeping this built-in loss to a minimum.

The XO stopped at the British PX, bought me a pair of Royal Navy Captain's bars, and presented them to me. He said I had earned them, especially by making the decision not to go into Sicily!

First order of business when I got back on the LST 325 was to call my friend in Houston, Texas at BP. I explained to her my problem; I needed another twenty thousand gallons of diesel fuel ordered by the U.S. Navy.

She told me, "I am positive I cannot give you any more fuel, Captain."

"I totally understand." Then I asked, "Is it possible for BP to supply the fuel and we pay you when we arrive back in the States?"

She said, "We can work out something, maybe at our cost. Our problem is we do not have fuel facilities in Gibraltar! Let me call you back tomorrow with some kind of solution."

BP called back. She had arranged for fuel with the Spanish Company that BP did business with, gave me a person's name and phone number to call. I called this company immediately and discussed our needs; they could deliver it to the ship Tuesday, December 12th. I was to pay BP when I got back to the U.S. It was a great feeling knowing that BP thought we would make it home!

We had all kinds of press people, plus radio and some TV reporters coming aboard the ship. One was Tom Brokaw's team from London, England. They filmed our muster at Quarters at 0800 in the morning, and then interviewed some of the crew. The ship had its share of camera hounds – always in front of it, and a few like Chapman who were not interested in any of it. One of the female reporters, a very good-looking black haired beauty with a dynamite shape, started to interview Cookie. He was a good talker and had been with the first seven men to go to Greece. She asked him, "What do you feed the crew most often?"

Cookie was given the opportunity he relished, a chance to interject his warped sense of humor to a question asked. He answered with a straight face, "Well I always give them *Viagra* when in a storm or rough water."

She fell for that and inquired, "Why?"

Cookie, now with a smirk answered, "It keeps them from rolling out of their bunks!" Cookie's interview was abruptly over! This comment did not see the light of day in Mr. Brokaw's segment of the 'Greatest Generation' when he aired our story!

The LST reached an untouchable plateau after Mr. Brokaw aired our story on Prime Time TV. His show, along with the other ten or so newspapers and magazine articles published right after we left Gibraltar, gave us untold fame. The magazines doing articles included the Navy times, Army times, and Stars and Stripes which are all military publications. I should have kept a list of everyone who published stories on our effort.

Because of Mr. Brokaw's show and those articles, and the mounting number of '*LST FANS*' around the globe, the State Department and the Coast guard backed off and moved out of our way.

This notoriety deterred anyone from doing or saying anything negative about the LST and especially its older crew of veterans trying to sail her home. Any thumbs down pessimism or threats were not taken lightly by our growing fan club, and e-mails and phone calls rained down on the guilty ones with seemingly no end. Some of these agencies, like our State Department, had already learned the hard way, having their communication systems jammed up by the mass of Americans protesting their actions holding up our paperwork. LST fans were all great patriots; they supported our military with a passion. They also like the underdogs of this world and in general want 'Big Brother' to disappear. The public broadcasting radio station started calling me periodically on our satellite phone while in port in Gibraltar, and later when we reached the open water of the Atlantic. These interviews were live on-air interviews and asked for up-dates and how things were going.

Meanwhile the shipyard was having its problems. They had removed and put in a new liner, piston and head, in three cylinders and the cylinders still leaked! They did a pressure test finally. First they permitted the water in the engine to come up slowly to the top of the cylinders and observed no leaks. Next, they raised the water level higher up into the water-cooled exhaust manifold above the engine. Water started dripping down the cylinders! The problem was the manifold, not the engine cylinders! There evidently was a crack in the exhaust manifold in the inside, which allowed water down into the valves and into the cylinder, which had caused the hole in the top of the piston. The yard took the exhaust manifold off the engine, raised it up through the access hole above the port reduction gear into the tank deck, and transported it to their shop for repair.

A Greek Orthodox Priest had blessed the ship in Souda. In Gibraltar a British Army Chaplain and a Catholic Priest came aboard, blessed the crew, the LST, and our Atlantic voyage. With three blessings, I knew we were OK. I had thanked all three of them. Having just one blessing in Crete, God had to be with us to bring us through the storm in the Mediterranean by Sicily and keep the old lady running all the way into

Gibraltar. With two more blessings, the LST 325 would be able to take anything the *Old Atlantic* could throw at her! However, she was not asking to challenge *Mother Nature*!

Captain Melhuish also came up with a couple of good luck charms. One was a piece of wood from the extensive overhaul of the *USS CONSTITUTION* in Boston which he said would bring us luck. The second was a small stone off the grave of an American buried in the Gibraltar cemetery. He said, "When the ship makes it back to the USA, you need to throw that stone back in the ocean to preserve the stone's good luck. It will bring the ship fair seas and good sailing for a safe crossing." The 325 was well equipped with prayers, blessings, and good luck charms.

My wife and I talked mostly about the farm and of course our dog Tai, named after the Island of Taiwan from my visit there. The crops were in and yields were good. She mentioned that our Minister and good friend, Del Kielman, had added my name to the morning's prayer list at church after she had told him I was about to start across the big pond. He began by explaining, "This is a special extra prayer for Bob, because I pray for Bob almost every day even when he is right here in town and at home!" He must have gotten a good laugh from my fellow parishioners on that one.

Lois also said one of our friends told her he had bought a computer just to monitor my progress with the ship on the web page. He told her there were quite a few people in Earlville who wanted to have an update about our problems, or success. There was a waitress, Sandy, in our local café that did a good job of keeping the locals informed with a report from our web page every morning. It was a popular coffee stop for the townsfolk.

One of our British friends organized a day's bus trip to Spain for the entire ship's crew at twenty dollars each. This turned into a nice trip, well worth the money. We learned there was only one foot of neutral ground between Spain and Gibraltar. Before WW II the neutral ground had a span of several thousand feet. It seems the British needed an air field to help in the war effort, so they built it in the neutral zone! This caused hard feelings with the Spanish, and kept the gate between the two countries closed until 1996. Once in Spain, we had to change American money into Spanish money, pesetas, to buy anything. Euros would have been easier but were not in use yet. I learned that Spain was a very modern and progressive country with friendly citizens.

Don Chapman, who had made us a brand new steering system that worked one hundred times easier than the old one (I hoped more reliable,) lost his American Passport out of his jacket pocket. The weather had warmed up so he removed his jacket, folded it up, and the passport must have fallen out. I was told an American passport could fetch one thousand dollars, so it was probably not going to show up.

Don needed to show a passport to re-enter Gibraltar. We had a guide of sorts, a bus driver. I told him one of my crew had lost his passport and he offered a solution. "A border guard will come aboard the bus and ask everyone to show his or her passport by holding it up. As long as everyone has one in their hand, he will not check to see if it is your face on it!" The driver volunteered to loan Don his passport saying, "They know me and never ask me to show mine. Just have him sit in the back so customs will not be able to see it well." Don did as he was told, and we all got in the gate. Another crisis solved. I told Don he should keep that passport; the bus driver's picture looked so much better than his!

Ernie Andrus' ankle was not much better. He made another appointment with the British Army Doctor. When he came back, he handed the quarterdeck watch a letter from the Doctor to me. The envelope was already opened when I received it. I took out the letter the Doc had written, "Mr. Andrus's ankle is still not good. He could easily get an infection without proper medical care. I strongly advise you not to take him with you across the Atlantic. He should fly home and seek medical advice."

I looked up Edwards who had just gone by my office. I asked if he had seen Ernie, or did he know where he might be? He said, "Yes, most of the crew has the bad news. Ernie is down packing his bags. I believe we should get him a cab to go buy an airline ticket to fly home."

I replied, "All of the crew will want to see him before he leaves." It was a heart breaker because Ernie had worked very hard, mostly as Cookie's helper from September up until a few weeks ago when his ankle swelled up and I made him lay in his bunk except for meals.

We lost two other men as soon as we pulled into Gibraltar: Ray Mai, who took Bartlett's place as fuel and water king, and Jim Young, who worked a lot on the sound powered phones; both were engineers. I pleaded with them to stay, and emphasized our need for engineers; but both said they had commitments back home. I answered, "Men, your first commitment should be this ship and getting it back to the US. We all have demands from home. What if we all left?" Nothing that I could say changed their minds. I never did learn the real reasons.

Another man, G. A. Robinson, had just arrived; flew in just before Bartlett. He was an air conditioning and refrigerator expert and someone we could surely use. After only five days on board, he came to me and said he could not sleep. He had heard all the things that went wrong, and he couldn't seem to shake the bad news. I told him I did not want anyone ruining his health. Have a good trip home.

Then I was surprised when our Marine and lover boy came to me and said one of his daughters was sick and had no one to take care of her. I asked if she was married. George said, "Yes, but her husband can't be counted on to be around to help her all the time. I have to go home, sorry." Ship's crew now down to twenty-eight – each as tough and mean as an old momma sow when one picks up one of her baby pigs and it starts to squeal.

While on the trip to Spain, I got to thinking about a young camera operator, Glenn Gregg, who had climbed aboard stating he was to ride on the ship to the U.S. and take pictures for the documentary that Linda Alvers was making for the *History Channel*. I first told him no way was he coming along. "Sorry, I don't need a camera in my face and you would be a big distraction to the crew."

He said, "I'll stay out of the way." I also pointed out that if I took him, how many more cinematographers and reporters would want to come, too. I had left him with a NO. He said, "I will do anything, please give me a chance."

Lois had told me on one of our phone calls that I was making a mistake by not letting him go along. I had explained to her my loss of crew and about this young man I had told NO!

Thinking, as I rode back from Spain on the bus, I must be out of my mind. I had told a forty-year-old male in good health no, he could not ride with us across the Atlantic! We were down in numbers to twenty-eight men counting myself, with an average age of seventy-two. What if some of the crew came down sick or somehow were hurt, just how could I rationalize turning down this young healthy guy? I could not wait to board the ship and see if he was still around. As soon as I arrived back at the ship, I asked the quarterdeck watch, "Is that video guy still aboard?"

The watch answered, "Yes, a little while ago he was back in the galley, a big eater you know. He spends most of his time there." I asked the Quarter Deck if he would find him and tell him I wanted to see him in my stateroom. Soon, Glenn Gregg showed up.

I asked, "Do you still want to ride with us back to the States?"

Glenn answered quickly, "Yes sir, yes sir, I really would, can I?"

I said, "OK, but first you must pay the $2,200 like the rest of us." He quickly said that he could do that.

I explained a couple of rules, "You will have to stand watch in the engine room and learn all about the engines, ballast, fuel systems, and generators. I am short on Engineers. You take pictures on your own time, off watch." He nodded his head yes and said he could handle that.

I added, "One more thing."

He was now worried and burst out with, "WHAT?"

"You cannot take any bad pictures of the Captain!" A big smile spread across his face and he said he would never do that and I could see every bit of video he took. If I didn't like it, he would erase it. I told him to stay out of sight when the ship was leaving until we were out in the harbor. I did not want other newspaper, TV, or video people seeing him or they would want to come along, too! He left. I sat back in my chair and said, "God is good."

The ship's roster was set at twenty-eight men plus one, Glenn Gregg. We planned to leave tomorrow, Tuesday December 12th, all systems go!

The fuel barge came very late in the afternoon. He handed us up a sample of the fuel. It was a round glass cylinder about eight inches long and two inches in diameter. When a ship takes on fuel, a sample was taken at the beginning and one at the end and sent up to the buyer. We placed them in the ships safe and wrapped them with foam rubber to keep them from breaking. The sample was clean and clear. Edwards said it looked like good diesel fuel, and I agreed.

In Greece, all fuel sold was by liters, so we had to convert to gallons. In Gibraltar, we bought fuel by the specific gravity of the fuel, or by weight. The specific gravity of diesel varied from batch to batch a small amount. I had my old physics book with a chart which converted everything to pounds, grams, liters, and the U.S. gallon.

Phillips Petroleum Company also agreed to furnish us fuel, but BP beat them to it. Instead, Phillips donated twenty thousand dollars U.S. Ms. Barbara Price, a Vice President at Phillips, told me later one of her employees, a daughter of an LST Veteran, came into her office with a request for a fuel donation. She presented her case with expression and passion, and described the need of Navy veterans for fuel to bring back an old ship which had been at D-Day. Price asked her, "What kind of ship?"

Barbara was surprised when her employee answered, "A WWII LST." Ms. Price explained that behind her desk in her office was a large picture of her mother christening an LST just before it launched at the Evansville, IN Shipyard. Do you think this employee found the right person at Phillips?

The British Army donated boxes of their emergency food rations - sort of like our WWII 'K' rations, only these were boxes six by twelve by eight inches! They were very generous; I believe we had enough boxes to feed us for a year if needed. Cookie ordered more supplies and food and had them delivered.

Then Doc and Perruso appeared at my door with more requests. Doc wanted more disinfectant cream and a host of other medical supplies. I suggested he go to town to a drug store and buy what he needed. He made out a list and persuaded a couple of crew to do it for him. We were set on medical supplies necessary to handle most emergencies. Perruso wanted a larger capacity suction pump in case the ship developed a large hole in the Atlantic. He must still be having nightmares of finding the water in the tank deck, I thought to myself. He told me he was not going with the ship if I didn't buy one or two more pumps.

I replied, "Dom, please don't get your pants in a wrinkle. I am confident that we have enough pumps on board, but if you feel that strongly about it, see Edwards. Have Jim give you some cash, take someone with you to help carry, and go downtown, and buy a couple of pumps. Be sure and get the discharge hoses and a long 3-wire drop cord of at least number twelve size electric wire to hook them up."

He got a smile on his face, and said, "Aye, Aye Captain," and away he went. I thought to myself, there certainly was no need to hurry; we plan to leave later today!

Having received the final bill from the shipyard, I started over to pay the bill at the shipyard office only a couple of blocks away. I passed a large dry-dock that could have handled one of our battleships; maybe it had at one time.

I had a cashier's check from the Greek National Bank in Chania for thirty thousand American dollars, the balance left from fifty thousand dollars that Linda Gunjak had wired to me after I threatened to fly home and shoot somebody if they did not comply! I had used eight thousand buying diesel, lube oil, and life rafts in Crete early on. When closing out the ship's account, the bank manager would only give me twelve thousand in American cash. He said if he gave me more, it would run him short for others. This forced me to accept the balance in a cashier's check. I had tried since I arrived in Gibraltar to get it cashed. I had several important British citizens try at their different banks. I told them we would guarantee it. I had Boats try, he was after all an ex-Bank President; he had no luck either.

I wanted the shipyard to take out their bill of eighteen thousand and give me back a company check for the balance. One would have thought that check was on fire the way they threw it back at me! Therefore, I paid them in good old American green backs, and thanked them for getting us repaired so fast, in eleven days! They thanked me and uttered, "Please come back!" We shook hands and I went back to the ship. I gave the cashier's check back to Edwards to return it to the ship's safe, wondering if I could cash it in Earlville, Illinois!

The United States Coast Guard sent us a self-deploying *Eperb* to mount on the ship. An *Eperb* was a radio distress beacon. This self deploying beacon automatically deployed leaving the ship at a six foot depth. It would rise to the surface and start sending out a continuous radio signal so search planes and ships could find us or know at least where we went to the bottom! We had two 'hand carry' *Eperbs*, one for each canister raft. The CG must have thought we would sink so fast we might not have time to snatch our hand carry ones on the way to the rafts.

The CG thought we should have two more life rafts. They wanted us to position two on each side of the ship in case the ship developed a large list to one side when it sank into the murky depths. In this case the crew could only use the rafts on the ship's lowest side.

I had learned from my friends on the Black Ships, with a flat deck all we needed was two rafts deployed in the center of the deck. They could slide either way to the low side of the ship and be placed in the water. This saved us three thousand dollars. I didn't mention Boat's guarantee to the Coast Guard!

Mobile, Alabama came to our rescue. We had a port and a place to tie up the ship! I had called Captain Hal Pierce, Navy Port Coordinator for the city of Mobile, Alabama. I talked to him several times about coming to Mobile with the LST, but did not have a definite answer from him. On a call right after we arrived in Gibraltar, he said he did not have a place for us yet, but bring her on. "I will have a dock by the time you guys arrive." I guess he knew how fast we were and he would have plenty of time! This was the best news yet!

All the others I had called asking for a place to dock had said no. One can't dock an LST in just any boat Marina. The New Orleans Coast Guard Sector had informed me that if I came to their city, they were going to make me anchor out in the Gulf until the ship met all their safety standards. I rather wondered how one would fix things out in the Gulf of Mexico? The entrance to the Mississippi River is 100 miles from New Orleans! Captain Hal's acceptance to make a spot for us was an answer to my prayers; one more huge problem solved. There was a light at the end of the tunnel.

Mobile called again, this time from the Mobile visitor center by a young-sounding woman, probably in her early twenties, who wanted to know the date the ship would be reaching Mobile! She was in charge of coordinating a small welcoming party for us. She said, "We are inviting your wives, family members, and other LST veterans to be here to see the LST 325's triumphant return from way across the sea! The welcome includes you and your courageous crew of course. The boat, I mean ship, has generated a lot of publicity. Please, I need to know the date when you are going to arrive here in Mobile Bay."

She did not even say, expect, hope, or even plan to be. I tried to tell her we had a long way to sail and that this LST was an old worn out ship. That did not seem to get through either. I continued my rebuttal by telling her the facts, "I am not sure of the week, the month, or possibly even the year! You want the day? I have no idea, but we are coming your way!"

She informed me that in order to have a welcoming party, she needed a date. People were planning on her to arrange it, "Come on Captain, and please tell me when you are going to be here. You know or can simply figure it out."

I told her, "Yes, I have a rough estimate of when we might arrive. Would you mind calling me back in an hour? I will talk with my Executive Officer and come up with a possible arrival day just for you."

"Oh! Thank you Captain!" she wailed with delight.

The XO, Quartermaster Nickerson, and I did some figuring with different estimates in how far it was to Mobile. The only constant in this equation was the twenty-four hours in a day! In Jack's report to the web, he used five thousand miles and, at eight knots, it would take twenty-eight days!

I re-calculated the miles going straight out of Gibraltar on an angle down to the North twenty-five degree latitude and following it west. I came up with four thousand three hundred miles in distance. Seven knots times twenty-four hours, the miles per day, divided into four thousand three hundred miles was twenty-five and six tenth days, WITH NO BREAKDOWNS OR PROBLEMS!

I turned toward Jack, asking him, "How many days steady did your LST run in Korea?"

He thought some, then stated, "Maybe ten days to two weeks!" I said that was close to the same as with my LSTs in the sixties.

"Jack, I said, what about adding three days to our estimate?"

He chuckled, "Captain, sounds like you are using the old SWAG system, (simple wild ass guess)."

I confirmed, "You have that right! However, I have used an old adage many times in calculating the time of arrival for an LST - one can always slow an LST up, but it's impossible to speed one up!"

With great eagerness, she called back right on the hour and inquired, "Captain, do you have a time you plan to arrive in our great city for me?" I answered her as if I would be driving on a new interstate highway with no stop signs all the way to Mobile in a brand new Cadillac.

"It will take us exactly 29 days to cross the Atlantic and arrive at the Sea Buoy at the entrance of Mobile Bay, on Wednesday January 10, 2000. Would this fit your welcome celebration time?"

She expressed that the tenth of January would be perfect, added, "Captain, what time will you arrive on that Wednesday?"

Now I wish Jack Carter had been on the phone listening, because he laughed when I used the SWAG system to come up with the day. What should I now use to come up with the exact time? I just decided to give myself most of the morning as it is 32 miles from the sea buoy to the Civic Center. I pulled the time out of the air telling her, "I will be there at 10:30 in the morning. You can sleep in, have a nice breakfast, and be at the Mobile Civic Center to see a great ship with a greater crew blowing the ship's whistle and sailing past!"

I guess I had made her day as she excitedly screamed into the phone, "You know I will be there Captain; I wouldn't miss it! See you in Mobile, good-bye now."

Captain Pierce never admitted to me how much he laughed when she told him what I had just predicted. I not only told her the day, but also the exact minute this grand old lady with an older crew would pass the Convention Center after almost a month in the Atlantic Ocean during the winter season! I wonder how many others shook their heads.

I like to make people happy when I can. Since she wanted nothing to do with reality, it just seemed OK in this case, to make up a day and time! I looked out at the Greek good luck charm, that blue and gold sunburst, and wondered if I should go up and rub it some!

We now had a goal to meet. I wondered if the bookies in Souda would have odds for or against our arrival on time in Mobile. Who would dare bet against this old ship?

There were still those doubters back home, maybe thirty percent now!

Someone did give us a Pirate's black flag, with white skull and cross-bones. There was a few times when we probably should have hoisted her up! There could be more!

With the CG letter filed and the inspector off the ship, the crew went to work and fixed sixteen of the twenty-three safety items listed by the inspector. There were seven items impossible for the crew to fix in Gibraltar:

    1. Covers missing off electric boxes - these were gone!

    2. Missing light bulbs - we did all have flashlights!

    3. Glass and wire guard protectors missing that go over the light bulbs mostly to protect the bulb if one hits it with his head! Where did one find these?

    4. Some loose electric wires that needed securing - work in progress.

    5. A few lights in storage compartments were hanging by their wires, a temporary fix by the Greeks.

    6. Some electric switches didn't work.

    7. A porthole was missing in the chart room, behind the wheelhouse. The hole was actually where an antenna base had been bolted to the bulkhead outside and evidently removed by the Greeks that took off all of the modern radios.

    It was next to impossible to fix these things in Gibraltar mainly because of time restraints.

    I asked the inspector why the missing light bulbs were on his list. He answered that one of my crew might stick their finger in the empty socket! I said, "Sorry Sir, but I wouldn't have anyone that stupid on my crew."

We knew that crossing the Atlantic could be dangerous no matter when or what ship anyone sailed on, but we were going to do it! They had nothing to say about the soundness of the hull or all of the compartmentalization the LST has, with voids, ballast, and fuel tanks. Having these tanks almost empty would lend a lot of buoyancy to the ship. LST ships were very hard to sink. This is a fact, not my opinion. I had the whole second deck on the port side dogged down as we weren't using it. I also planned not to hit any icebergs.

TOMORROW THE BIG POND

**** ABCNews.com 12/10/2000 - The hull is rusting and the gray paint is peeling. Today, the only thing older than the ship is the crew sailing her. Undeterred, their goal is to sail the ship 4600 miles across a wintry Atlantic.

**** Ottawa Times 12/12/2000 - LST Vessel launches for America.

**** Daily Herald – 12/13/2000 – WWII Vets challenge the Atlantic.

**** Chicago Tribune 12/14/2000 – Aging vets on LST reject advice.

**** Mobile Register 12/17/2000 – 'Ancient mariners weave new tale.' Ancient muscles man the levers, turn the wheels, and negotiate the steep ladders. The LST 325 has known better days; so have the men who urge her to bring them home.

CHAPTER 23

HEADING OUT INTO HARMS WAY

We had a lot of people and press on the pier and also on the *USS Arleigh Burke,* hoping to get a picture of our departure. I had the pilot lined up for 1730 hours. The fuel barge pumped fuel but it was slow due to a small fill hose to draw off the fuel. Twenty thousand gallons took a while. The pilot came aboard; we had the engines warmed up, sea detail set. The deck apes were ready to pull in the lines. The fuel person said it would not be long, but it went on and on for seemingly forever. The pilot said he had another ship to take out and would have to leave. Did that sound familiar? The sun was gone, as the days were now much shorter. Some spectators on the pier said, "Stay another night, leave in the morning." I told the XO, not a chance, we were leaving!

Finally, the fuel hose sucked air, the final fuel sample was in Edward's hands, and I signed the paperwork. I yelled to pass the word, "Pull the lines aboard. Let's get underway!" It was almost 1800 hours when the Pilot called for the tug to pull our bow out; when at forty degrees, he unhooked the line to the tug and Boats and his men hauled it aboard. He ordered both engines one-third ahead and the 325 jumped out and away from the pier into dim light as night was coming on fast. We passed the American Destroyer, the British Atomic Submarine moored to port, and the *Brambleleaf* on our starboard side. The *Arleigh Burke* blew their whistle as a farewell - a big mistake because now they would endure the sound of a real horn! The XO gave a hefty yank on our whistle's handle. The cob-webs came out first, then the deafening roar which echoed off the *Rock* and the Destroyer's crew clamped their hands over their ears. I was glad the *Rock* was still standing afterwards! We also got a toot from the *Brambleleaf.* We had gone through the narrow entrance of the shipyard when the pilot said, "Sorry, I have to catch my other ship" and off he went. So far, we haven't been able to keep a pilot on this ship!

We were still deep in the Gibraltar Harbor and I once again had the CONN, heading out in the dark for the Straits of Gibraltar and a right turn towards home; a mere four thousand three hundred miles away! It only took about forty minutes as we went up to standard speed and had both engines running. I might add they sounded very good to my ears, too. I asked how the steering was doing and the helmsman's answer, "Just great."

I turned right to 240 degrees at the half way mark across the straits. The straits were not straight! It was from eight to twenty-three miles wide and thirty-two miles long. It was a very dark night out there, black as pitch. We did not see any ships coming at us; our speed, a good six knots. Carter indicated there was always a current coming into the Mediterranean through the straits. A call came in from the *Arleigh* wishing us a safe trip. We answered back with a thank you and good luck with your deployment. The Captain and XO were on the LST twice and I hadn't stepped foot on their Destroyer even once!

I cannot put into words what a great feeling this was to be underway and headed home. I for one was really starting to get homesick. I believed every one of the crew had that feeling. I quickly thought back to the many months that we had been working and fighting to get this ship going; all the red tape, the delays, breakdowns, the good men that I had to send home. Right now, right at this time, I was thankful for the best crew that EVER sailed an LST!

A stranger came up on channel sixteen!

The person was calling for LST 325 in perfect English and expressing the fact that he was a *Spanish Battleship* off our starboard side, and he had the distinct privilege of escorting us through the 'Spanish' straits tonight. I asked Jack if he could see a Battleship anywhere. "Well Sir," he answered, "I see a small boat sort of bouncing around coming up on our starboard side." I looked over the starboard side; the boat was showing a red running light.

I picked up the radio and said, "Spanish Battleship, are you that Patrol Boat coming up on us?"

He answered back with, "Sir, in America I am a Patrol Boat; but in Spain, I am a Battleship!" He went on to say he was told by Spain's highest authority to pass on this message and I quote, "Spain has authorized the LST's admittance into any Spanish port in the world and apologies for the Spanish authorities who denied your Ambassador's request for the LST to enter Rota for repairs. If you were to visit Gibraltar again, please stay on the Spanish side and not with those English!"

I told him thanks. I would like to come back, but not necessarily on a WWII LST!

Jack said, "Captain, don't be hasty. We may have to turn around if we have engine trouble!" The Spanish Patrol Boat stayed with us until about 0100 hours, and then turned back. He came up on the radio again. Gave us a 'Bravo Zulu,' and wished us a safe journey home. We were all alone in the huge Atlantic. We had a long way to go and I wondered what lay ahead. I was relieved of the watch by Jack and down to my cabin I went, jumped in my bunk, and so quickly I was asleep.

Jack and I wanted to stop in the Canary Islands as we planned going right by. At quarter's yesterday morning, I had asked for a show of hands. "How many want to stop at the Canary Islands?" Jack and I raised our hands, no one else did. I then asked how many did not want to stop. The entire crew raised their hands, some had two up.

I looked at Jack and he looked at me, and then stated, "You are the Captain."

Most of the crew heard that remark and I envisioned a mutiny but quickly said, "I don't care how many of you guys want to go to the Canaries. As Captain of this ship, we are not going! End of story." Again, smiles were back on their faces. Their loved ones at home were on their minds.

The ocean was as smooth as a hardwood floor. The Navy men out of Rota, Spain told us it would be flat for about one thousand nautical miles. I did not turn south towards the Canaries as the Navy wanted us to. It was so nice that I told Jack it would be a shame to turn south and not keep going west and lose this great weather, flat sea, and time. We angled slowly down to the twenty-fifth parallel, and then turned west.

The Navy weather team from Norfolk had called before we were out of the harbor and told us not to leave for another five days. They said the weather was bad right out past the straits for a long way! This was totally different from what we had been told previously. Actually, I was not sure what someone had up their sleeve. This did not add up. Was it to delay us or stop us? The slow down tactics just kept popping up. Had anyone else noticed?

We sailed right by the Madeira Islands - a little too close I thought and I swung out a little bit as we approached them. Boats' was on the CONN saying, "Let's stop here. The Madeira Islands make very fine wines!"

"Next time, Boats, we will stop twice," I remarked. Boats continually asked me if I saw the Miller Lite sign on the shore when we were close enough to observe lights. I realized that once past the Madeira Islands, it would be a long stretch before he or I saw any Miller Lite signs or any lights at all.

Things were going too good, I thought. I had my fingers crossed. I made the rounds down to the main engine room, the engineers had the two horses in absolute harmonization, and the generator ran so smooth.

The men were all happy, telling their old stories over and over. Boats and I had taken on the champion euchre player from Marseilles, IL. That would be Don Lockas with one 'S.' The old glass blower himself. Boats and I just fit together and we always managed to win; it was uncanny. Don had several different partners. Don accused us of all kinds of things such as having word phrases, facial expressions, hand signals, the cards marked in order to beat him, but we were just lucky and maybe even a little good at this game.

I started playing a modified version of Euchre called 'Rabbit' in grade school every morning and after school when I rode the school bus. I played a little at my college fraternity and again while going through Navy OCS. There I found it was strictly a Midwest game. We had the east coast guys in complete awe as they watched.

There is a saying for the people 'telling stories' in the wardroom - *the Cows may come and go, but the Bull just stays forever!*

The days were warm and sunny and the nights pleasant and cool. There was nothing like the cool breeze sliding in over the ocean at night. The ship hardly rolled and only a few waves were thumping against the bow. Strobel told me he had not made a rudder change for over an hour one night.

Then one morning I felt it, even high on the CONN; the starboard engine had stopped. The ship was not shaking as much and an eerie quiet took over the ship. Chief Bartlett came up on the CONN. Generally, when he appeared on the CONN, the only problem he had was he misplaced his big coffee cup, or maybe wanted to get some fresh air and sunshine! He said, "Captain, you best sit down in your chair." I knew instantly we had a problem. Something very bad had happened or would very soon. All had run smoothly for a full week. It was Wednesday morning December 19.

Bartlett said, "We have shut the Starboard engine down! We have a hole in the top of piston #11. The #11 cylinder was missing (not firing,) so we shut down the engine. You will have to make it home on the Port or turn back."

It would be a long way to go on one engine, but going back almost a thousand miles was simply out of the question. I said to Jim, "Do we have to shut the whole engine down? I read the book a long time ago, and I am certain it indicated we could shut the fuel off to an individual cylinder on the 12-567 engines and run the engine on the other eleven cylinders."

Jim responded with, "That is true, but you didn't read far enough down on the page where it says do not run the engine any longer than you have to."

"Mr. Bartlett, I would not think of running that engine one minute longer than necessary." A smile came on Jim's face until I continued, "We have about three thousand miles left to go, and we will shut it off in Mobile!"

Jim without hesitation expressed, "Sir, with all due respect, it will never make it!"

I replied, "Jim, we are going to find out just how far this great GM engine will run with one cylinder shut off. It will be a great experiment."

"OK if you say so. I will start it up again." He grumbled something as he left the CONN. One can put in his own words what Jim may have said! I suggest include a word to describe one's lack of intelligence and another referring to one born without a known father!

The next day, I received a call from the U.S. naval weather people in Norfolk or so they said. Evidently they had not given up on stopping us. The man stated right out, "There is a mammoth storm dead ahead of the LST. Captain, we recommend turning the ship around and heading back to the Canary Islands!"

I politely told him, "I am sorry but this ship and this crew will not turn back."

Disturbed he declared, "At least you should turn IMMEDIATELY south and try to go around this storm."

I tried to enlighten him some on our type of ship and replied, "Sir, an LST does not do anything immediately! But I will turn the helm and go south for a while."

He replied, "That Sir is very prudent of you. Good luck."

I was in communications with a man by the name of Bill Kaupas from Plano, Texas. His business involved purchase of poorly operated hospitals mostly in the South, then doing whatever is necessary to bring them back to profitability with good management. One of these hospitals had a computer with a special weather program. It accessed weather reports from Merchant Marine ships steaming in the oceans, first hand information. He was already feeding us weather reports from ships in the Atlantic for our information. I called Bill and asked him if he heard of this gigantic storm out in the Atlantic fourteen hundred miles straight out of Gibraltar? I explained, "The US Navy has ordered me to turn immediately south to avoid it." He hadn't seen any data, but would do some checking. In a little while, Bill called back and told me he had a report from a Merchant ship about 200 miles ahead of us. He reported there was no storm; the weather was great, nice, and sunny even. Bill wanted to know what our navy was smoking! I talked with Jack and we agreed to turn back west and back to course 270. I had gone south for over twelve hours or about 100 miles. We turned back west, sailed for several days, and never witnessed the storm. I added this to my unexplained happenings.

Bartlett showed up on the CONN again and I had to sit down. He informed me, "We have a small hole in the ship's bottom in the Auxiliary engine room right ahead of the electric switchboard."

I asked if he tried to plug it. "Yes" he said, "This caused a quarter size hole to enlarge to a fifty-cent hole! However, we put a rubber gasket down, a two by four on top, placed a four by four on end over the top, and braced it to the overhead adding a few shims to make it tight. We have the leak down to a slow dribble."

"Good work, Jim," I said. "Please don't spread the word around. Someone will call on the satellite phone, tell his wife, and she will tell another and another and pretty soon we will have a three foot hole and we are going down!" Bartlett agreed, but told me some already had the word.

That very evening, when I went by the 'spy shack' I heard Ed Strobel telling his wife Eileen, "Honey, we have a hole in the bottom of the ship!" So much for our secrecy, the whole world will know now. We also lost the #2 generator and were running on #3.

I was asked to call in to the Navy Headquarters every morning to give them my position and status. First, I checked in with our Navy Department in London, and about half way across was switched to Norfolk, same navy - different number, and different officer. Both men were Commanders and very nice to talk with. When I reported the #2 generator down he wanted to know if I was going to repair it. I said, "No, not at this time."

He calmly said, "Why not?"

I simply answered, "I am short on men, but long on generators! If another generator breaks down, we will repair the one we determine to be the easy fix."

He said, "Sounds like a plan to me," and that was that.

Everyone who has sailed on the oceans would inform a person who has not had this experience that the stars appear much closer at night because of the darkness with no light from other sources to dilute the heaven's brightness. All of the crew, not having sailed for many years, took more time enjoying the vastness of the sky and the multitude of stars at night.

In the daytime we had dolphins running alongside the ship - always one or two riding the waves at the ship's bow. We witnessed several rainbows and at sea, one can observe both ends, the complete semi-circle, bright and full and beautiful.

Now compare what I just said to this report from my wife at home. Lois described in detail the tons of snow we had in the front yard by the garage. She told how the temperature fell below zero the last two nights; she was snowbound more days than the days she could get out. The wind blew and howled every day piling the snow higher. The dog would not even go out! Then she asked how it was in the Atlantic?

I said it was terrible. The temperature had fallen to about seventy-two the last few nights and I put a light blanket over me. The sun was shining big and full during most days, and the moon at night, well it almost filled the whole eastern and southern sky. Then she said, "Stop! I don't want to hear about it!" She had a hard time getting the crops in. Now she was working with the government farm program called the 'Pick' program. That program caused some farmers to start drinking. She wanted to know if she should sell some of the corn or beans. I said go ahead; it was anyone's guess if the price would go up or down.

She had a hard time getting me to think about the farm. I was on the ship, in another world with ship problems, and I couldn't get my mind off them. Lois was also selling seed corn and seed beans to my customers for next year. She just told all of them that I was somewhere in the Atlantic on a leaky old boat and if they wanted seed for next year, tell her what numbers and how much. She sold more corn than I had sold the previous year!

NEXT, THE HALFWAY MARK SLIDES BY

**** British Navy Oiler RFA Brambleleaf -Paul Stephenson, crewman –Obviously, it's going to be a hell of an achievement.

CHAPTER 24

HALFWAY ACROSS

On a beautiful day, December 23rd, about 2,500 miles out of Gibraltar, I was on the CONN with Jack and this big Albatross (or maybe a big variety of Sea Gull) suddenly appeared and started circling the ship about mid-afternoon. This bird circled us for twenty minutes, just going up the port side and back down the starboard side as we steamed along. I asked several crewmembers what kind of bird it was and nobody really knew, and that included the old salts like Boats and Calvin. The large, somewhat brown bird finally came in for a two point landing way up forward, just aft of the elevator hatch, smack on the main deck. He walked around for a while, but did not leave the bow area. Nobody was working on the main deck or even walking around. Finally, he lay down close to the starboard doghouse and slept there all night.

The bird was still there on my morning watch. About 0900 he stood up on his feet from his restful night's sleep and, well, did his business right on the Boats' deck. I knew who had to clean that up! He walked slowly over to the port side about three feet out from the lifelines and tried to take off but hit the top cable and fell back on the deck. He did this maybe five times before he backed up far enough to clear the top cable. He flew around the ship again about three or four times and then headed for Gibraltar or parts east! I wondered if he knew he had lost 100 miles last night and just how far he could fly. Birds must think this ship was an island because of our slow speed. We also carried a very small bird that came aboard when we passed the Madeira Islands.

Cookie spotted her in the aft twin 40mm gun tub while peeling potatoes out in the sun and fresh air. She just sat there, sometimes flying up to one of the forward gun tubs then back. I believe Cookie fed her some breadcrumbs from time to time.

When we left Greece, I had to set up a watch bill. At the top of the list was the OOD (officer of the deck) watch. Normally in the Navy, the Captain and the Executive Officer would not stand watch underway. Since Jack and I were the only watch officers qualified, and the only officers on board, we would have to stand 'Port and Starboard watches' which would be four hours on and four hours off, or maybe six and six. Since I already knew the voyage was going to be at least 26 days of straight steaming, this was way above the call of duty for my XO to do or me for that matter. We both had other duties to take care of from time to time. Boats volunteered to stand an underway OOD watch. He had to be qualified as a boat coxswain on the LCVPs to make second-class petty officer. He said he would like to be the third OOD. All he would have to do if we had a lot of traffic was to have the messenger get hold of the XO or me. I put him on as our third OOD.

Next was to assign crewmen to each watch. I was not familiar with the abilities of most of the crew. My only insight to individual crew member's skills was simply based on my observations over the last two and a half months on how they worked, and the initiative they exhibited. These twenty-seven sailors on board were the 'cream of the crop.' With this knowledge I picked who I believed at the time were the best three men and assigned them to Boats and the third watch section. The second best three, I assigned to the XO who had the second watch, and the last three to me and the first watch. We had two men on the helm or wheel that took turns steering and one on the CONN as a lookout. All three were to rotate, so no one was stuck for four hours doing the same job or maybe have the easy job of messenger, coffee fetcher, etc. He would also relieve for 'Head' stops. I thought this was as good as any way to assign crew. Everyone except Cookie and his helper had to stand watch.

For my watch, I picked Don Lockas, 'Doc' Jones, and Hike Nedeff. Hike was a History teacher and wrestling coach from Dayton, Ohio and we often asked each other history trivia questions. I liked history, and because of that, I remembered quite a few dates of historic importance. Hike was a great guy, but could not seem to comprehend the procedure for getting the ship back on course; in essence, he could not steer! Lockas had done everything to get Hike to turn the helm in the opposite direction to bring the ship back to course. Lockas would tell him which way to turn the rudder. Lockas told me one time that he asked Hike what he would say to a student that could not get something through his head. Hike told him that he would tell the student to get serious. Lockas then told Hike to get serious! That did not change the mental block Hike had formed in his mind. To me it was a natural thing like turning a corner in a car. Hike was a hard worker, but had real trouble in this one area.

I had assigned our photographer, Glenn Gregg, to the engineering department. He stood watch in the main engine room and caught on quickly with his ability to record gauge readings, adding oil to the engines, and learning the important things to watch such as water temperature, oil pressure, RPMs, and the engine order telegraph for speed changes. When we were close to halfway to Mobile, Gregg asked me if he could come topside and learn to steer the ship. This also would allow him to take more pictures of day-to-day activities as they unfolded. He was an extra man in engineering, mostly on standby in case someone got sick or hurt. I gave my OK to come up, stand a wheelhouse watch, and learn to steer.

Gregg turned out to be a real asset. He joined in on his own to help the guys whenever he saw the need. Our two life rafts worked loose on the main deck during one of our storms. I called for Boats to catch them as they rolled from side to side, thinking they could slip through the lifelines and fall overboard. Glenn stopped the rafts from going back and forth, then held on to them while Carter and Strobel with Voges' directions tied them back in place in the center of the deck forward of the cargo hatch. He helped in similar situations the entire trip. Glenn also worked hard taking pictures and videos for his employer, Linda Alvers of National Audio Video. Linda was producing a documentary for the History Channel, *Return of LST 325;* Glenn did not take any bad pictures of the Captain (that I know of.)

My electricians, Maranto, Edwards, Chapman, and Lyon had things under control in the auxiliary engine room. They had other duties crop up from time to time. Gary Lyon had made several armature brushes for different motors from scratch out of a drawer full of Greek brushes, none of which fit anything. He had to find some close in size to the worn out brushes, then shape and cut them to fit. In most cases, the armatures needed turning. The armatures were rough so the new brushes in the motors didn't last, and he had to carve out more sets.

Back in Mobile, Captain Pierce worked at lining things up for our arrival. He told me I should talk to a CMC Bill Norris, who was arranging for a pier for us to moor the LST after our arrival. Pierce said we could stay at the State Docks near downtown Mobile for only a few days. He said the Chief was arranging for a Dock in Chickasaw, a small town a few miles north and west of Mobile with a Mr. Slade Hooks, the owner. I also knew that my Marine Attorney, Mr. Connaughton, was working with the CG and with Mr. Hooks. Things were coming together for our arrival. I am sure our arrival party was also!

We lost the gyro again, so we were on magnetic compass, set by my GPS as to the true course. Lockas had decided not to correct Hike this one night, figuring he would have to move the rudder at some point. It was a dark, clear night, so all of the stars were out. I was standing watch and enjoying the night air and the sounds of the sea as this heroic lady moved through the water. I had confidence in my helmsmen, Lockas and Nedeff, and my lookout, Doc, would not miss a contact no matter how far off it was. My job was much easier knowing these men were doing their respective jobs, watching out for the ship and the crew aboard her.

We had a bright star about fifteen degrees off the port bow or about two hundred fifty-five degrees true. That star was there every night unless cloud cover kept me from seeing it. This night the star appeared as bright as ever as I walked around the CONN and then went out-board to see around the spy shack, checking aft for any ships overtaking us. Nothing was out there. I checked inside the spy shack to see if the light on the satellite phone showed a green light or a red light. Green meant it was still connected. Red meant it had lost the satellite signal and needed to be re-programmed, which I did several times in my four-hour watch period.

Doc was not happy unless from time to time he could report a contact to me, and the few he saw were mostly a long way off. We could see their white mast lights at night as they came and went or as one of us dropped down in a swell.

When I got back in the CONN and recorded another GPS fix, I looked up and the bright star had moved over to the starboard side about fifteen degrees off the bow. I yelled down the voice tube to Lockas, "Lockas, what are you doing down there?"

His answer was, "Sir, we are off course, but we are coming back."

"Lockas, why are you off so far?" I yelled again into the voice tube, "Did you guys fall asleep?"

Lockas explained the situation to me. He had told Hike in simple words that he was not going to advise him which direction to turn the rudder tonight. Hike was going to have to do it all by his lonesome. Lockas continued, "At five degrees off course to the left, I told Hike better turn the rudder. At ten degrees, I told him to get serious and turn the rudder. At twenty degrees I yelled at him. Hike, turn the rudder; you are way off course. At twenty-five degrees going on thirty, I told Hike in complete disgust to turn the helm to the right. That was when you shouted down, Captain." After a few minutes went by and the LST came back on course, Lockas shouted up the voice tube to me, "Captain, I have a question, just how did you know we were off course? You don't have a magnetic compass."

I jokingly said to Don, "If I told you how I knew, I would have to kill you." Then I explained, "Lockas, when the stars go around this ship for the second time, I know the ship is off course!" I continued to add insult by saying, "If we had good helmsmen, this ship would be almost home! This zigzag course has destroyed our forecasted arrival time!"

Lockas was one person I underestimated when picking a duty section. I thought Don the best or at least one of the best helmsmen on the ship. He had to keep Hike on course by telling him which way to turn the helm. In essence, he was steering the ship for the full four hour watch.

Doc from the beginning refused to steer the ship. He was not keen on having to stand watch at all, as he indicated he had to be free to give aid if someone got hurt or sick. I told him the best place to find him in an emergency was on the CONN. He would be free to go to any emergency on his watch or off. He had eight hours between watches to have sick call. After talking with Lockas and Nedeff, they agreed to steer the ship, and Doc could be lookout for the entire watch. Everyone was relieved when necessary to go to the head or to eat meals.

For breakfast and lunch, the oncoming watch could eat first, and then relieve the watch. All watch standers could cut in to the head of the line for chow so they could eat and relieve the watch in good time. Cookie kept track of the number of crew that had eaten by the number of plates left unused, out of 29. Nobody ever missed a meal and most did not miss ice cream at 2030 hours as the messenger or another crewmember would bring it up to the watch. I took good care of my men! Is it time to feed my apes? Please read on!

The first morning after leaving Gibraltar, I had found out the British "K" rations had a large bag of individually wrapped hard candy in each box. I had found the rations stacked neatly forward of the ship fitters shop (pipe shop,) off the tank deck. I retrieved a few bags of candy from several boxes plus the big dark chocolate bars. The entire wheelhouse watch was deck crew. I started dropping two or three of these hard candies down the voice tube, after warning them the hard candy pieces were coming down. I was feeding my 'deck apes' as I explained to Carter and Boats. The word spread, of course, to the other watches and one or two times a watch, the apes would ask if the OOD had any candy. These round hard balls of candy would go down the voice tube like bullets. The Helmsman had to place his hand on the end of the voice tube pointing in their direction. If he didn't, I could hear the candy hit the back bulkhead after whizzing by their head and ricocheting to the deck with several loud bangs. The CONN is located two decks or eighteen feet higher than the wheelhouse; the candy, induced by gravity, gained an untold amount of momentum before reaching the journey's end!

Don Lockas and his twin brother left high school a few days before graduation on the encouragement of a friend to join the Navy. The three of them drove to Chicago to join up. When an individual joins the Navy, one must first pass an extensive medical physical. Don and his brother passed, but the friend did not and was designated as 4F (not physically fit for service.) Donald was in the US Navy at a ripe age of seventeen.

At an inspection in boot camp, when the inspecting officer came and stood by Donald, he observed his name 'D. Lockas' on his locker behind him and could not help but note another 'D. Lockas' written on the locker next in line. The officer asked Don how he rated two lockers. Don answered, "Sir, that locker belongs to my brother."

Don's brother, Darwin, was 6' 3" and 220 pounds. Donald was 5' 10" and 170 lbs. maybe. The officer looked at Darwin, then at Don, and exclaimed; "Now I suppose you are going to tell me you two are twins?"

Don said, "Yes Sir, we are!"

The Officer thought Don was not telling the truth, and ordered, "Sailor, never ever try to pull that on me again!" He then moved on down the line looking back at Don and Darwin several more times as he continued his inspection.

Don and his brother went to different ships. Taken to his LST in the South Pacific by a troop ship around 0300 hour, Don climbed up to board his assigned LST via a rope cargo net, and announced his name.

The officer replied, "We have been expecting your arrival. Go find a bunk and store your gear and find a place to hang on. We are scheduled to hit the beach at 0400." Don's ship was about to make a landing at the invasion of Leyte Gulf! Imagine doing that at the age of seventeen and nine thousand miles from home!

Considered the last big naval battle with us against a still strong Japanese Navy, the battle at Leyte was the final attempt made by the Japanese to turn the tide in the Pacific. The US Navy did so much damage to the Japanese ships in the straits of Leyte, the Japanese never mounted a major fight against our ships again.

The Japanese finally determined the LSTs were the means the Sherman tanks magically appeared on the beaches. Until this time the Japanese just thought LSTs were supply ships, not extremely big, and therefore not important compared to the other larger ships. On the priority scale of importance, they mostly left them alone. However, from that time on the Japanese pinpointed the LSTs, making them priority one, and sent their kamikazes and bomber planes after them. The LSTs had reasonably good anti-aircraft guns, and when in a group of thirty or more, could put up a formidable screen of fire. One LST during the Okinawa invasion received credit for shooting down six kamikaze planes.

This Sunday morning, another nice day, I heard this request from Lockas shouting up the voice tube. He said he needed an echo!

I said, "You need what?"

Don answered me, "Sir, it's Sunday and I want to sing *'This is the Day that the Lord Hath Made'* but I need an echo."

I stated a very well known fact. "Don, I cannot carry a tune in a basket as big as our tank deck or hit the right note even if my life depended on it. In a group of tone-deaf monotones, I would be last."

He continued to beg, "Sir, you just repeat after me, and as your voice vibrates down the voice tube, it will make your echo sound OK." I knew better than that, but he insisted and pleaded, so I went along with him. He sings in his church choir and I could tell when he sang the first line, Donald knew how to sing!

So up the voice tube came this great sounding voice – **This is the Day** – then me back-This is the Day - **That the Lord Hath Made** – that the Lord hath made. **This is the Day** – this is the day - **That the Lord Hath made** – that the Lord hath made - **This is the Day that the Lord hath made,** this is the day that the Lord hath made - **let us rejoice and be glad in it,** let us rejoice and be glad in it - **this is the day** -this is the day - **that the lord hath made -** that the Lord hath made.

Don thanked me and said, "Could we do just a little more?" We did it several times. We then did this every Sunday on watch for the rest of the trip. I would do just about anything to keep my crew happy! Instead of just saying the words, I even moderately tried to sing just for Don. One Sunday he forgot, but I gleefully reminded him, just to embarrass him for forgetting it was Sunday!

We had discussions about discipline before going to Greece, what we could do to someone that refused to take orders, or if one of the crew got angry enough and it turned into a fight. We were not in the Navy and everyone was a volunteer. I maintained that this should not be a problem, since everyone wanted and volunteered to bring back an LST. Secondly, none of us were kids.

One day our Quartermaster, Mr. Nickerson, complained about not having fresh coffee, hot chocolate, and snacks (called mid-rats) for the watch going on duty at midnight to 0400. He thought that the cook should provide these extras. Cookie overheard him grumbling, and took it personally. He now cooked two meals a day plus a dessert and snack for later, rising at 0430 to make breakfast. He worked long hours. Cookie went out on the weather deck right to the porthole of Nickerson's stateroom, which was the most forward one on the port side, and yelled, for Mr. Nickerson to come out and face him. He said he would pound some sense into his thick head. He told him if he wanted 'mid-rats' to get up and make them. Nickerson did not come out of his stateroom, so the matter for the most part went away except Nickerson was put on a forced diet by Cookie for the rest of the voyage!

One of the crew was reported to me for drinking before his watch. I quickly confronted him and he told me he had not been drinking. Since I didn't see him, and with only one man's observation, I took his word. I warned the individual that if I saw him drinking before or on watch, or he was reported again, I would have to take some action and maybe put him off on one of the islands. He must have believed I would do that, and there must have been some islands out there! Anyway, I never had any more reports of him drinking. Maybe his good behavior was a result of my harsh punishment given out at my two Captain's masts!

I had set a firm rule; one could have two beers after his watch, but none six hours before the next watch. I never drank at all once underway. I told the guys that if we had any trouble, no one could say that I had been drinking, even one beer. The *Oiler Valdez* comes to mind! Most all the time, the crew was so tired they just headed for bed after standing their watch. Very little celebrating took place. All of us worked long hours.

Near the halfway point of our voyage across the Atlantic, we cruised between two fishing buoys, both all white in color and easy to see in the bright sun light. They were maybe a little more than one hundred feet off both sides of the ship, in perfect alignment. I did not change course, we just proceeded right between them sort of like a football going between the goal posts. Doc Jones suddenly appeared inside the Conn. He stood watch on the outside walkway unless rain, cold or some other adverse condition brought him inside. He had seen the buoys go by and wondered why they were out here in the middle of the Atlantic.

Having been around Boats Voges too long, I explained, "Doc, have you ever played golf?"

He responded, "No I haven't."

I said, "Well Doc, on a golf course you have markers placed at different points on a fairway to tell a golfer about how many yards you have left to reach the green. As a rule, they mark the halfway point.

Those buoys you just saw mark the halfway point across the Atlantic Ocean!"

Doc replied "Oh, OK!" He turned right around to exit, reached the hatch going out, turned back, and replied, "I don't think so!" He continued out to his post and avoided me for the rest of the watch.

One of the men assigned to Boats was Ed Strobel. He gained a nickname as 'Trough' Strobel. In rough water, Ed thought he knew better than the OOD, and would change course a few degrees, left or right, to have a smoother ride for the ship. More than once, he steered the ship into the trough between the waves, which caused a much bigger roll, thus his nickname. On one occasion, Cookie had a big kettle of oatmeal on the stove for the crew's breakfast. When the ship rolled in a bigger wave, the kettle went sliding off the end of the stove, hitting the small stop at the edge, flipped over and landed upside down squarely on the deck. I learned that I had acquired several new names, shouted out by Cookie, names one cannot repeat. He blamed me for not getting on a smoother course! Cookie went over to the kettle and reached down while explaining my origin, and picked up the kettle. To everyone's (and his) surprise, the oatmeal had not come out of the kettle! The floor was clean; the oatmeal was stuck firmly to the bottom of the pot. He placed it back on the stove and with a sheepish grin, asked one of the men to announce breakfast on the PA for the crew.

Trough also had the distinction of losing the steering system more than anyone else while at the helm. Since he came on watch relieving Carter's section, I was sound asleep before the signal, one long blast on the whistle. I relieved Boats on the CONN, so he could get to aft steering. Chapman ran down and with a hammer handle, reset the contacts in the steering controller. This happened more in the Mediterranean than in the Atlantic. When we had docked in Gibraltar shortly after arriving, another ship's whistle sounded, and Don Chapman jumped out of bed and in a hurry started placing a leg in his pants. Jim Edwards had the stateroom right opposite and aft of Don's and could see him. Jim asked, "Don, what's the hurry?"

Don said, "I have to run down and fix the steering."

Edwards had the fun of telling him, "Don, we are tied up to the dock!"

When I investigated why 'Trough' was losing steering so much, I stood back in the radio room and watched Mr. Strobel while he was on the helm. I had quizzed him on what he did to lose the steering all the time. He had answered, "Nothing." What I saw was Ed patting the steering control lever in an effort to get the exact number of degrees of rudder or so I believed. Most of the men would hold the lever over, let go and if it went to seven degrees instead of five, so what. Not Ed; he was going to get exactly five degrees or know why. When he tapped the lever, it might go to six or four degrees. Then he would tap it again. This could take Ed three or maybe six times before the rudder stopped at five degrees! This action caused the rudder contacts in aft steering to go in and out, in and out, and eventually caused a steering failure similar to the old hydraulic system Don had circumvented. I told Ed to stop beating up on the steering system please. This for the most part, corrected the problem and I got some sleep and so did Chapman.

At this point in the journey, I reported to our Navy headquarters in Norfolk, Virginia. My morning report was about the same as the XO's web page report, except I did not put in all the verbiage. My report was mainly the ship's position. Carter occasionally, out of the clear blue, made up stories in his daily report.

We entered into our second Atlantic storm. I had purposely not ballasted all of our tanks to full capacity. I wanted speed and fuel economy, so I kept the ship about half ballasted, with a draft of about 4 feet at the bow and 12 feet at the stern. In Gibraltar, we had filled all the fresh water tanks, which held close to 100,000 gallons. All of these potable water tanks were located toward the stern. As we used fresh water, the stern came up. Because of this shallower draft, the ship's roll was more excessive in a storm with higher waves pounding the sides of the ship. We had a ship's clinometer, built by Strobel, outside of the CONN entrance hatch, right on the bulkhead of the spy shack. This showed twenty-three degrees of roll at times in this storm. As the bow dropped and encountered an oncoming wave, water went flying over the bow, splashing up high and then dropping on the deck, which gave several of the crew reason to say a prayer. That water ran aft on the main deck until the bow went down, and then raced off the deck on the next roll. This storm lasted through the night before it let up.

Somewhere in the Atlantic, the question came up (probably in a phone interview) if I was ever afraid in this kind of situation? I answered NO, adding it was a great photographic opportunity to take a picture of the huge waves breaking over the bow! A short time later, after the wave story made the rounds, someone criticized me for leaving my post in a big storm and going forward to take pictures. My comment was made to re-enforce my statement that I was not afraid, nor was the crew! I never actually took any pictures or left the CONN, even though it really was a great photo op for the scrapbooks. Our photographer, Glenn Gregg, took full advantage of these waves!

My second censuring came in a newspaper article placed in the Mobile Register Star by a man claiming to be a retired Navy Captain. He said that as Captain, I should never have taken these men into harm's way by attempting to bring this LST back across the Atlantic in the wintertime, especially against the Coast Guard's opposition and warning of the ship's unsafe condition.

I wanted to answer him and defend my actions. However, as has been my position and confirmed by most, best not to answer critics directly. If I'd had the opportunity, I would have said I did not take these men into harm's way – THEY TOOK ME! The crew was going to bring this ship home with or without me. The critic had not inspected the ship or seen the hull report and I would guess had no idea of the great flotation of an LST with all of its empty tanks. The crew had all reached an age capable of making their own decisions to go or not go. They had encouraged me to be the Captain, and we were bringing this ship back together. They were not bringing it back for me or because of me!

During one slow period, the XO had not sent out his normal e-mail of our position or any other tidbit that our LST fans expected to see daily. George Werneth, a writer for the Mobile Register Star, had been assigned to write an article on our journey every single day, but had run out of things to talk about. In desperation, he called Lois, and with his distinctive slow southern drawl announced to my wife, "This – is – George - Werneth."

Lois generally cut him off after "this is" and said, "Hi George." This time George asked if she had any news on our progress. She didn't, but said she would call me and call him back. On hearing his plight, I told her to tell George we were moving along at a steady pace, going six and one-half knots up the waves and seven knots down! He wrote in his article the next day those exact words. He went on and compared the LST to the battleship *USS ALABAMA* if one can imagine that! George did a great job of keeping everyone informed of our progress during the entire trip. Comparing an LST to a battleship was like comparing a one-room schoolhouse to the empire State Building!

Another writer for the *Mobile Register* was Gene Owens. He also wrote several articles on the ship. One article I particularly liked was entitled, '*When vintage ship has problems, the vets aboard can pop the hood.*' In the article, Mr. Owens compared his old 1951 Buick (which he called 'Big Bertha') to the LST with one big difference. He could not fix his Buick when something broke, but the crew of LST 325 could fix their LST! Newspapers had a heyday with this ship. A writer for the *Navy Times*, Christopher Munsey, who visited the LST in Gibraltar, talked to me many times on our phone. He wrote some great articles. One was "*The Old Men & the Sea.*"

CHRISTMAS, NEW YEARS, AND THE BAHAMAS

As we approached Christmas on the high seas, Boats and I discussed the many things that we missed or would miss by not being home. So far, I had missed my mother's 90th Birthday after which mother fell, broke her kneecap, and Lois had to put her in a nursing home, and my niece's wedding (my sister's youngest.) I missed combining 1200 acres of corn and beans and Lois reminded me I missed many days of bad weather! Daughter Kim had her second baby, a girl named Alexis. Thanksgiving had already gone by, as had Lois' birthday. Christmas and New Years were on the horizon. I had also missed voting for a President for one of the few times in my life. However, I could not top Boats - he missed a football game, but not just any game! His two sons had bought tickets for the Green Bay Packers vs. Minnesota Vikings game in Green Bay to take place right after Christmas! Everyone thought we would be home!

The XO put his version of "The Night before Christmas" and more in his e-mail:

"Twas the night before Christmas and all through the ship
Not a faucet was leaking, not even a drip
The sailors were all snug in sacks
Resting from a day's work of breaking their backs.
The watch standers steering the ship through the night
Alert for any warning, whistle or light.
When down in the tank deck there arose such a clatter
The bos'n ran down to see what was the matter.
There stood Santa in red coveralls, covered with grease,
I thought the crew's laughing never would cease
The crew fell silent as Santa came near,
Telling us that our Christmas was now here.
He told us, "You boys have had a mighty rough time,
But you all did your jobs, and everything turned out fine.
My gift to you all this holiday season,
Is the joy of knowing that you have done a job
Well for a very good reason. "

"The ship's company wishes to extend our warmest season greetings to all our family members, loved ones, friends, and supporters."

This has been a difficult period for all of us and the continued support of those at home has been a source of strength and support for us. The realization that we would not be together with our families for the Holidays was truly painful. We hope that the joys of our forthcoming homecoming will in some way make up for the disruption of the Christmas season. J. R. Carter CDR USNR (Ret.), XO M/V Memorial Dec 24, 2000.

Christmas was like any other day on the ocean with a couple of exceptions. Boats Voges came through the crew's quarters with his reindeer playing Jingle Bells in Greek. Many of the crew called home. Our weather was favorable so the satellite phone worked better than usual. Cookie prepared ham, sweet potatoes, string beans, hush puppies, and pumpkin pie for dessert. It was delicious; not quite like home, but I didn't tell Cookie! Linda Alvers had produced a short video of each of the crew with their Christmas greetings to their wife/family. These videos were completed while still in Gibraltar. She mailed them to each of our homes just before Christmas. Lois remarked how great that was to receive and she shared it with the family on Christmas day. It really was a great gift!

We had another storm two days after Christmas, December 27th. The crew considered it the wickedest storm yet, worse than one we went through in the Mediterranean. I don't agree, but we did rock and roll.

This storm heaved its vengeance on us for nearly two days. Some of the guys even got a little sick so I heard. We changed course to encounter the waves on an angle instead of dead on. If the wave hit dead on, the old girl would shake and we could see a ripple make its way down the main deck. We were glad when it finally let up and Cookie could actually cook hot food and we could enjoy a hot cup of coffee again without holding it from sliding the entire time we were drinking it. During a storm, one had to put his pants on with his back to the inner or outer bulkhead; no one could stand erect facing the bow or stern or they fell over. Put one leg in, wait for the next roll, and then put the second leg in. It was pretty tough on aging bodies. Shaving was definitely a problem during a storm of any kind.

Rocky Hill found how deep the bilges were when a big wave caused him to lose balance, miss the deck plates in the engine room, and fell in. Skinned his leg up and hurt his pride. Rocky always maintained he had the best looking legs on the ship. One day he challenged the bos'n mate on whose legs were the best. As I watched from the CONN, two men were on the deck, pants down, and a couple of the crew served as judges! I hope the Navy was not watching at that time or anyone else for that matter.

We made hash marks on our navigating chart, one for each day on the big Atlantic. We had changed the clocks only a few times, several hours each time. We had decided rather than confuse our watch list by moving the clock an hour as we entered each new time zone, we just kept the old time until it was light at 0400 in the morning and dark earlier at night.

A little ahead of schedule at this point, we contemplated what we should do to delay our arrival into Mobile. We were a good thirty-four hours ahead of schedule, but then we still had a good one third of the trip left. We navigated by the great circle method saving a few miles. The

XO had a program he had devised on his computer. All one had to do was enter our present position and destination, and it told us the course we needed to take for the shortest route on the great circle. The good Lord had to be assisting with our navigation, as LST 325 continued grinding out the miles. Go west young man, go west; but in this case we were heading for the East Coast!

We had some Saturday quarterbacks giving our arrival predictions in Mobile based on our position reports. They were all over the spectrum. None agreed with the other or with us!

Engineer, Chief James Bartlett, who was born in the State of Maine, but moved to Texas after his stint in the Navy, tromped up the ladder to the CONN. The "T" had run fine for the last ten days; it must be that time again! Without even saying good morning, Jim blurted out, "Captain, you had better sit in your chair." I knew what that meant. He followed with, "Captain, you did not order enough Lube Oil!"

"Jim," I shouted back, "You know I ordered more than you asked me to!"

He said, "I know, but you did not order enough! We are almost out."

I contended, "We should have plenty of lube oil to make it to Mobile. I figured those old engines would use about five to maybe ten quarts a day." Jim then informed me we were using thirty gallons a day! The engines were leaking most of it out of the rear mains for some reason. He then told me I had to get us into the Bahamas, Nassau.

I reminded Jim that we were a *Pirate Ship*, and we couldn't just go into Nassau. Smiling, I believe because he enjoyed my frustrations over the problems he dumped in my lap, he told me that as Captain, that was my problem and not his. He added we would probably run out of oil for the mains before Nassau! More great news; thanks a lot Jim!

We did run out of new lube oil before reaching Nassau. However, the engineers had changed oil in Souda and had stored that dirty old oil in a tank on the ship. When we ran out of the new, they just started using the old oil to add to the engines. I called my Pro Bono Marine lawyer, Sean Connaughton, and asked him if he could get us permission to go into Nassau. He said he thought he could, and a day later called me back and said we had permission. Our worldwide publicity had paved the way. I knew Mr. George Werneth was doing his part.

CARTERS 28 Dec. Web Page Report

Position: N28-33, W056-06.

Now we are scheduled to make a quickie stop in Nassau on 3 January to pick up supplies, etc. Then it's onward to Mobile for the return of LST 325 to the US on Jan 10, after over 35 years of absence. We know that the citizens of Mobile are waiting to welcome us warmly with open arms. The big question is what kind of arms will the all too numerous bureaus and agencies of the Federal Government use to welcome us. We are determined to make sure that our good Captain leaves the ship with honor even if he is in hand cuffs and leg irons. If that is the case, the entire crew will form as 27 side boys and a Bos'n. As the Captain leaves the ship the Bos'n will pipe and the 27 side boys will salute and sing that old favorite "for he is a jolly good Felon." It should be great for the National news.

My very good friend, shipmate, and my XO, went off the deep end. I told him if he kept that up, they might actually arrest me! The Coast Guard Captain called me a couple of days later and asked if I could straighten out our followers. He said, "Sir, we are not going to arrest you, but we are receiving so many calls and e-mails, all our systems were jammed." This is a repeat of what happened with the State Department earlier. I told Jack to get the word out that the CG was not going to arrest me, and please, Jack, leave the CG alone.

Next problem, how do I get lube oil bought and delivered to the ship? My electrician, Don Chapman, has a son, Mike, who had worked with a man in Nassau a few years back. They had become friends and Mike had kept in touch with him. Don had Mike call his friend to order the lube oil - five hundred and fifty gallons, ten fifty-five-gallon drums - to be delivered to our pier on our arrival in Nassau. In fact Mike flew from his home in the Quad cities in Illinois to Nassau and made sure this would happen.

I also needed a diver to get under the ship and stick a bolt with a rubber gasket on it through the hole in the Auxiliary Engine room. After they screwed the nut, washer and rubber gasket to that bolt, the ship would be watertight again. For this, I offered the diver a ride from Nassau to Mobile on a WW II LST!

We came into what I had been told was *The Hole in the Wall*, but in reality, it was the 'Providence Channel.' The *Hole in the Wall* was a narrow place at the north end of Great Abaco Island. The Providence Channel we came through was a narrow break on the east side of the Bahama chain of islands, several hours north of Nassau. It was a narrow inlet, but plenty deep. There are areas around the Bahamas that are quite shallow. We came in early in the morning under very poor visibility, with misty rain and patchy fog. If we had not had my Garmin 12 GPS, we would have had to stop and wait for the weather to break, maybe a full day or two or more.

After we passed through the break in the island chain, we turned south straight for Nassau. It was now Jan 3, 2001. We took several hours to reach the breakwater at the harbor entrance. Then it took a while to raise anyone and get a pilot out to the LST. I had shut down the starboard engine, as its vibration had become worse. Taking the CONN, the pilot turned the ship to the left against the port engine. Eventually the old girl came around, and this did put us in a good position to go through the narrow harbor entrance. In the harbor a very sudden stiff wind to starboard came up and one of the tugboats fell off the port bow. LST 325 took off like a dog going after a rabbit. I thought the ship would end up over against a couple of smaller ships, but the tug recovered fast and saved the day! The pilot gasped and volunteered, "This ship is harder than the *Queen Mary* to maneuver around!" Finally, we were against the pier moored to the starboard side. I could see the oil drums on the pier and two men standing close by. I said to myself, we were at the right place.

THE PIRATE SHIP IS MISTAKEN FOR A U.S. MAN OF WAR

**** Navy Times 12/18/2000 – 'Old Men & the Sea' – A Last adventure for an old ship and her crew. This is your grandfather's Navy: steel men and a steel ship.

CHAPTER 25

THE 325 ENTERS NASSAU
AS A NAVY SHIP

The diver came aboard as soon as we put over our ladder, the one with rungs about two feet apart. Made from aluminum, it was fairly light. We explained what we wanted done. I had Bartlett show him the hole and gave him the bolt, with washers, to put through the hole. The diver needed to tap on the bottom of the ship when he was close. Bartlett then removed the makeshift patch he had in place and aimed a flashlight down through the hole, as water poured in the engine room. Off the diver went to slip into his scuba gear.

On the pier were several well-dressed individuals, women and men. I went down to see what they wanted. To my surprise in the group was our US Ambassador to the Bahamas! He had his office staff with him. He welcomed us to the Bahamas and requested to come aboard with all of his people. Several were a little on the heavy side and I explained that the only way to get on was up this wide rung ladder. He said it was OK, and slowly they climbed the ladder and were aboard. A Navy Captain, a liaison officer for American ships that visited Nassau, a similar position as Captain Melhuish, also climbed aboard to see if there was anything he could do for us. I gave them all a tour of the LST, as everyone wanted to see this old gray lady.

The Ambassador invited me to his home for cocktails and dinner that evening. I had to tell him no! I said we were leaving as soon as the oil and a few supplies were aboard. He was surprised, maybe even shocked, by my answer and the fact we were not staying a couple of days in beautiful Nassau. I told him how much it hurt me to have to decline his gracious invitation. How many times was a person invited to an Ambassadors home, not just to his residence, but also for dinner and cocktails! This small town boy never has, and I question if I ever get the chance again! I explained that my crew would leave without me. I wish I had his name; all I know is he was from Texas, and scheduled to be relieved in a couple of months.

A customs official of the Bahaman government summoned me to come to his office on the pier. The US Navy Captain went along with me. I had my letter with the red seal on it in my hand. The Customs agent said that I had to pay a duty tax for stopping in Nassau. I showed him the letter and he handed it back to me. He said he was sorry but all visiting ships had to pay except Navy ships. With that added knowledge I disclosed, "Well, we are a Navy ship and the crew and I are all US Navy veterans." I thought to myself that two out of three should be enough. The Navy Captain gave me a very hard look.

The Customs official answered, "Sir, show me your ship. We went out of his office and down to the pier. As we came out from behind the big yellow warehouse buildings that lined the pier, there with all its rust and glory was LST 325 with the 40mm and 20mm guns pointing out over the bow and over the side of the ship. She sat high above the pier, as the dock was only a couple of feet out of the water. The 325 had twenty-five feet of free board at the bow and even to me, she looked impressive!

The official looked up and declared, "By God, you are a Navy ship – you are exempt from the duty tax." He turned around and went back to his office.

The US Navy Captain said mockingly and in disbelief, "You are a US Navy vessel and a Navy Captain!" Then he smiled and said, "I have now seen everything, and Captain, you did great."

The barrels of oil were aboard and Boats had a detail dumping the oil out of them into the small opening right by my cabin, which drained the oil into the main engine lube oil tanks three decks below. The diver had found the hole and Jim had tightened the nut on the bolt. When completed, the leak stopped. The diver refused my offer of a ride on the ship after he fixed the hole. Wonder why!

Several of the men had made phone calls home and, from their reports, the excitement was building. Mike Chapman was aboard for a ride to Mobile, offered as a token of appreciation for arranging our lube oil purchase. Besides he was young, knowledgeable, and could be of great assistance to the crew.

We had hoped to receive the ashes of crewmember, Bill Hart, in Nassau. His family had requested him to be buried at sea, but sadly the urn had not arrived.

Cookie, I found out, had ordered twenty loaves of bread and four cases of beer! I was too late in finding out; he had it aboard and pigeon holed. I jumped Cookie about ordering four more cases of beer since we had ten or twelve still on board in the cooler. He just said, "Captain we must keep up our image!" and turned and walked toward the Galley. I wondered what image?

We also had an LST veteran, Bob Madden, and his wife, Poppy, fly over from Miami to see the LST. He had volunteered for the very first crew to sail the ship back from Taiwan some ten years earlier, but having lost most of his eyesight, he was not able to be on the crew. He was a friend of Nickerson's.

Mr. Madden was quoted in a newspaper article saying: "S*eeing is believing! We have an LST and it is now close to home."* With tears in his eyes as he walked up and down the pier, saying *"She is beautiful, she is beautiful!"* She did look beautiful even in her present state.

The same pilot came aboard and with two tugs maneuvered us out of the harbor. I tried to convince him to donate his pilot services and the tugs, but with no luck. It cost us two thousand five hundred dollars for his approximately two hours of work. Nassau was the only place that cost us money. However, the pilot did stay aboard until we were out of the harbor! I was still thinking about those cocktails and the dinner I missed as the pilot departed. I pointed the ship north to swing around the Bimini Islands. I was dead tired, turned the ship over to the XO, and went down and crashed in my bunk. I would be back up for the midwatch.

GULF STREAM AHEAD

CHAPTER 26

DAMN THE TORPEDOES – FULL SPEED AHEAD

It seemed like a long way around, but we had to go north for several hours and then turn west to get around the small islands and shallow water off to the east with the LST. Nickerson who had been there before from Miami, had told me about a passage through this area, but to navigate through it at night was suicide. We made good time, but some of the Florida boys (Nickerson, Taylor, and Calvin) wanted me to take the ship nearer the Florida Coastline in order to use their cell phones. I said no. We would have more traffic over there and we have the satellite phone on the ship. We turned south and skimmed down along the Bimini Islands.

The *Compass Bank* based in Birmingham, Alabama, had a big branch bank in Mobile. They were to send a helicopter to take pictures of the ship. The helicopter, spotted about midday on January 5, flew around the ship shooting pictures. I looked down from the CONN and there was the crew out on the deck shooting pictures back! I yelled for them to get off the deck. We had all seen choppers before and the bank wanted pictures of the ship, not the crew! They all realized their error and left the main deck.

I planned to go south far enough to turn the ship on an angle to parallel the Florida Keys, and pass through the Straits of Florida. I forgot the exact course we turned on, but it was about 250 degrees true. We could not sail very close to the Keys as they protected the reefs and marine animals. The Keys curve more due west, and we had a straight westerly course to the Dry Tortugas. We received a call from a man who belonged to a private boat club that wanted to escort us as we passed their position in the Keys. We were ahead of schedule; I must have called him a hundred times, but never reached him on the radio. We passed the Keys in the morning hours, and went by Key West about noon. We thought about stopping at the US Naval Base there, but could not be assured the CG would not tie us up if we did. We had to be in Mobile in a few days.

I was concerned the Gulf Stream, which can have a current of three knots or more, might cause us problems. The Gulf Stream started right about Key West, goes around Florida and heads north up along the East Coast of the US. It is the second largest ocean current, only the Antarctic Circumpolar current is greater. It can be fifty miles wide and 3,000 feet deep. With the LST churning out a seven-knot speed, I thought the ship might end up in Palm Beach, Florida. However, we never knew we passed over the Gulf Stream. I believe, because of our shallow draft, the current had little effect on the ship.

We were finally past the Dry Tortugas and turned northwest towards Mobile. I hoped the wind would get off the bow of the ship to the port side for a change, but no luck. The wind turned northwest and was again precisely on our bow as we made for Mobile. The dark blue seas turned rough for the usually calmer waters of the Gulf and our speed stayed the same. The tepid temperature dropped to an unpleasant coolness. I looked at the Garmin 12 GPS, set the Mobile Sea Buoy coordinates, and at our present speed, we had about eighteen hours to the good. That seemed like a lot of time, but downtown Mobile was about 35 miles from the sea buoy. Subtract five hours from the eighteen and we were down to just thirteen hours to play with.

I forgot to mention our resident ghost, Jonathon. The Greeks claimed the 325 had a ghost on board who was an American sailor who died by being pulled into the anchor hawse pipe. The ship's anchor chain on the bow goes down through this pipe out to the side of the ship, and the anchor housed with its shank pulled up into it. The Greeks believed the ghost was still aboard and did some crazy things aboard ship. They said that many of their sailors had seen him from time to time. Some of our crew believed he was still with us; many strange things happened to explain any other way!

Early on January 7th we lost electricity with a plugged fuel filter on #3. Everything was quiet except for the sounds of the waves as they hit the ship. The main engines idled and the wind tried to turn the ship around to its direction. This happened when all of the equipment comes to a dead stop and the engines idled with no air to the clutches. The port engine could be heard but not the starboard engine. The lights came back on, the radar, heater fan, and the port engine picked up RPMs. Our propeller pushed us ahead again, but no starboard engine. The engine room called and said they could not get the starboard going. I could hear them turning it over, but there was no firing of a cylinder; we only had eleven active ones to begin with.

BARTLETT BACK ON THE CONN

On the CONN came Chief Bartlett. I am not sure if he was upset, or behind that stern face was a little bit of triumph. Maybe he had won; the starboard engine had not made it home with one cylinder shut off. Anyway, he informed me (after I sat in the Captain's chair) I had to finish this sea adventure to Mobile on one engine! I quickly pushed in my trusty GPS and with a speed now of four knots, and headed into a stiff northwest wind, I was going to arrive twelve hours late. This translated into maybe 2300 hours or eleven PM on Wednesday at the Civic Center. The party was over; the celebration would have to be changed. Who was going to call that sweet girl in Mobile and give her the bad news? I talked out loud as I thought, so Bartlett could hear my distress with the situation - all caused by the engineering department!

Well, I was not calling her yet, not enough nerve. I said a little prayer for the wind to die down so we could maybe increase our speed to five or five and one-half knots. We had four big days left and the loss of the extra hours would not be bad, if we could just arrive in the daytime. All that day and all that night, we plugged along. No one in sight, no one called, and I knew I was not going to call anyone! I could just see the panic with all the plans made for our successful arrival. I knew from all reports we'd heard that America was waiting and listening.

I had the 0400 to 0800 watch on January 7th. It had been a cold night on the CONN and the sun never came up. The sky was cloudy, looked like rain, and the wind from the northwest had not let up one bit. It blew right in the face of this grand old ship, but she gave it her all on one engine. Oil leaked from places I never knew even had oil. I noticed from the port exhaust the #3 generator had started to smoke. I was sure we would be switching to the last good one, old #1, before long. The XO arrived on the CONN to relieve me. He was hurting, with a lingering pain in his stomach. He had used all of the antacid pills on board, mine and the crew's, but there he was ready to stand his watch.

He asked me if I had decided to make the call. I said, "No, I have not. Instead I am going down below as soon as I get some old clothes on. Jack, I am going to start that starboard engine!"

He hesitated, and then, "You are?"

I said, "Yes, I am going to prime the fuel to that engine, open up the blow down valves like the old two cylinder John Deere tractors had to do. Then we hit that starter and get that old girl turning, while someone keeps priming the fuel to her. I know she will have to run, because she will have no other option but to run. We need that engine. I will not be late!"

Jack said to me, "Captain, good luck, I hope it works."

I told the wheelhouse the same thing as I passed through, when they asked if I'd called yet. I went down the ladder to officer's country and my stateroom and started to change clothes. I had just changed into my old pants when I heard the familiar sound of the starboard engine turning over. I heard the starter kick in and the engine's solid groan, very slowly at first, then faster, and then I could hear a cylinder fire, then two, three, and then she was running! The old engine ran very slowly at first, but then picked up speed when the engineers engaged the clutch. The shaft and propeller started to turn. What a feeling! I felt and heard the throttle open, and we had both engines again propelling this old girl towards Mobile Bay!

Jim Bartlett showed up in my stateroom hatchway with this grin on his face saying, "Captain, we have the starboard going."

"Jim, I heard it start up. What was the problem with it anyway?"

"Well," he said, "I was not there when we lost electricity, but evidently without the air compressor running, we lost air pressure to the clutch disengaging it from the engine. The engine, with no load, revved up to high hitting the over-speed safety trip and kicked out the safety switch, which shuts off the fuel and kills the engine. I didn't know, so I didn't check the trip. Whiting, after he re-read the start procedure, saw that the first thing to do was check the over speed trip. He did that and found it had kicked out. He reset it, hit the starter, and you know the rest! They heard you were coming down to start the engine, and they didn't want you to show them up I guess."

Almost everyone believed it was God who started the engine or maybe Jonathan! I said, "Jonathan probably kicked out the over speed trip in the first place, but I seriously doubt if he would put it back."

I ran up to the CONN, punched in my GPS and was happy to find we were exactly one hour ahead of our appointed arrival time. A Coast Guard plane flew over at this moment, went behind us, then turned around and came back along the port side. He dipped his wings and flew away heading for Mobile. He would give the word on our position and speed to the LST fans in Mobile, that we were right on schedule. Several of the tired crew were revitalized by the plane sighting and went out and waved at the plane as it swooped down over us. They were all running on adrenalin now. I went down to my stateroom and hit my rack. I did not have to make the dreaded call to the girl at the Mobile Convention Center and ruin her homecoming plans. What a relief!

Day eight of the New Year was sunny, but still cold for this part of the country. I received calls from just about everyone who has helped us in some way. Captain Hal Pierce checked in now with regularity; he had lined up a pilot and tugs to bring the LST in. He had asked the first men he ran into if they would help bring the ship into Mobile. He said, "Each, without hesitation, said yes. Then I told them at no charge! This placed me in a bad position, as my other friends were mad for not being asked first!"

I talked with another volunteer, the ship's agent, Carl Black. He had lined up the Immigration, Customs, Agricultural, and the Health department people. All of them agreed to come aboard and donate their time. He had trouble arranging transportation to the sea buoy for them to come aboard with their forms to fill out and inspect the ship. Finally the tug coming out to help guide us into port permitted them to ride with him.

Carl then advised, "Pass the word to the Cook, throw overboard all of our meat and fresh vegetables." I told Cookie and he promised to do it right away. Someone else suggested I should pump our bilges at this time. We had close to a thousand gallons of 30W lube oil swimming below the deck plates. I knew I could not in good conscience dump the oil in the Gulf. For one thing it was against the law, and secondly, it was just plain wrong. I ordered no pumping. We saw several CG helicopters fly over; I knew the authorities were checking on us.

MOBILE SEA BUOY STRAIGHT AHEAD

**** Rockford Register Star 1/7/2001 – Their story should be told, followed with pride, and they should receive a hero's welcome when they reach home port.

CHAPTER 27

THE IRON MARVEL HAS THE BIT IN HER MOUTH

Like a horse biting down on her riding bridle bit and his rider can't stop him galloping towards the barn, I believe the 'Gray Lady' knew she was close to home. I could almost feel that added power in her engines as she surged towards the finish.

The vibration in the starboard engine had cracked the exhaust manifold, this time on the outside. This allowed water to trickle out and run down on the engine. The enginemen had first tried to caulk the split seam with no luck. They called Perruso into action. He improvised a sort of 'rain trough' to funnel the water off to the side of the engine, allowing it to fall harmlessly into the bilge. The flow seemed to be about the same as when it started. When we lost electricity due to a plugged fuel filter, the engineers had just started #1 generator and placed it on the line. This action proved faster than changing a fuel filter on #3, then re-starting it. They now had changed the filter and had generator #3 ready for service, if needed. We had a very good engineering department. Many of these engineers had lost most of their hearing since hearing plugs or ear muffs were not used in WWII. In fact, when I was engineering Officer in the early 1960's, engineers still did not wear hearing protection. I was fortunate; I did not have to stay for long stretches of time in the engine room. The few times I did, I could hardly hear right after I came out.

On the ninth Day of the New Year, I had the 0400 to 0800 watch. Doc was happy. He pointed out ships heading in all directions, some towards Mobile. It was still quite cold, in the middle 30's. None of the crew brought clothes along for cold weather. The crew had gone from 115-degree heat in Crete in August, to this unusually cold temperature in January where it is normally warm. We placed a small heater in the CONN. With the hatch shut and our two air conditioners (windows) closed, it was tolerable. I wore multiple layers, about everything I owned, on my body and was warm except for my feet.

The XO was tall at six feet two inches and had pasted a piece of duct tape across the entrance to the CONN about three inches down from the top. He had written "Duck" across it! He had several marks on the top of his head, as did most of us, but his duct tape knocked my hat off almost every time I went through the hatch.

The ship, rigged in wartime for darken ship, had two curtains at each entrance going in or out to prevent any light from escaping. These curtains hung from rods fastened to flat sheets of steel extended from just below the curtain rods up to the overhead, sealing off any light.

The XO came in from the weather deck by the galley and had ducked for the first flat steel sheet, but had risen up and caught the second one with the top of his head. Those who witnessed the collision said he placed his hand on his head, ducked outside, picked up the fire axe cradled on the bulkhead, and came back in and hit the flat piece of steel as hard as he could. He hit it twice, then looked at where the axe met the steel and realized he had not even chipped the paint! He put the axe back and went to his stateroom without saying a word. I bet that hurt!

Doc had moved inside the CONN for some warmth. Hailing from Michigan, I thought this was spring weather for him. He did not like my sense of humor! Everyone came up on top in hopes of seeing land as long as it was daylight, then came later to watch for lights on shore as the sun waned. I thought visibility of land or lights would not happen until later that night; we were a good seventy miles out yet.

The vibration in the starboard engine increased since we had to start the engine when the over-speed trip flew out; something made it worse. No one knew the real cause. The Greeks had said the starboard had a bent connecting rod. It seemed it developed a rougher vibration every time we restarted it, and when we slowed the engine RPMs down. When we ran it at five hundred RPM, it seemed to smooth out. To compensate and keep our seven knot speed, we increased the port to six hundred RPM to arrive at our appointed time.

Things were busy all day. Everyone knew we were close enough to say the "Gray Lady" had made it! About the only news was Bailey had talked to his girlfriend, Christine. Several of the crew asked him what she said. He finally relented, "She told me we have a lot of lovin' to catch up on, and if those old guys don't like it, well they can just go sit on a stump!" Bailey had lost his wife and Christine, her husband, but as couples had been good friends. Through the years, Bailey and Christine had developed a close friendship, but lived separately.

I should have tried to get some sleep, but like everyone, was wound up tighter than a tennis racket and looking forward to completing this odyssey. I had completed my 1600 to 2000 watch and Jack relieved me right on the dot, actually 15 minutes early. That was the Navy's protocol - to be early to relieve the watch. Nickerson was with him and they worked on our position and set a course correction for the Sea Buoy. My GPS did not always work correctly inside the CONN because of the steel cutting out the satellite signals. Nickerson had rigged his GPS outside forward of the CONN and made a position fix with it.

We had a group coming out to ride the ship into port tomorrow morning. They were:

Dan Waterfield, of BP and one of the persons instrumental in obtaining our fuel in Athens.

Carl Black, our ship's agent, from Mobile.

Gene Owens, newspaper writer, from the "Mobile Register Star."

Mike Gunjak, President of the US LST ASSOCIATION. He and his wife Linda had been supporters and contacts throughout our mission. I had called them and kept them up to date.

John Niedermeier Jr, son of the man who designed the LST. He had never ridden on an LST. I looked forward to meeting him.

I went down into the engine room to see firsthand how everything was running and received a few high fives in recognition of our completion of the mission. I stood by the starboard engine, placing my hand on her. I felt the vibration, noticeably rougher but seemed tolerable.

Bruce Voges had the 2400 to 0400 watch, and when he relieved the XO, we were very close to reaching the 'Mobile Sea Buoy.' Since

Nickerson left the CONN with Jack, I decided to stay up and help Boats. I was sure that we could see the buoy and the lighted channel markers that led north into Mobile Bay with the naked eye. The oil rigs and platforms started to show up. These platforms had a thousand bright lights that masked the running lights of ships as they passed and overtook us. It was dark, but clear; we had traveled along watching as best we could for the channel markers and that elusive sea buoy. I turned the LST west, thinking I must be too far east of that buoy; nothing visible. I could not believe we had missed it! I got a fix on the GPS and found that, in fact, we had gone right past it; we were too far out evidently to see it or we were heading the wrong way.

There were shrimp beds marked on the chart, and we were right over them. I ordered Boats to turn to the right and get out of the way of several shrimp boats. These shrimpers had nets strung out to the sides of their boats as they swept back and forth. I figured they would not appreciate our interrupting their shrimping! One boat came very close and we swung left to get away from him. Then we circled back to the right. He was now off the starboard side of the "T" and had changed course right for us. I called him on the radio saying, "Shrimp Boat off our starboard, I am trying to get out of your way, what direction should I steer?"

He came back and answered, "You are not in my way. I am just trying to see if you are that old WWII ship that is coming in today. I see you have running lights placed far up front on the bow where old ships have them."

I told him, "Yes, we are the LST 325." I told Boats, "We must be expected today!"

The Shrimper came back with, "You must be some old salt to bring that thing all the way across the Atlantic in the winter!"

My answer was, "You have the 'old' part right!"

Boats and I had managed to return very close to the Sea Buoy and it just happened a big tanker ship was coming out of Mobile Bay using the very shipping channel we were searching for. I could see his green running light and mast light. His pilot had overheard my conversation with the Shrimper.

Suddenly, the radio came to life. "LST ship, this is your pilot, Wildon Mareno. I am going to take you into Mobile this morning. The

Sea buoy is straight ahead of you. Sit tight. I have to go back into Mobile first but I'll be back in a little while." He also said he would notify the Coast Guard that we had arrived at the buoy and he would pass the word to the other people that were coming to board the ship. "You just hang around the sea buoy."

I answered up, "Aye, Aye sir."

We continued on an east-southeast course, and sure enough, there was the sea buoy. When Boats and I reached the buoy, I noticed channel markers straight into downtown Mobile or so it seemed. How could we have missed them? To kill time we ran up the channel a mile or two, then turned around and came back. We made big circles around that sea buoy, round and round. It was right at 0200 on January 10, 2001!

It seemed like an eternity before a boat came alongside. I put the port into reverse, but kept the starboard running, slowed to four hundred RPM to keep the vibration down. If I stopped the starboard, it might fail. With the one engine in reverse, we came almost to a stop. Voges went down, helped get the bos'n ladder over the side, and secured to the life rail. People boarded from the ladder. It was not easy. We still had a wind and rough water. Their boat bobbed against the LST. I tried to maneuver the LST in a west to east position to shield the people climbing aboard from the wind and waves. The first aboard was Coast Guard and he asked Boats, "Do you know you rigged the ladder over the starboard engine's exhaust?" Boats had a little egg on his face, but quickly yelled for all to wait and he moved the ladder forward.

All of the CG came aboard followed by our ship's agent and the civilian VIP riders. Mike Gunjak did not come. Carl Black told me they tried hard to contact him, first by phone then knocked on his hotel room door, with no luck. Carl could not wait any longer.

Next were the government entities. Carl told me to pass the word to tell the crew not to declare anything on the customs form. We did what he asked and nobody said a word. We didn't have any illegal immigrants on board either! The agriculture people went down to the meat locker; guess what they found! They found meat there! Meat we had gotten in Gibraltar, which came from Argentina. Meat that the cook had assured me would not be there! They triple bagged the meat, tied it, and put a USDA seal on it. They told Cookie they would be back to take it off when they had proper gear and could dispose of it. The XO and Doc reported that we had no sickness of any kind on the ship. This satisfied the Health department.

The CG showed up on the CONN and the one in charge introduced himself as Lieutenant Sutton of the U.S. Coast Guard, then said to me, "Sir, I have my orders."

I quickly shot back, "What are your orders, Sir?"

He said, "We are to leave you alone! We are going to go around the ship and make it look like we are doing our job. As soon as we finish and your pilot arrives, we are going to allow you to proceed into Mobile." How sweet were those words?

Our pilot, Captain Mareno, climbed aboard and Boats escorted him up to the CONN. Carl had told me we had the senior pilot for Mobile Harbor, a real honor. He was the best. Captain Mareno entered the CONN and I said, "Captain, welcome aboard" and introduced myself and Mr. Edwards to him. He asked what the status of getting underway was. I told him what Mr. Sutton had said. He nodded his head.

A call on channel 13 came from Lieutenant Sutton, who asked, "Did I know we had the manual steering system engaged?"

I quickly answered him, "Yes I do. I ordered it hooked up as an added safety measure while entering the harbor. If we lose steering, we can go directly to manual steering." That seemed to be OK with him. Shortly, the Lieutenant was back on the CONN and told me I was free to proceed into Mobile. I asked him if I should stop and let him, his men, and the others off.

He quickly answered; "No, we want to ride a WWII LST into Mobile!"

I replied, "Well, you know we are not safe."

He smiled, "You cannot be very unsafe. You just travelled forty-three hundred miles across the Atlantic and are still floating and sailing!"

The pilot took over. We had a tug along the port side and with the order of port and starboard engines ahead standard, we started making headway up the channel. It was now about 0400 and the LST 325 was on schedule. How about that!

EAGERLY THE LST FANS WERE WAITING

CHAPTER 28

AN AMERICAN HERO COMES HOME

We passed Ft. Morgan and Ft. Gaines on opposite sides of the entrance to Mobile Bay, when loud cannon fire from each fort erupted and broke the morning silence. The pirate ship was under siege! If only we had our guns operational. I asked Edwards to give them a shot of our only weapon – blow that damn whistle. Let them know we are here! It was 0430 in the morning. This was the beginning of the welcoming ceremony and we had six hours to go!

The XO came up and relieved me and I went down to fill out my Custom's card and pick up a hot cup of coffee. The temperature had dipped to twenty-three degrees. I have only been this cold to the bone a few times before in my entire life. The cold temperature caused some water fog to develop, triggered by the warmer Bay water against the cold crisp air. I went back up on the CONN and asked the pilot and Mr. Sutton if they would like some coffee. The Lieutenant thanked me, but said he would like to see our galley anyway. He would get his cup then. The pilot said, "Yes, I would love some." I called down to the wheelhouse and ordered a black cup of java for the pilot.

A CG Cutter now maneuvered in front of us and one had already stationed himself directly behind to follow us; both were there to escort the LST into Mobile!

"Hey, LST!" a voice came up on the radio. "LST, come over here by us. We could use you for parts!" Speaking was the Captain from the *Columbia,* a dredge that now worked in Mobile bay year around. The dredge, I learned, was a former (but modified) WWII LST. Modified was an understatement.

I grabbed the radio mike and called back, "Why don't you follow us. We left our parts ship in Greece and we could use ANOTHER ONE!"

Shortly after that, the Coast Guard Cutter ahead of us called back. The female Captain informed us she was having engine troubles and was going to pull over, but said we should keep going. I grabbed the radio mike and, without thinking, asked if she wanted us to throw her a line and tow her into Mobile? She instantly answered with, "No, not in my lifetime." This was on Channel 13 and most all of the ships, tugs, shrimpers, and amateur boaters were listening and heard this exchange. I guess she received a lot of ribbing for the entire next year. I was on her list!

Every one of the marine businesses knew the CG declared us unsafe. I believe most had heard our State Department was sure we would never make it across the Atlantic. Then of course, there were the non-believers who said it couldn't be done. Now we had offered to pull a CG Cutter back into Mobile. Though the captain was not happy with my offer, I thought it was the right thing to do. We had looked all the way across the ocean for a boat or ship to rescue. I never dreamt of rescuing a Coast Guard Cutter!

As we came into the Mobile city limits, the shipyards allowed all of their workers to come out and sit on their docks along the Bay. As we passed by, they took off their yellow hard hats and waved them in the air. People in the small boats that ran along both sides of the LST waved American flags. Most yelled at us, but I could not hear what they said in the CONN.

On shore on the port side, we passed by the Brookley Center that used to be an old Air Force base. It had a big open area and was packed with people! It was reported that over ten thousand people watched the LST come in. From my observations from the CONN, it looked like far more than that!

It was now about 0930 and I told the pilot we could not be early. We must go by the Convention Center as close as possible to 1030. He said, "OK, go ahead and slow her down." I called down to the wheelhouse, and said, "All ahead two-thirds." We had clipped along at Standard speed doing a good eight knots. Soon after that I decided to cut her down to one-third ahead and also shut the vibrating starboard engine down as the LST seemed to be in a hurry to cross the finish line, downtown Mobile!

The sun had moved a little higher in the morning sky and the fog that had been around us dissipated into more of an eerie mist. The crew was out on the decks, some up on the sides of the CONN. They were having a blast. They had to stay back of the conning structure or lose their hearing as Edwards tugged on that handle. I had turned that pleasure over to Jim Edwards when he came up on the CONN to see over the morning fog. The men would yell at some of the small boats and wave back to them. The fog was not thick (visibility was a half mile) but more of a haze that started right against the water line and up thirty feet. From our lofty position on the command center of the LST, one could see quite a distance over the top of the fog. We had more small boats join the procession as we inched closer to downtown Mobile. Many of the boats had signs that read *welcome home LST*, *welcome back*, *we love you guys*, *welcome back American Veterans*, or *we knew you could do it*! Some had businesses with their name on the sign and read, *"We are glad you are home LST 325,"* or *"Mobile welcomes you home."*

THE GHOST SHIP EMERGES OUT OF THE FOG

There were several helicopters overhead. Every few minutes the CG announced the Mobile Channel closed to shipping. "We are bringing in the LST 325!" They also warned all boats to stay at least one thousand feet away from the LST, but little attention was paid to the warnings. We had too many small boats for the CG to control. The Mobile TV station helicopters shot videos of our arrival; one station had covered us all morning

When Lieutenant Sutton reappeared, I asked him why they had closed the entire Mobile Channel to bring us in. He answered, "Well, you have sailed over six thousand four hundred miles across the Mediterranean and Atlantic with no difficulties. We do not want you to be run into by a freighter or have a boat turn into your path, especially as you get closer to downtown Mobile."

The Mobile Tug Companies, every last one of them, placed their tugs side by side in a straight line on our starboard side with bows pointing right at the LST as we slipped by in front of them. We had been blowing our whistle every few minutes. My enginemen told me they were afraid we might lose the air pressure to the engine clutches, especially when Jim held the blast of the horn for a long time. The tugs evidently had a plan to reciprocate. All at once the loudest whistle sounds I've ever heard by far came roaring out. Some twenty or so tugs blew their horns at exactly the same time. They gave us first a long blast, then several short ones, then repeated this wonderful salute. How they all timed this I have never learned. We answered them back with one long blast, but they had won the day.

A couple of Mobile fireboats joined the parade on the water, one reported to be older than the LST. Red, white, and blue water sprayed out of their nozzles as they led the way towards downtown. A large two-mast schooner slid up on our Starboard side. Was this a homecoming or what? This was some kind of day - one of the greatest days of my life - and a great day to be an American.

I told Jim to cut back on the whistle blowing until we reached the south end of the convention center ten minutes away. Half of the people of Mobile and our families waited on the convention's bay front. An elongated raised platform filled the space between the Convention Center and Mobile Bay. We were about to pass it on the port side. We saw our families waving to us, plus LST vets and friends from all over the country waiting to welcome us home. This area must have been three hundred yards long and sixty feet deep. We were all waving at them. They were waving back. Not one more person could have squeezed into this area. I wondered where the young lady responsible for this 'small welcoming' stood and watched. She had to be smiling and so pleased. I wondered if she had any idea her welcome home shindig would mushroom into this colossal event.

I said, "Jim, pull the handle as hard as you can, but don't break it!" He held on to it for a while letting it resound off the back wall of the convention center. This crew had accomplished the impossible. They had overcome so many obstacles that would have caused most to give up and quit. These crewmembers were not quitters. I simply cannot put adequately into words how relieved, excited, and elated I was. I was happy for my crewmembers, happy it was over, happy we were home, happy to see my wife and family, and very happy we brought a WWII ship home with us.

We all could go back to our towns with our chests out and our heads held high! As Cookie crowed while holding out his fist, "We said we were going to do it, and we did it!"

One of the signs Ed Strobel had made (and retrieved from the trash bin many times) read, "Over this gangway pass the oldest sailors in the world!" I told him he should redo the sign to read, *the oldest and greatest sailors in the world!*

We sailed right by that young party planner who demanded a day and time we would arrive in Mobile so she could plan a welcoming party. We passed by our families waving flags. We passed by exactly, and I mean exactly, at 1030 hours on Wednesday morning, January 10, 2001! Not only had the old gal brought us home, battled storms and breakdowns, but she got us here on time.

THAT'S MY STORY AND I AM STICKING TO IT!

Bob Jornlin, Captain of LST 325 -- Souda to Mobile, 2000 to 2001

The End.

EPILOGUE

We continued on to pier #5 at the Alabama State Docks. Two tugs came out, helped to turn us around so we were starboard side to the pier in order to use our accommodation ladder. The pier was high and we only had a two-foot drop from the ship's main deck. We did not use our ladder but a short gangway from the dock. There were four thousand people on the dock, the MAXIMUM they would allow.

A countless number of school kids were there waiting and holding up signs with each of the crew's names on them. Their teacher, Ms. Kirkpatrick, had used our crossing as a history tool for WWII for the kids and made them use the computer to find out about each crewmember and about LSTs. They also had to read the Mobile Register newspaper where the writers I have mentioned gave them more information than they probably needed.

Dignitaries of all kinds gathered on a make-shift podium. There were two Congressmen; Ralph Hall from Texas, with his aid Priscilla Thompson-Roberts; and Congressman H. L. 'Sonny' Callahan from the Mobile area of Alabama; Mike Dow, the Mayor of Mobile; Mr. Rodney Smith represented the Governor of Alabama; Don Siegelman; Mike McAdams, the President of American operations for BP; Mobile Postmaster James Salter who with Postal Service Officials, gave the ship a box of envelopes bearing the stamped cancellation: "The Proud voyage of LST 325 –January 10, 2001, Mobile, AL 36601" - along with the Greek Embassy representative, Capt. Konstantinos Saflianis who gave a short speech; Captain Pierce; all of the crew's families.

I personally had my wife Lois, son Kirk and wife, Valerie with granddaughter Lori. My daughter Kimberly, her husband Anthony, and granddaughters, Kia and Lexi, now just two months seven days old! Lexi, a few days later would be the youngest person to ride on an LST ever! In addition, there were the Mobile Magnolia girls all dressed in beautiful dresses with matching parasols, several school bands playing patriotic songs, and numerous news media including some major networks.

I did not quite understand all of the hoop-la until later. I was given a scrap book by a young man, Michael Richard Brannon, four inches thick, with a copy of every newspaper article that was in the Mobile Register and other newspapers over the last two or three months. For various reasons, which I still do not fully understand, we had captured the hearts of many different age groups, along with many veterans (not just LST veterans) and service men on active duty. The press had transformed us into David fighting Goliath, the Marines defeating the Japanese on Iwo Jima, Patton with his tanks coming to the rescue at *Bastogne* in the *Battle of the Bulge,* or maybe just McHale of *McHale's Navy* getting the best of his Commanding Officer! Whatever the reason for the excitement, I will be the last to fight it!

Captain Pierce was Master of Ceremonies and gave the welcome address. Then he introduced the celebrities who were to speak. I did not get a chance to even say "Hi" to my wife until after Captain Pierce introduced me. The Magnolia Girls had escorted me to the speaker's stand and to a chair alongside the VIPs until it was my chance to say a few words. I received a key to the city of Mobile, and a picture plaque from Compass Bank from the helicopter that came out to the Bimini Islands to snap the photo from overhead. There were several plaques, one from the Battleship Alabama, all presented one by one to me. The crew received duplicates of most of these plaques as well.

My talk was short for two reasons: I was now without any sleep for thirty-six hours and exhausted, and the arrival reception had already been long due to the large number of speakers.

Here was the gist of my speech:

"We did not go for glory; we just wanted an LST brought home for the veterans who served on them and for their families to see one. I thank everyone who helped us accomplish this feat, especially Mr. McAdams for the fuel and Captain Hal Pierce for believing me when I said I was bringing an LST home and needed a place to dock it. I thank everyone here who supported us, because that was what kept us going when things seemed hopeless." I gave credit to God for letting us do this and for keeping everyone safe.

I had purchased small gifts for Linda Gunjak and Priscilla Thompson from the 'Brass Shop' and presented them. I felt they had helped me as much or more than anyone. I then introduced the men of the crew, not individually, but as a group. I had them stand and wave at the crowd. Most were still on the main deck of the ship. I said, "They were the ones who brought the ship home. I did not bring this ship back alone. This was a joint effort and accomplished by the whole crew, each in his own way with his individual talent got this job done. When they heard someone saying they would never get this done or maybe laughing at our pursuit, they just worked harder. These men were the greatest crew to sail an LST!

"This is one of the greatest days of my life - to be home in the good old USA, and to have brought an LST back with me! I was just fortunate to be part of this crew. It is great to be an American and to receive such an outstanding welcome you folks have given us. I thank you all. I have never experienced anything like this. Thank you all so much. Thank you."

I really do not remember exactly what happened next. I know there was a lot of hand shaking, a hug from Priscilla, who I had talked to often but had not met, and seeing my family again. The press went directly to the crew, dropped everyone else as fast as one drops a hot horseshoe.

After the ceremony, a WWII LST sailor told me with tears in his eyes, that when the fog started to clear, he was standing at the railing of the Convention Center. He thought he could see the LST, he saw her bow break through as it emerged out of the mist, then some of the super structure, the ship looked like a ghost ship that had been in a time warp, she was just coming back from the war! He said wiping his eyes, "I was so happy to see that ship and know that you guys were safe and accomplished your mission. Man was she a beautiful sight coming out of the fog and into the sunshine. I never believed I would see an LST again."

I told him, "We are one of the ten percent who never received the word the war was over!" That brought him to laughter as he wiped more tears from his face. We learned today many here at home were every bit as happy and thankful as we were that we made it and brought a 'Hero' with us.

Somehow my wife got me to the hotel. The hotel upgraded us to a suite with two bedrooms and a big parlor in the middle, but we had to pay for the bedrooms! The worst part was Lois had to move from her room several floors down, up to the suite. My son-in-law and daughter stayed and paid for the one bedroom. The hotel was right across the street from the convention center. The big BP reception was on schedule for the hotel ballroom this evening. I went directly to our hotel room and was ordered by my wife, the Admiral, to go to bed and get some sleep, which I did. The time to get up for the reception came way too soon! My son-in law, Anthony took phone calls and messages and wrote them on a tablet. He had close to three pages of phone calls by the time I awoke, with time, names, and phone numbers, and noted if they wanted a call back or not. He had asked what each wanted if they had not told him. Some were friends that simply wanted to say, 'glad you made it,' or 'good job.' Most were TV and newspaper people. I had most of the following day scheduled at the ship for TV appearances beginning at 0600! It seemed we were all celebrities.

I was late to the reception, but it was packed. I made the rounds and, said "HI" to the crew, and as many people as I could who helped us. One person I wanted to see was my Executive Officer, Jack. He told me he was going to the hospital as soon as we arrived. I wanted to know the results, if possible. He told me the doctors thought it was mostly his nerves, that he should go home, see his doctor, and get a thorough check up. I would later learn it was much more serious.

The Admiral pulled me away and we left the reception so I could catch up on some sleep and gear up for the TV people the following day.

The LST is featured at Normandy and Slapton Sands (Exercise Tiger) since our return. The only operational LST, it has been mentioned or pictured in numerous books, magazines, and newspapers. Two History Channel documentaries have been made, *The Return of LST 325* and *Hero Ships the LST.* One Japanese documentary was filmed on the 325 about the use of our LSTs to retrieve their soldiers off the remote islands in the Pacific after the war. The LST 325's LCVPs were used in Iceland and are both in the movie *Flags of our Fathers.* In May, 2014 a documentary was shown on the *Exercise Tiger,* filmed on the 325.

Capt. Bob

**L to R – Jack Carter, Captain, Commodore,
CDR Nickoldakis and Capt. Petrakis**

Having a toast with Greek Officials after signing papers giving us the LST 325 Nov. 14, 2000

Captain Bob and wife Lois

CDR JACK CARTER, EXECUTIVE OFFICER

(I am still buying BP gas)

L to R – Carter, Calvin, Edwards, Capt.

Edwards is pointing to BP Logo

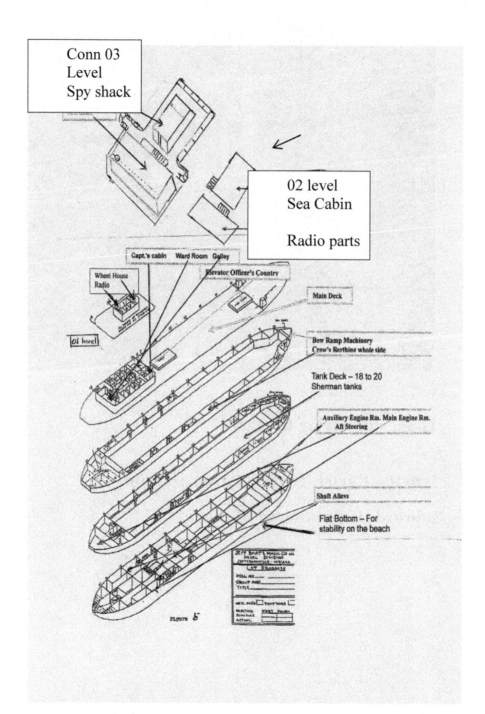

Figure 6

Embassy of the United States of America

Athens, Greece
November 15, 2000

To Whom It May Concern:

The LST-325 was built in 1942 -- in Philadelphia, Pennsylvania -- and served with distinction as part of U.S. Navy operations during the Second World War.

It was transferred to the Hellenic Navy in 1963.

In 2000, the U.S. Government approved the transfer of the LST-325 from the Government of Greece to the USS LST Memorial Inc., which is a fully registered organization under U.S. law and is entitled to all the protections therein. The LST-325 has significant historical value and, upon reaching the United States, will become an important maritime museum.

We ask that you extend all appropriate courtesies and privileges to the captain of this vessel, Mr. Robert Jornlin, and to his fellow members of the USS LST Memorial Inc. -- all of whom are citizens of the United States of America.

Thank you for your attention.

Sincerely,

Betsy Anderson,
Consul General
of the United States of America

Red Seal

GOLD CREW
BRASS SHOP: MOTHER, CAPT.,
**   DAUGHTER, BOATS, AND FATHER.**

LST 325 AT BIMINI ISLANDS JAN. 2001

Photo taken by Compass Bank

Those attending the party in Souda

    Ambassador Burns is in the center, white open collar shirt, between two ladies

USS LST SHIP MEMORIAL, INC.

A PENN NON-PROFIT ORGANIZATION
TAX ID #025-1581762
Repr. Ralph Hall
*** PRESIDENT***
Rayburn Bldg. HOB 2221
Washington DC. 20515
202-225-6673

October 3, 2000

Robert D. Jornlin C/O LST-825
*** Vice President ***
4763 E. 10th Rd.
Earlville, IL. 60518-6203
815-627-9077

James H. Edwards LST-28
*** 2nd Vice President ***
1214 VZ County Rd 2143
Canton, TX. 75103-3432
903-848-1171

Jackson R. Carter X-O LST-887
3rd. Vice President
28911 S. Golden Meadow Dr.
Rancho Palo Verdes, CA. 99275
310-377-3586

Edward Strebel LST-1020-1141
*** Secretary ***
324 Shoreline Place
Decatur, IL. 62521
217-423-6521

Freeman A. Ballard LST-447
*** Treasurer ***
6901 Veterans Hwy. Suite 63
Metairie, LA. 70003
504 887-8348

To: Congressman Ralph Hall
    Mr. Peter Leasca
    Mr. Mike Gunjak
    All US LST Association Members

From: Crew of LST 325 Crete, Greece

We the undersigned, crew of WW2 US LST 325 in Souda Crete, do proclaim our support to the officers of this ship, and in Robert D Jornlin The Captain.

We also proclaim that Ambassador Burns, the ODC, our US Navy and especially the Hellenic Navy has supported us in our quest to bring back the LST 325.

The Crew:

With State, Federal and IRS recognition under 501-c-3 and 509 all donations are tax deductible

Crew's support letter for Capt. Jornlin

**** Portsmouth, Va. 12/7/2000 - 29 veterans plan to sail a WWII LST home.

**** Navy Times 12/18/2000 – 'Old Men & the Sea' – A Last adventure for an old ship and her crew. This is your grandfather's Navy: steel men and a steel ship.

**** 'Mutiny on the LST' –The huge task of getting the LST ready for sea was hampered early on by the crew's dislike for the first skipper.

**** Toasting the LST 325 crew with a shot of 'raki,' the Greek Navy turned over the ship Nov 14, 2000. The LST set sail for home.

**** From Greece to Gibraltar took 13 days. First the starboard engine went down, and then the gyro went out forcing steering with the magnetic compass. Then the steering went out and the crew steered by a manual steering system into Gibraltar.

**** To the 'Great Americans' aboard LST 325: All of us aboard Admiral Burke's destroyer knew you would handle this trip in style. **CDR Alan Eschbach, Commanding Officer *USS ARLEIGH BURKE* (DDG 51).**

**** 'Distinguished Mariners' Award' We present to Capt. Robert Jornlin for his tenacity, dedication and perseverance in the face of unsurmountable odds in crossing the Atlantic in that oceans most raging attitude, toward the historic preservation of the WWII fighting ship LST 325. **Conferred by the Sec. of the Salmon River Navy**

ABOUT THE AUTHOR:

 Bob Jornlin, Capt. LST 325, born and raised in the small town of Earlville, Illinois on a family farm, was 61 in 2000 when he was made Captain of LST 325. He had served in the U. S. Navy from November of 1961 to April of 1969 reaching the rank of LT. He never thought it possible to be on a navy ship again underway but thirty five years later, he was called back to service by Navy Veterans of WWII and the Korean War. They needed a Captain to lead them in restoring an LST, with the hope to sail this fifty-eight year-old ship from Greece to the USA, something never done before. He answered their call. He is the only Navy Line Officer to command sailors from three wars, WWII, Korea, and Vietnam on the same ship, and especially with the combined average age of 72.

Jornlin worked for four major seed companies in Sales positions, earning numerous awards before returning to the family farm. He has served as a trustee in his church, as President of the Rochelle, IL Rotary Club 1978-79, and President of the Rochelle Wildlife Conservation Club 1980-81. He is a Past Commander and lifetime member of the American Legion, and a Life member of Ancient Free and Accepted Masons Lodge No. 558. He was President of the USS LST SHIP MEMORIAL from 2001 to 2008; Director of the Memorial and Captain of LST 325 for 14 years. LST 325 has traveled to more than 45 cities under his command.

Awards received: Rotary 'Service above Self' Award, the International Lions Club 'Lion of the Year' Award, the 'Audie Murphy' Award from Decatur, AL, 'Patriot of The Year' Award in Mobile, AL and the 'Veterans Freedom' Award from Charlotte, NC. In 2014 presented the William J. Diffley Award and Casper J. Knight, Jr Award by the Historical Naval Ships Association.

He and his wife, Lois, were married in 1965 and have two children and five grandchildren. He belongs to several other organizations and is a member of the Earlville Presbyterian Church.